The Canela

Kinship, Ritual, and Sex
in an Amazonian Tribe

Second Edition

William H. Crocker
Smithsonian Institution

Jean G. Crocker

 Case Studies in Cultural Anthropology: George Spindler, Series Editor

THOMSON
™
WADSWORTH

Australia • Canada • Mexico • Singapore • Spain
United Kingdom • United States

THOMSON

WADSWORTH

Anthropology Editor: *Lin Marshall*
Assistant Editor: *Analie Barnett*
Editorial Assistant: *Amanda Santana*
Marketing Manager: *Diane Wenckebach*
Project Manager, Editorial Production:
 Rita Jaramillo
Print/Media Buyer: *Rebecca Cross*
Permissions Editor: *Kiely Sexton*

Production Service: *Mary E. Deeg,*
 Buuji, Inc.
Copy Editor: *Cheryl Hauser*
Cover Designer: *Rob Hugel*
Cover Image: *William H. Crocker*
Text and Cover Printer: *Webcom*
Compositor: *Buuji, Inc.*

The logo for the Cultural Anthropology series is based on an ancient symbol representing the family: man, woman, and children.

For more information about our products,
contact us at:
Thomson Learning Academic Resource Center
1-800-423-0563

For permission to use material from this text,
contact us by:
Phone: 1-800-730-2214 **Fax:** 1-800-730-2215
Web: http://www.thomsonrights.com

Library of Congress Control Number: 2003100341

ISBN-13: 978-0-534-17491-0
ISBN-10: 0-534-17491-4

Wadsworth/Thomson Learning
10 Davis Drive
Belmont, CA 94002-3098
USA

Asia
Thomson Learning
5 Shenton Way #01-01
UIC Building
Singapore 068808

Australia/New Zealand
Thomson Learning
102 Dodds Street
Southbank, Victoria 3006
Australia

Canada
Nelson
1120 Birchmount Road
Toronto, Ontario M1K 5G4
Canada

Europe/Middle East/Africa
Thomson Learning
High Holborn House
50/51 Bedford Row
London WC1R 4LR
United Kingdom

Latin America
Thomson Learning
Seneca, 53
Colonia Polanco
11560 Mexico D.F.
Mexico

Spain/Portugal
Paraninfo
Calle/Magallanes, 25
28015 Madrid, Spain

To George Spindler
And to the memory of
Louise Spindler
For their inspiration
And friendship over the years

Contents

Foreword

ABOUT THE SERIES

These case studies in cultural anthropology are designed for students in beginning and intermediate courses in the social sciences, to bring them insights into the richness and complexity of human life as it is lived in different ways, in different places. The authors are men and women who have lived in the societies they write about and who are professionally trained as observers and interpreters of human behavior. Also, the authors are teachers; in their writing, the needs of the student reader remain foremost. It is our belief that when an understanding of ways of life very different from one's own is gained, abstractions and generalizations about the human condition become meaningful.

The scope and character of the series has changed constantly since we published the first case studies in 1960, in keeping with our intention to represent anthropology as it is. We are concerned with the ways in which human groups and communities are coping with the massive changes wrought in their physical and sociopolitical environments in recent decades. We are also concerned with the ways in which established cultures have solved life's problems. And we want to include representation of the various modes of communication and emphasis that are being formed and reformed as anthropology itself changes.

We think of this series as an instructional series, intended for use in the classroom. We, the editors, have always used case studies in our teaching, whether for beginning students or advanced graduate students. We start with case studies, whether from our own series or from elsewhere, and weave our way into theory, and then turn again to cases. For us, they are the grounding of our discipline.

ABOUT THE AUTHORS

Bill Crocker graduated from Yale College in 1950 and was the first of George Spindler's students to earn his M.A. in anthropology from Stanford in 1953. He completed his Ph.D. at the University of Wisconsin at Madison in 1962, having made the first of many visits to the Canela in 1957. In 1962, he joined the Smithsonian Institution as Associate Curator for South American Ethnology in the Department of Anthropology of the National Museum of Natural History. He continued his study of the Canela, making 20 trips to the field over the years, totaling 74 months of living with the tribe. Although Crocker has missed teaching, he appreciates the opportunity for intensive and long-term research his career at the Smithsonian has provided. He is the author of numerous articles on the Canela, and in 1990 his comprehensive monograph, *The Canela (Eastern Timbira), I: An Ethnographic Introduction* appeared as number 33 in the Smithsonian Contributions to Anthropology series. Bill's work also contributed to the 1999 video on the Canela, *Mending Ways,* and to an extensive Canela Web site, launched in 2002, that is linked to the Smithsonian anthropology's web system. In 2001, Bill spent three months with the Canela, and he hopes to spend a few weeks every other year with them, continuing the study of long-term cultural change.

Jean Galloway Thomas married Bill in 1987 and has since collaborated informally with him as an editor. She earned her B.A. in English from Stanford in 1960 and her M.A. in English from Georgetown University in 1971. She taught literature and writing in college preparatory schools for 20 years. Jean accompanied Bill on his 1991 trip to Brazil and lived with the Canela for three weeks. For the original case study, and this revision, Jean used her teaching experience to orient the text for the college student. She helped organize the material and wrote some sections. Since Bill is the anthropologist, Jean has preserved his voice as the single narrative "I."

ABOUT THIS CASE STUDY

It is impossible to do justice to this case study of the Canela in the short compass of a foreword. Bill Crocker began field research with the Canela in 1957 and has continued intermittently to the present. He has lived with the Canela for an accumulated total of more than six years during 20 field trips. There are few anthropological field studies that surpass his in duration and intensity.

This long-term approach to the study of a culture enables Crocker not only to mount a time-stretched interpretation of culture change and adaptation, but also permits him to achieve an intimacy of interpersonal relationships with the Canela people that is often voiced as an objective of anthropological fieldwork—but rarely achieved. Bill Crocker is among kin, locked into an intricate pattern of terminology and reciprocal behaviors, when he is with the Canela.

Though "one of the family," he must retain perspective as an anthropologist—a viewer and interpreter of behavior into which he has been socialized. He does this, in part, by acquiring "research assistants" rather than "informants." They share knowledge and their interpretations of behavior with him. They also share responsibility for culturally correct reporting and analysis. Crocker acknowledges their input but still retains his obligation to produce alternative perspectives and interpretations flowing from his anthropological training and his position as a cultural "other" to the Canela. The result of his special, long-term relationship with the Canela is a complex, detailed description and analysis of a spectacular way of life.

Canela culture is radically divergent from European-based cultural expectations, values, and perspective, even though their common humanity is apparent. They live a joyous life of festival, ceremony, and ritual that is inconceivable from the perspective of a work- and time-oriented Westerner. The Canela spend hours and days engaged in symbolic reenactments of their cultural meanings, and parts of each day engaged in what seems like plain everyday fun—such as racing around the village perimeter carrying heavy logs on their shoulders (a great way to keep in shape, it seems).

The theme of bonding runs throughout this case study: bonding through kinship, through ritual, and through sex. The first two are to be expected, given our anthropological understanding of social life, symbolism, and the reinforcement of community through ritual and ceremony. The third, bonding through sex, is unexpected, though not unknown in tribal cultures of some parts of South America. It is not that sex is unexpected. Sexual activity and sexual restraints are everywhere, in every culture. Its regulation is what is interesting. In the United States, we stimulate it with tantalizing imagery, dress, and innuendo, and then deny and punish it. This ambivalence is a major theme in European-American culture. Among the Canela, sex is a joyous expression and reinforcement of community bonding. The story of this bonding is too complex and startling to more than mention in this foreword.

Two major challenges to Western perspectives and sensibilities are sequential sex—when one woman may receive as many as 20 men—and the induction of young girls of 11 years of age, and even younger, into sexual experience involving full intromission. What is most interesting, anthropologically, is that sexual behavior that seems to involve the ultimate of licentious freedom from a Western point of view is stringently regulated by Canela custom and mores. It is just as easy to become disreputable among the Canela as it is in any Western community, but for quite different reasons. Among the Canela, one who is "stingy" with sex is scorned, for such a person does not contribute to community well-being.

The implication of this case study for understanding cultural relativism, as well as the sources of a common humanity, are of great importance for teachers and students everywhere. We are fortunate to have it available and fortunate that it is clear and thoroughly readable, despite the complexity and detail of its subject manner. To this end, the present edition has been cut here and there, simplified, rewritten, and updated. A complex and changing culture is made more understandable and interesting for all to read and enjoy.

George Spindler
Series Editor
geospinner@aol.com

Preface

HOW I CHOSE ANTHROPOLOGY
AND THE CANELA FOR MY LIFE'S WORK

"How did you pick the Canela to study?" is a question frequently asked of me. This account of how I picked a particular tribe, and before that the field of anthropology, is an attempt to answer these questions. In order to encourage students to persist until they have found their life's work, I will trace some of the circuitous paths I took before devoting my professional life to the study of the Canela Indians of Brazil.

My family in California descended from railroad and banking "barons" who played a role in California history. It was not comfortable growing up on the "top of the hill," in Hillsborough, California, during the 1920s and 1930s. This perch was isolated both geographically and socially. Although there were naturally happy moments in a childhood full of plenty, my nannies and parents had virtually no understanding of child psychology, and their social set was impervious to developments in the new social sciences. Added to the more than ordinary childhood frustrations was an element of fear. The Lindbergh kidnapping impelled my parents to hire a bodyguard, a figure in a green hat who lurked in the woods behind my house where I was allowed to play with my sister. As a child during the Depression, I was traumatized when the car my mother and I were riding in was stoned by people on the street in San Francisco. Somehow I developed the conviction that the way to defang the danger was to descend the hill and get to know the world that resented us.

Although my boarding school years at Groton School outside Boston were a cultural shift of sorts, with the Spartan communal dormitories and the ethic of self-denial and service, the first real exposure to another subculture was the summer I worked in a lumber camp near Redding, California, between my junior and senior high school years. The year was 1942 and some toughening up seemed like a good idea for a young man who faced a wartime draft. A young innocent, I tagged along after my rough, working class companions as they frequented the bars in Redding on their days off. No one but the supervisor knew of my background, and I relished the anonymity. As a husky youth, the physical conditions were no problem for me.

Upon graduation from Groton in 1943, I was drafted, but was shuttled from one training program to another. By the time these training episodes were over, World War II was over as well. I found myself on a "liberty ship" steaming out of San Francisco Bay and heading for the Philippines. After 28 days at sea, we steamed up the west side of Luzon to Lingayen Gulf. We set up tents on a San Fernando beach where we established a modicum of domesticity. I promised extra pay to one of the Filipino women who took our laundry if she would help me with the vocabulary of the language I heard around me. This was a mix of English, Spanish, and Ilocano, a native language of peasant people around northwestern Luzon. This curiosity about languages would later contribute greatly to my choosing anthropology. To this day, I can settle down with a long list of Canela vocabulary and study it in perfect contentment.

Eventually I was assigned to a company guarding a staging area for nurses and other service women leaving for the States from the Far East. On our days off if three or four of us got together, we could borrow a jeep. One soldier more experienced in the Philippines took us to an Ilocano wedding. I had never seen anything like it, a combination of Christian and native elements. On these drives, we also saw hill tribes on the sides of the road, probably Igarot—real mountain people who were headhunters. I didn't really know at this point what anthropology was, but I was drawn to the other cultures I saw in the Philippines. At Christmas time I had a five-day pass and spent it wandering all over Manila, still covered by war's rubble, just observing.

A Filipino family in Buang befriended a group of us soldiers. The father was a Protestant clergyman with several daughters. We were not allowed to take them out, but we could visit and talk with them. Their brothers were still fighting Japanese in the hills. One time we arrived at their house to find the girls beautifully dressed and made up, unlike their more modest appearance at our usual visits. It turned out they were going out with officers. Only with officers would they be deemed safe, because only officers were armed and could protect them. In spite of these restrictions, I loved the warmth of the Florendo family and also that of the Bustamante family, who were hospitable to some of us soldiers.

The warmth and hospitality of these families were part of their Latin culture, which was evident in every little town with its plaza and Catholic church. My attraction to Latin culture was reinforced the summer after my discharge from the Army, the summer before I would enter Yale as a pre-med student in 1946. Two friends and I decided to drive to Mexico and visit some social contacts we had through our families. When after two months my friends returned to the States, I stayed on to study Spanish, boarding with a Mexican family. My experiences in Mexico validated the feelings for Latin culture I had developed in the Philippines. The emotional expressiveness was a welcome release from the repressions of my Victorian upbringing.

At the end of the summer I headed off to Yale with hundreds of other veterans. Although I followed a pre-med course of study, I had an undergraduate concentration in literature—English, American, Spanish, and French. I loved comparing the cultures through their literatures. I was sensing that by comparing cultures one could gain some perspective on one's own. The summer between my junior and senior years I went to France with The Experiment in International Living. I have often said that the home stay with my French family in Bordeaux foreshadowed the many "home stays" I would have with my Canela family.

Pre-med was a struggle because of the required chemistry and mathematics. I did not do very well, and the only medical school that might have admitted me required that I take some more courses before potential acceptance. So I headed toward home and Stanford University. There I came under pressures to go into the family bank. I felt like an outsider to the world of my family, however. This feeling, and my curiosity about peoples of different classes and cultures, really constituted the temperament of the anthropologist, though I didn't realize it at the time.

Conflicted about career choices, worried about my academics, and bothered by other aspects of my upbringing, I decided to undergo psychoanalysis. Of course, this was anathema to my family, who believed that psychoanalysis was for "demented" people and that the social sciences were for "communists." But fortunately I had my own resources and was financially, if not emotionally, independent of my family. At this point, I hoped that my medical training would lead to psychiatry, so psycho-analysis was part of a career interest as well.

In the 1940s and 1950s, sociological, psychological, and anthropological inter-ests were closely related. This was true of the work of Margaret Mead as well as oth-ers. Before long my analyst told me not to come back to him until I had taken the Stanford course catalog and read the course descriptions under anthropology and eth-nology. There I found courses about culture, psychological anthropology, culture change, and linguistics—the very topics that fascinated me. I knew immediately that I had found my field. I went to the Department of Sociology and Anthropology the very next day. The head of the department admitted me on probation. If I did well, I could enter the master's degree program. After a quarter of A's and B's, I was launched.

All my courses inspired me, but one young professor, George Spindler, thrilled me with a course on the dynamics of culture. I also was able to take a course from Gregory Bateson at the Veteran's Administration in Palo Alto. I became fascinated with culture change, which I really was undergoing myself, leaving one culture and moving into another. Culture change became my interest for life.

I was George Spindler's first master's student in anthropology and was invited to go on for my doctorate. But I needed to get away from home. I wanted to get com-pletely away to somewhere I could be anonymous. Cornell and the University of Pennsylvania accepted me, but I chose the University of Wisconsin at Madison because they would allow me to teach. At the private universities, the teaching assis-tant positions were reserved for those who needed the stipends. I wanted to prove myself as a teacher, and indeed I loved being a teaching assistant at Wisconsin. Ironically my final destination, the Smithsonian Institution, gave me a research rather than a teaching career. Although I have missed the teaching, it is fortunate that my Smithsonian career encouraged the long-term research that I desired. It also allowed me to follow my strengths, which lay in fieldwork. Anthropology fortunately requires field workers and ethnographers as well as theoreticians and writers. Most of the social sciences have room for people of quite different abilities.

When I passed my doctoral preliminary examinations at Wisconsin, it was time to choose the topic of my dissertation. Naturally I gravitated toward South America because of my love of Latin culture and desire to be far from home. Even Central America was too close and possibly susceptible to family influence. Then I wanted to choose a society that had already been studied and do a restudy of it oriented around cultural change with the earlier book as a time base. I did not want it to be a society that had been Christianized, so that eliminated the Andes, the highlands, because the Spanish had been there for four centuries. This meant the lowlands. I went through various bibliographies and found three monographs, which might be restudied, one on a group in Guyana and two on groups in Brazil. I sought out Cliff Evans and Betty Meggers at the Smithsonian, who had been to Guyana, to ask them about the group there. They pointed out that there was no village continuity through the years. As the inhabitants married out of the small villages, the villages often ceased to exist, making a restudy difficult. Also the language of Guyana, then British Guiana, was English, and I really wanted the challenge of studying in a different lan-guage milieu. One group in Brazil, the Bororo, had been studied by Catholic missionaries, but the study of the Canela, by Nimuendajú, seemed more promising. Nimuendajú's monograph had been translated into English, so it was more immediately accessible. As far as tackling Portuguese instead of Spanish in order to work in Brazil, that was fine as long as I was in a Latin culture far from home. Probably many ethnologists are motivated by a desire to get away from their own cultures and find a new identity.

To go to Brazil, I used my contacts from Wisconsin to visit Charles Wagley at Columbia. He agreed to be my mentor and write the necessary letters to contacts in Brazil. Going to the field and getting a job back then was quite different from today. When I returned from the field in 1960, I visited Evans and Meggers again. They had been following my progress and invited me to apply for a new opening at the Smithsonian when my dissertation was accepted. Although I had wanted to teach in a university, I loved Washington already from my visits there as a soldier and was ready for an Eastern environment.

The search for my life's course may have been circuitous, but I feel the delays were worthwhile considering the gratification the Canela experience has provided. Over time I realized that in choosing the Canela, I had chosen a group that had survived exceptionally well. Many other Indian nations in the same Timbira family had become extinct, most of them between 1800 and 1830, and none that has survived preserved its culture as completely as have the Canela. Moreover, my hopes for a long-term study of culture change were fulfilled. The record of Canela survival reached back to the beginning of the 18th century and the accounts of the Portuguese Captain Francisco de Paula Ribeiro. After these historical accounts of military encounters with Canela ancestors and the Canela elders' tales of their activities during 19th century, their story was resumed in the 1930s by Curt Nimuendajú, Brazil's foremost anthropologist of the first half of the 20th century. When I arrived in 1957 to study the Canela, I could draw on the experience of Indian Service agents and the memories of the Canela themselves. Since the memories of the old people in 1957 reached back to the 1890s, my study has covered over 100 years. Finally, I was fortunate in choosing a people I liked and found compatible and in having the help and active participation of the Canela themselves in my work. My long-term partner in research, Raimundo Roberto Kaapêltùk, has shared my interest in analyzing and recording Canela culture, as have many other Canela. I am grateful to these personable and intelligent people for granting me a life's work of extraordinary interest and satisfaction.

ACKNOWLEDGMENTS

George Spindler and the late Louise Spindler helped me find my life's work by inspiring me to go into anthropology. They encouraged Jean and me in the writing of this case study, always countering our many doubts and delays with a hearty "let's get on with it." Their enthusiasm and wise counsel were indispensable.

Betty Meggers and the late Clifford Evans have supported my career at the Smithsonian in many ways. The late Charles Wagley also encouraged and advised me over the years. I have indeed been fortunate in having these distinguished mentors.

Gail Solomon became my research assistant in 1976 and held this position until she retired in 1998, continuing after that as a volunteer. As the archivist for all my data—field notes, photographs, films, artifacts, and recordings—her help has been indispensable. She spearheaded the project of computerizing and digitizing these collections. Barbara Watanabe is now my equally talented assistant. She has had a major role in selecting the photographs and preparing the figures for this book and in creating the Canela Web site. Carl Hansen, Don Hurlbert, and James DiLoreto of the National Museum of Natural History improved the photographs digitally with their usual skill.

The wise perspective of Kenneth Kensinger, formerly of Bennington College, was a valued resource. I am grateful to my colleagues in the Conferences on Lowland South American Indians, which Ken organized and led, for their constructive criticism. This group continues to be a vital forum as the Society for the Anthropology of Lowland South America, or SALSA.

In Brazil, the late Berta Ribeiro of the Museu Nacional made the 1991 and 1993 trips possible through her energetic resolution of the many technical requirements for permission to visit and do fieldwork among the Canela. For the trips between 1994 and 2001, Professor Júlio César Melatti of the Universidade de Brasília made these same arrangements. His friendship and our discussions before and after field experiences have helped immensely.

Over the years, many others in Brazil have extended to me great warmth, kindness, and practical assistance. Darcy Ribeiro helped me obtain my original permission to conduct research among the Canela in 1957. Heloísa Alberto Torres gained the critical support and permissions during the 1960s. Eduardo Galvão was my mentor and advisor in the years 1957 through 1976. Expedito Arnaud was my representative for the extremely difficult and trying field stays during 1978 and 1979.

In Barra do Corda, Olímpio Martins Cruz managed my financial affairs from 1957 through 1963 and became a great friend and advisor. Special thanks must go to Jaldo Pereira Santos. Between 1964 and 1979, Sr. Jaldo was my representative in Barra do Corda, handling all my finances and extending limitless hospitality to me and my family. Sr. Jaldo used his prestige and ingenuity to help me solve countless difficulties. His family's warm hospitality, his competence in handling my finances, and his clearing the way for a safe passage through the politics of the town were an extraordinary asset.

Júlio Alves Tavares of Barra do Corda has handled the complicated logistics of my trips in 1991, 1993, 1994, 1995, 1997, 1999, and 2001. Sr. Júlio has managed my finances and acted as liaison with the Canela. Between my trips he receives and pays for the Canela diaries. He and his wife Rósimar have made my continued research not only possible but enjoyable through their assistance, warm hospitality, and friendship.

For the revision of this book we are particularly indebted to the helpful advice of professors William H. Fisher of William and Mary, Dolores Newton of SUNY at Stony Brook, Janet Chernela of Florida International University, and Nancy Flowers of Hunter College.

The field research in Brazil has been carried out under the auspices of the Museu Paraense Emílio Goeldi, the Museu Nacional, and the Universidade de Brasília. Financial acknowledgments go principally to the Smithsonian Institution for the various years of field and office support, but also in 1964 to the National Science Foundation and the Wenner-Gren Foundation for Anthropological Research and in 1993 to the National Geographic Society. Permission to carry out research among the Canela was granted before 1968 by the Serviço de Proteção aos Índios and afterward by the Fundação Nacional do Índio. For most of the trips, permissions were also obtained from the earlier Conselho Nacional de Pesquisas or the later Conselho Nacional do Desenvolvimento Científico e Tecnológico. I am deeply grateful to these cultural and governmental institutions of Brazil for authorizing my work.

Most important, however, is for me to express my great appreciation to my Canela family. My sister, known as Waterfall in this book, her daughter Single, and her granddaughter Three Streams, have all been so hospitable and friendly that I truly feel at home and comfortable when I am there. I lament the recent death of my brother-in-law, Macaw's Bone, at about 83. His constant good cheer and enthusiasm enlivened my stays with the family.

Finally, I wish to pay homage to my predecessor, Curt Nimuendajú, the great Brazilian anthropologist of the first half of the 20th century. His work, *The Eastern Timbira,* originally inspired me to pick the Canela as the subject of my research and enabled me to carry out my goal of a long-term study of culture change and continuity.

Introduction to the Second Edition

In the original version of this case study, we presented a people who had survived better than most other Brazilian indigenous tribes. We wanted to inform the reader about the positive aspects of Canela history and culture, since so many Amazonian peoples were being threatened by loggers, gold miners, or other intrusions. This relatively positive view of Canela survival grew from the preponderance of early data used in the case study.

Most of the data for the first edition were collected while I was among the Canela for 66 months during the late 1950s through the 1970s. I was absent during the 1980s, but present among them again with Jean for three weeks in 1991. This revision takes advantage of new data collected during six more visits during the last ten years, amounting to eight additional months of field research.

We also wanted to bring the revision abreast of the material presented in the video on the Canela released on June 1, 1999. (The video was originally titled *Mending Ways: The Canela Indians of Brazil*, but was renamed *Intimate Truths of the Canela Tribe* by the Discovery Channel. The video reverts to its original title for distribution by Films for the Humanities and Sciences of Princeton, New Jersey.) The latest data for *Mending Ways* were collected in 1997, when the view of the Canela's present and future could still be presented quite positively. However, data from my month spent among the Canela during July and August 1999, my three months during September through November 2001, and from taped diaries made as recently as January 2003, depict a culture that is going to change dramatically in the near future.

The new preface attempts to answer a question we hear frequently from readers of the case study and viewers of the video: "How did you come to study the Canela?" We eliminated overly detailed sections throughout the book in order to make the material more accessible to students and, we hope, to the general reader. The chapter on the balance between the sexes was eliminated with the main points being integrated into the other chapters. The last part of Chapter 2, the section "The Demise of the Extramarital Sex System" in Chapter 5, and the Epilogue are devoted to bringing the reader up to the present.

A potential criticism of the first edition and my work in general is that of male bias. We have tried to address that by including more female Canela voices and by consulting with female colleagues. There is no way to overcome totally my male point of view, however, especially since anthropology was not as concerned with gender and other biases during the years of my training and early career as it is today. In retrospect, some "affirmative action" to bring in more female research assistants early on would have been wise. Fewer Canela women than men in the early days knew Portuguese or were able to write. And, of course, the women were occupied with their households and children. More recently, however, Relaxed-One has become an excellent research assistant as was Teresinha before her, starting in the 1960s. Relaxed-One was one of my diarists, and with that experience joined my research council in 1979. Her opinions add weight to this revision. In hindsight, I wish I had encouraged more women to take this role.

Not only was it necessary to bring our study up to date in the light of new findings, but we wanted to attempt to answer in the Epilogue the question most readers ask: "What is going to happen to the Canela?" We went to the Canela themselves for answers as well as using our own analysis to consider the Canela's future. It depicts an increasingly rapid rate of culture change, change that we will continue to follow with great interest and, inevitably, mixed emotions.

1/A First Visit
to the Canela[1]

As we coasted down toward the distant landing strip, my new wife, Roma, and her three children—Tara, 11, Hugh, 9, and Philip, 8—showed the tension of awaiting their plunge into a strange culture. I told them to keep smiling no matter what happened, though I knew nothing dangerous could occur. The Canela had learned to get along with outsiders after over 200 years of contact. Besides, I had already lived with them for 35 months and spoke their language well enough, so I was returning to good friends and "relatives."

The thatch houses of the village, Escalvado, began to take on their rectangular shape as we descended. The tiny people pouring out of the houses onto the circular boulevard grew larger, and we could see that some of them were waving to us. Other Canela began jogging down the straight pathways from each house to the round plaza in the center of the village where fireworks were being set off in our honor. As shown in Figure 1.1, from the air the village looked like a great wheel: the plaza its hub, the radial pathways its spokes, the boulevard its rim, and the houses its cogs. (See also Figure 1.2)

The single-motored missionary plane rattled to a stop at the end of the dirt runway and was soon completely surrounded by Canela. They had come to see my new family and to give me a proper homecoming. Once on the ground, I groped for names and terms of address while shaking many hands. Soon my Canela "mother" Tutkhwèy (dove-woman),[2] pulled me over to the shade of a plane's wing and pushed me down to a mat on the ground. She put both hands on my shoulders and, kneeling beside me, her head by mine, cried out words of mourning in a loud yodeling manner. Tears and phlegm dripped onto my shoulder and knees. According to a custom now abandoned by the younger women, she was crying for the loss of a grown daughter, Tsêp-khwèy (bat-woman),[3] as well as for my return. When my old mother had finished, my "sister" Kô-roorok (water-fall) caught my attention and said I looked too thin, that I must have eaten very poorly while away. Her responsibility was to feed me well. Then her three adolescent daughters, my "nieces," started pelting me with questions, asking me how many women I had "seen" while away—besides my wife, of course—and if I had made them "cry."

Ray Roberts Brown, 1970

Figure 1.1 The Canela village of Escalvado from the air in 1970

This lively uncle-niece sex joking made me feel I had fully returned and was once again at home among the Canela, just as having my first *cafezinho* and *queijo com goiabada* (cheese with guava paste) made me feel I had fully arrived in Brazil, my second country. The ribald exchange made me remember when I was learning Canela. My nieces had said salacious words for me to repeat and hurl at Tũm-ti (experienced-very), my elderly aunt, who in turn had assaulted me with equally crude expressions.

When my nieces were finished with their fun, my primary informant and helper, the younger[4] Rãrãk (thunder) approached me with a serious demeanor. After a long handshake and courteous questions about each other's wives, he pointed out that my wife and three children were waiting under the plane's other wing, getting hot and impatient. They had asked for water and were pointing to themselves and to the houses indicating they wished to be out of the heat. Recalled to my family responsibilities, I asked Paul, the missionary[5] pilot, to unlock the vacant missionary house, where we would spend a few days until we could establish our own quarters in the house of whichever Canela family was willing to adopt Roma and her children. Then I would live with Roma in her adoptive house and visit the house of my own "kin."

After lunch we settled into our hammocks for naps, but I was sleepless with the excitement of my return. I had to absorb all the news of the Canela that the Indian Service[6] in Belém had given me. There had been an epidemic of measles among the Canela and the neighboring Apanyekra (Piranha) Indians. Out of a Canela population of 397, only three children were lost. The Service's vaccination program, administered in the village by Service personnel from the town of Barra do Corda, 40 miles to the north, had been effective. The Service agent, Sr. Sebastião Pereira, had helped immensely. In contrast, among the 227 far less accessible and still unvaccinated Piranha—a sister tribe to the Canela and only 30 miles away—31 individuals had died, including three adults. During my insomnia, I kept wondering who was lost

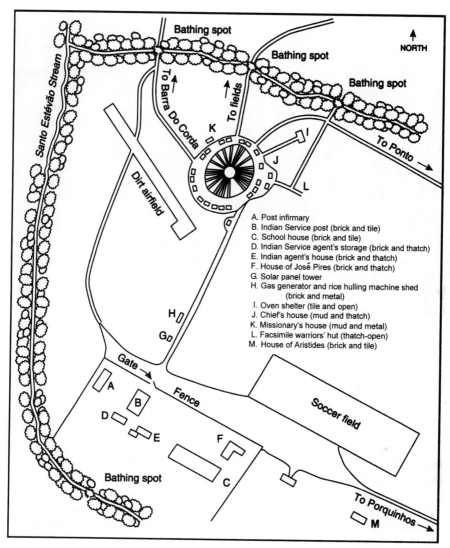

A. Post infirmary
B. Indian Service post (brick and tile)
C. School house (brick and tile)
D. Indian Service agent's storage (brick and thatch)
E. Indian agent's house (brick and thatch)
F. House of José Pires (brick and thatch)
G. Solar panel tower
H. Gas generator and rice hulling machine shed
   (brick and metal)
I. Oven shelter (tile and open)
J. Chief's house (mud and thatch)
K. Missionary's house (mud and metal)
L. Facsimile warriors' hut (thatch-open)
M. House of Aristides (brick and tile)

Figure 1.2 Escalvado village and Indian Service post buildings, 1975

among "my" two tribes. After spending 29 months with the Canela and six months with the Piranha during the 1950s and 1960s, I knew most tribal members.

I gave up trying to nap and listened to the familiar sounds of women pounding rice in wooden mortars, children crying until quieted with a breast, and chickens clucking near the wall of the missionary house. Roma and the children slept on, weary from the trip. I was glad, as plenty of culture shock awaited them.

At about 4:00 in the afternoon, I roused myself to the sounds of distant shouts and the pounding of feet drifting over the mud walls and through the palm-thatched roof of the missionary house. A log race was approaching. I climbed out of my hammock, put on my sneakers, and rushed over to Roma and the children, urging them to get up. The log race would be a joyous introduction to Canela life. (See Figure 1.3.)

Figure 1.3 A Canela relay log race. The runner will turn and shift the log to the shoulder of a teammate.

© Myles Crocker, 2001

Out on the boulevard, we stood watching a crowd of at least 80 Canela men approaching along the sandy road from Barra do Corda. Two logs rode smoothly above a sea of brown and red shining bodies, the farther log slowly moving up to a position abreast of the leading one. These tree trunk sections sometimes weighed over 275 pounds. Pãn-hi (macaw's bone) was chanting to urge his leading team on, and Chief Jaguar's Coat was shouting at his team to try harder and carry their log past the other team and to the village boulevard first. The repeated blasts of several horns rose over the shouting of the runners and onlookers. As the men came closer, we could see that about every 25 yards a runner with a log on his left shoulder turned to pass the log onto the left shoulder of a racer just behind. Young women ran alongside the mass of jogging men, offering certain men, their lovers, water from small gourds.

As the teams approached the boulevard, the excitement and cheering intensified, and crowds of onlookers swirled around the mass of runners, making way as they advanced. "They don't even know we're here," shouted Roma in my ear as I was trying to look over the mass of bodies to see which log was dropped first. But the outcome really didn't matter, because the Canela were racing for the fun of the sport. I explained to the children that the redness of the racers' bodies was urucu paint put on them by their wives and sisters, and the horns they blew were ordinary cows' horns, smoothed by stones or metal files, with wooden mouthpieces.

With the race over, the crowd dispersed into the houses and the racers went down to the swimming holes to bathe. As we watched from the shade of a house, we could see old men walking slowly down the pathways from their houses to the plaza in the pleasant warmth of the late afternoon. When they were seated in the center, the village crier sang from the edge of the circle in my direction, instructing me to appear before the assembled Council of Elders. Then my naming uncle, Krôô-tô (boar-sticky) appeared and said he would escort me to the Council of Elders, as in times past, but reminded me that I needed a present to give them. So we went back to the missionary house, where Sticky Boar courteously motioned my family to sit on racing logs placed against its front wall, while I went inside to unpack a machete. Although Uncle Sticky Boar could speak to my wife and children only in backland Portuguese, his gentle manner was reassuring. He was the one of my three diary writers whose writings were often poetic.

Sticky Boar walked just ahead of me up the pathway toward the plaza, carrying a ceremonial lance and chanting loudly. He was playing the role of a returning warrior, declaring what he had done and seen while away. The Elder, Tep-yêt (fish-hanging), met Sticky Boar just before the entrance to the plaza, stopping his progress. Then Sticky Boar thrust the point of his ceremonial lance into the ground and, pounding his foot in the sand, screeched at Hanging Fish at the top of his voice. All movement and talking in the plaza ceased. Everyone focused on the returning hero, who was swearing he would always defend his tribe with his life when the tribe was attacked. After Sticky Boar was through expressing his fealty, Hanging Fish stepped toward me, so I gave him the machete. As my naming uncle, Sticky Boar was performing this traditional act in my place. I was really the returning warrior, but my screeching ability was not up to the role. Through Sticky Boar's act I had just been accepted for presentation to the Elders, and they would now interrogate me about my exploits among other "tribes."

Seated in the plaza facing me, Chief Jaguar's Coat asked how things were in the land of my relatives and if my country was at peace with Russia. Of course, he asked about my new wife and what I had brought the tribe. Did I have money to buy cattle for the festival? I knew he had to press me when before the Council, but that later, matters could be settled quietly in his house.

Nevertheless, I worried about the anthropologist's warning in Belém about the Canela's growing awareness of city prices and their persistent "begging" in the state capitals throughout most of Brazil. They were used to traveling free in small groups to Recife, Salvador, Rio de Janeiro, and other large cities. Once there, they would try to obtain goods for their people, such as shotguns, cloth, beads, axes, and machetes. Often the Brazilian Air Force would fly them back to Barra do Corda to get them out of the hair of regional Indian Service personnel. The Canela would beg from me as well; their traditional pride would make them reluctant to be taken advantage of by me or anyone else.

One of the young men listening on the edge of the circle of Elders, Krôô-pey (pig-good), 32, asked whether it was true that my relatives had been walking on the moon. He said he had heard this while in São Paulo and had seen it in a movie there. I answered that this was true and that Americans had built fireworks so powerful and big that they had shot one to the moon with three Americans inside. The Americans had landed on the moon and even walked around on its face. This story angered the old shaman I?hô-tsen (its-leaves likes), who chided me for not having remembered what he had taught me years ago: that Sun and Moon were both male persons and that they had walked in the savannahs on the face of the earth before the Canela and the *civilizado* had been made. Rather than draw further fire from the Elders, I admitted Likes Leaves was right and that what I had said about my "relatives" was merely a bad rumor that had amused me.

After the council meeting, I walked down the radial pathway to my wife and children to find them talking haltingly in Portuguese with Sr. Sebastião, the Service post's new agent. He was pointing out various features of the village, such as the well for drinking water the missionaries had drilled and the new barbed wire fence they had provided to keep the Service cattle and the Canela hogs out of the village. He also pointed to the new outhouses behind most Canela houses that the Service official in Barra do Corda had required. He said that while the fence kept the village largely clean of animal droppings, and the Canela liked this, they seldom used the outhouses. They found the savannahs cleaner and less smelly. Sr. Sebastião, an educated native of Barra do Corda, had come to invite us to dinner at the post, so I thanked him in my most courteous Portuguese and said we would be delighted to enjoy his company and to meet his wife.

My family returned to the missionary house, where I suggested they dress more warmly for the evening. In such grassy savannahs—composed of low, single-standing trees and bushes—situated 900 feet above sea level near the equator, the temperature descends into the high 50s in the July evenings. I said we would walk around the village boulevard from the missionary house to my "sister's" house, where she had invited us to appear after the Council meeting. Then, we would go to the Service's post house for dinner and return to the village by way of the house of the wife of Chief Jaguar's Coat. There we had to report in and pay our respects to the chief, since he was responsible for all outsiders spending a night in his village. This visit was a mere formality, because Chief Jaguar's Coat and I had known each other for so many years. We also were related to each other as Informal Friends who, in Canela tradition, always joke when they meet. Finally, we would return to the missionary house to unpack and sleep.

As we walked around the boulevard, I saw my primary Canela sister, Waterfall, sitting in front of her house with her sisters, her female parallel cousins, and almost all of their unmarried children. Several men sat next to or in back of their wives. This formidable array of people made up most of my extended matrilateral Canela kin. Waterfall, 31, was the one who had volunteered to adopt me on my second day among the Canela in 1957. She managed this extended household, while her husband, Macaw's Bone, merely cooperated.

Waterfall stood and welcomed us in a gentle and dignified tone. First, she pointed to the young babies and children who had been born in my absence, mentioning their names. Then I presented my wife and her three children. Waterfall, speaking to my wife and children as if they could understand, slowly and carefully introduced her sisters, their children, and their husbands. I whispered to Roma and her children to remain standing and to bear with the recital patiently.

Finally, Waterfall, with a graceful gesture of her hand, invited us to sit down on three mats laid out for us. Tara and Hugh abruptly dashed for the first mat, Philip took the second one, while Roma and I ambled over to the third. Almost immediately I noticed sounds of amusement and guessed what was provoking the fun-loving Canela. Tara and Hugh, though opposite-sex siblings, were sitting next to each other on the same mat, an incestuous act for the Canela. Only couples in a sexual relationship can do this. How well I remembered classificatory wives tempting me in fun to sit with them and eat on the same mat, and once when I had mustered enough courage to do so playfully, the woman had dashed away to the amusement of everyone present. So, I asked Hugh if he was married to Tara. When he answered with a wondering "no," I warned that the Canela must think he was married to her because they were sitting on the same mat. Hugh jumped up so quickly that the crowd roared with laughter, and the ice of formality was broken. Waterfall and her sisters came forward and shook hands with my American family and took them around separately to greet the rest of my Canela kin. Between the American and Canela children, curiosity and giggles overcame their shyness.

I told Waterfall that I would distribute the expected presents to our kin on some dark night (to avoid the jealousy of others) once my wife and children were settled in a Canela family. Then we said good night and started walking out of the village toward the Service post. The lights of the post buildings, from a gasoline generator, showed us the way in the dark. Electricity was also used to run the post's radio for communication with the Service personnel in Barra do Corda and São Luis. On the left was a large straw house built in the style of the interior backlands, which served to house backland merchants spending the night in the area. The Service prohibits outsiders, except anthropologists and missionaries, from spending nights in the village for fear such casual visits would lead to cohabitation and consequent adulteration of Indian genes. While the Canela disapprove of such contacts with outsiders, a few Canela women occasionally made some money in this manner.

Sr. Sebastião met us at the gate of the post's wire fence enclosure. He led us past the post building of whitewashed brick with a red-tiled roof to his own house of mud and wattle with a palm-straw roof. His wife, Dona Fátima, greeted us and introduced a small child and a baby. Sr. Sebastião seated us at a long table, with himself at the head, and passed us separate bowls of chicken, beef, and pork stews from which to serve ourselves. We ate off enameled metal plates. His family's generosity honored us greatly. "But where is Dona Fátima seated?" Roma asked me in English when Sr. Sebastião had gone to arrange something. I replied that in the backlands, the women do not eat with the men, though city women are treated as men.

On the way back to the village, I described for Roma and the children some of the cultural differences between Barra do Corda and the backlands. Some of the poorer backlanders lived in conditions no better than the Indians, in houses of mud and thatch with packed earth floors. The better-off ranchers lived more substantially, but because the land was marginal for cattle, most ranches and herds were small. But no matter how poor, the backlanders considered themselves vastly superior in culture to the Indians.

Once in the village, we approached the large mud-and-wattle house of the wife of Chief Jaguar's Coat, which was set back from the circle of houses for prominence. His wife, Pôôhù-ʔkhwèy (corn-woman), 50, beckoned us to enter and be seated on square hide-covered stools and offered us coffee and tinned cookies. We accepted to please her but hoped to drink as little as possible considering the hour.

Jaguar's Coat asked me if "our wife," meaning Roma, and "our children"—Tara, Hugh, and Philip—would consent to have haircuts in the tribal style. For a moment I was taken aback, because when he had said "our wife" on previous trips, he had meant his wife who was also my "wife." After the ceremony that had made us Informal Friends, I had the "right to" his wife, which in earlier times meant sexual rights. Though Jaguar's Coat was now referring to Roma as his and my wife, I knew he did not intend to take advantage of his people's ancient practice. The custom had almost died out, and Roma was an outsider. Roma and the children bravely agreed to the tribal haircuts, which would leave them with horseshoe-shaped pathways around the crowns of their heads, creating a bowl-shaped cut in the front and sides with the rear left uncut.

I asked Jaguar's Coat if he thought Corn Woman's mother and father would like to adopt and take in our wife and our children. I explained how well old Katsêê-khwèy (star-woman) and Kô-häm (water-standing) would care for them. Jaguar's Coat and I then wouldn't have to change terms of address for our wives, because if Roma were Corn Woman's "sister," these two women would be doubly "our wives," both as sisters-in-law and as wives of Informal Friends. The idea amused him, so he talked to our wife about it (this time meaning Corn Woman), and she went over to her mother's house to see if they would like the arrangement.

Jaguar's Coat asked me if our wife (meaning Roma) and I would like to get married Canela style. Going through such a ceremony would mean I would have to pay for an all-day festival during which the tribe would eat at my expense. This was typical Canela: get what is possible from the outsider, but do it kindly and courteously. Rather than say no—nothing should be direct with the Canela—I suggested that we talk about it later.

Suddenly Corn Woman grabbed my ear from behind, twisting my neck, and almost yanked me off the stool. "Don't you ever 'look at' other women than Roma," she scolded, "or I will pull your whole ear off." Now I knew, painfully, that Roma and her children had just been adopted and accepted into Star Woman's family line and that I would soon be living in an extension to her house with my American family. ("Look at" in Canela is a euphemism for having sex.)

We said goodnight and strolled toward the plaza where enthusiastic dancing was going on. About 40 women had formed a line across the lower side of the plaza and were all facing a man who was singing vigorously and marking the rhythm with a gourd rattle. These social dances used to take place three times a day, most days of the year, but now occur less frequently. Passing behind the dance line, where mothers with babies and children were sitting in the sand, we wandered slowly down the radial pathway of the missionary house, noticing the activities of the village. Two files of men were progressing around the boulevard in opposite directions, singing low and dancing undemonstratively. Most middle-aged and older people were in their houses; only younger people were still moving around outside.

In the missionary house, my wife and children took to their hammocks quickly, exhausted from the long day. But I still had work to do. I took out my small, hand-held Sony recorder and began to describe on my daily journal cassette the important events of the day, starting with the beginning of the air trip from Belém.

In the plaza the dancing was over, but a group of young women and men were still singing in the circular street in front of the houses. They walked slowly and chanted in long-held chords in a minor key—the Canela late evening songs. The soulful, relaxing, slow-changing chants of this hour always seemed appropriate to the end of the day.

I looked over at Tara, Hugh, and Philip. Fast asleep in their hammocks, they were already adapting to their new world. The calm strains of music moved farther away and then closer again as the singers strolled around the circular village street. The sound soon lulled me to sleep also.

NOTES

1. Although the year is 1969, some details from later visits have been included. For the archeology of circular villages of the region, see Wüst and Barrreto (1999) and Heckenberger (1996).

2. Personal names used in this book are real Canela names. However, to protect the privacy of individuals, the names have been switched. If qualified researchers need to follow the activities of specific individuals among my other publications, they may write me for a key to the names. In the video *Mending Ways,* names have not been changed, except Pedro's.

3. When I translate names and expressions from Canela to English, I use the same word order in the translation as in the original Canela expression. I also keep the same number of word units in the translation as in the Canela by using spaces, hyphens, and dashes appropriately. While this procedure may reverse the word order or make less sense in English, it helps the reader identify the meaning of each Canela term.

4. Canela males pass their names on to a nephew (usually a sister's son), so, in this case, the nephew is called the *younger* Thunder, and his uncle is called the *older* Thunder.

5. Summer Institute of Linguistics missionaries, also known as Wycliffe Bible Translators, worked among the Canela from 1968 into 1990, when they left, having translated the entire New Testament and some Old Testament stories into Canela (Popjes, 1990).

6. For simplicity, I use the expression "Indian Service" for the federal service that takes care of the Indians of Brazil. Between 1910 and 1968, the Serviço de Proteção aos Índios (SPI) performed this service, while from 1968 to the present time the Fundação Nacional do Índio (FUNAI) has performed it.

2/The Historical Context

Before we outline the historical events from the days of the Portuguese contacts with the Canela ancestors up to the present day, we should listen to the Canela's own version of an important part of their history. Their account of their subordination to the surrounding Brazilian society is embodied in the myth of Awkhêê.

According to the version narrated to me by Hanging Fish, Awkhêê called together the Canela Elders and the *civilizados*[1] to have them choose between the bow and arrow and the shotgun:

[W]hen the Indian saw the shotgun, the Devil, fully loaded, he thought that the shotgun was hostile and threatening. "It has its mouth open. It has a mouth. I'm afraid."

Awkhêê ordered the Christian to pick up the shotgun and fire it to show the Indian. The Christian picked up the shotgun and fired, and the Indian fell to the ground. He felt his back and the pain spread all over his body. The lead balls had not hit him; it was just the blast from the explosion which hurt him. The magical powers of the shotgun had penetrated the Indian's body. The stupid Indian had felt pain without having been shot. The Christian had shot without aiming and the Indian had fallen to the ground in pain.

When the Indian had recovered from the pain, he said: "We don't need this shotgun. It is wild; it has powers that we don't need." So Awkhêê ordered the Christian to pick up the bow and arrow, but the Christian did not know how to shoot the arrow from the bow. Awkhêê ordered the Indian to pick up the bow and arrow and shoot it. The Indian did so and shot off the arrow, which traveled through the air noiselessly. The Indian liked the bow and the arrow and spoke of receiving them. It was exactly this that Awkhêê did not like, and he became really angry with the Indian. Right then and there he ordered the Christian to take the shotgun and the Indian to take the bow and arrow.

Awkhêê spoke in the Indian language. "It is because of this that you are going away and will roam aimlessly through the world. You will travel around in the forests and dry brush, scratching and tearing your bodies, and doing little of significance. You will live any which way, any way you can, traveling throughout this world. Leave now! I'm very angry with you."

The great-grandfathers came walking here in the forests, doing pointless things, just like animals, traveling without direction. It seems it was at this time that the Indians came here, eating rotten wood.

This was the story that the old men always told there in the middle of the plaza. . . . I think the story goes like this and I never heard it told differently. Others told it the way I just finished telling it. So, it is only like this, the story of Awkhêê.[2]

This myth, believed also by other Northern Gê-speaking peoples, embodies the Canela version of the events that put them in a position subservient to the *civilizados*, now referred to as "whites." For the Canela, the myth explains their low position in Brazilian society. It also justifies their entitlement to handouts from the whites.

Nothing in my account can capture quite so well the Canela's understanding of their situation as they express it in this myth. Nevertheless, I will trace, from a Western point of view, the major steps in the Canela's pacification and their accommodation to Brazilian society.

PACIFICATION AND ADAPTATION

Timbira Nations: The Canela's Ancestors

Before I begin the historical narrative,[3] I need to establish just who are the Canela of today.[4] Around 1700, peoples like the Canela lived in relatively self-sufficient and isolated villages of 1,000 to 2,000 in population, between the Parnaíba and Tocantins rivers or not far beyond. Although no one knows exactly how many tribes of the Canela type existed, due to the scarcity of historical chronicles of the period, there were probably between 30 and 50. Portuguese settlers called these tribes the Timbira, but the Indians called themselves the Mëhĩ́.[5] By 1820, the Brazilian pioneer front had moved completely through the region of the Timbira, from east to west, having decimated most of them. By 1860, Brazilian quasi-military bands had totally pacified[6] these peoples. At that time they numbered about a dozen tribes, but now only seven survive as significant groups.[7] While some of the tribes live in several villages, the Canela occupy only one village, which has grown from probably less than 100 during the 1820s to more than 1,300 in 2001.

The Timbira tribes[8] speak a language in the language family called Gê, which is found only in Brazil and is very distantly related to Carib.[9] Today, the tribes that speak this language are divided into the Southern Gê (Kaingang and Xokleng),[10] the Central Gê (Shavante and Sherente),[11] and the Northern Gê (principally Kayapó[12] and Timbira). The Canela understand the Kayapó language only well enough to catch occasional meaning from a Kayapó debate in the plaza. They cannot understand Shavante or Xokleng at all, though linguists point out that these peoples' variations of words like fish (*tep*), rain (*ta*), meat (*hĩ́*), and mother (*nàà*) come from the same roots or cognates.[13]

Before pacification, Timbira tribes who were enemies fought each other during the dry months of June through August. Friendly Timbira tribes formed alliances and traded minimally.[14] These allies could not rely on each other at the time of enemy attacks, however, because raids were so sudden and because the nations lived too far apart to come to each other's aid in time.[15]

During a sneak attack on a village at dawn, the attackers would kill as many men, women, and children as possible with hardwood clubs or arrows. They used considerable shamanistic powers to overcome the enemy, directing arrows into victims' eyes and using magical clubs. When the heat of battle was over, the tendency was to leave the survivors alone, especially the women and children. However, those who could escape, or those who were momentarily not in the village, tried to run away and hide in the stream thickets in small, dispersed groups until the enemy had gone.

Bodies were rarely mutilated and women and children were not usually taken back to the attackers' village as spoils of war. These raids were not to take territory, stands of trees, women, or quarries of flint and chalk, but rather to avenge earlier attacks or just to keep the enemy numbers down. Youths, to show their prowess or to gain warrior's status and potential future leadership of the nation, went on revenge raids with their uncles to show their mettle. Raids of this sort spawned feuds. Tribal members tended to stick together in significant numbers for defense, because small foraging groups could be annihilated before help could reach them.[16]

The Timbira nations lived largely in the "closed" savannahs, grasslands with widely spaced low trees and shrubs, and their way of life was well adapted to this environment.[17] Their military organization allowed them to move swiftly at a moment's notice. They relied mostly on hunting and gathering, but they carried out some agriculture in the forests along the streams by clearing the brush and trees with stone axes and fire. The savannahs were too sandy to be cultivated. The Timbira were seminomadic, moving their villages every several years to locations that were better for foraging and limited agriculture. They had gourds instead of ceramic pots, which would have been too heavy and breakable to transport easily, and their cane arrows had only sharpened points, not arrowheads. Thus, they have left no potsherds or projectile points to aid archeological studies.[18]

Just north of Barra do Corda and Grajau, the "closed" savannahs end and the forests begin. In these dry forests[19] lived a type of Indian people who spoke a totally different language, Tupi. The Tupian Guajajara practiced more extensive agriculture, lived in smaller, relatively immobile communities, and were far less athletic and warlike. The current Guajajara even look different from the Canela, being shorter, stockier, and more Asian (Mongoloid). Timbira tribes traded occasionally with Tupian tribes, but rarely deigned to fight them. Instead of the seasonal skirmishes between the same hostile Timbira tribes each year, the warfare between Timbira and Tupian tribes was rare but drastic. The Guajajara remind the Canela of Asians. An American missionary woman of Japanese descent living in Barra do Corda during the late 1950s was said by the Canela to be very much like the Guajajara. The citizens of Barra do Corda distinguish the Canela from the Guajajara by the former's greater height, thinner and more delicate build, and less Asian appearance.[20]

The Canela currently believe they are descended from at least five different Timbira tribes. They still celebrate this belief in their summer-long festival, called the Facsimile Warriors (Pep-kahàk: warriors—as-if-they-were). In one act of this festival, male descendants of the principal tribe, the Mõl-tũm-re (going-along, enduring people), sit in the center of the plaza. The Mõl-tũm-re are Nimuendajú's Ramkokamekra.[21] The men of the tribes that joined the Ramkokamekra sit at the edges of the plaza in the geographical directions from which they are believed to have come. These are the descendants of the Mud (Karë?katêyê), Boar (Krôô-re-khãm-më-?khra-re), Piranha (Apanyekra), and Fox (Tsoo-khãm-më-?khra) peoples. The Canela have no name for the totality of the remnants of the former nations that make up their current tribe. Consequently, they accept "Canela," which was applied to them[22] by local Brazilian authorities early in the 19th century, as their tribal name.

However, a German nongovernmental organization[23] used the name Ramkokamekra with the Canela, so during the 1990s many Canela have revived this name.

Nobody claims to know the origin of the name Canela. Nimuendajú suggests that it comes from the earlier name of a hill, Serra da Canella (hill of the cinnamon trees), located in the greater Canela region, but in Piranha lands. Nimuendajú points out[24] that the early chronicler of the Canela, Captain Ribeiro, used the expression *"Canellas finas"* (shinbones fine: calves thin) to describe them, but that Ribeiro himself did not know the origin of this expression. My guess is that Brazilian authorities of the times, who were more used to the Guajajara, contrasted the Guajajara with the Canela by referring to the Canela's longer and thinner calves. While *canela* means either cinnamon or the calf/shinbone of a person's leg in local Portuguese, "calf" as the original name makes more sense to me than "cinnamon," given the context of the Guajajara-Canela contrast in body type.

Pioneers Decimate the Timbira Nations

To gain an impression of the ancestors of the Canela before pacification, we can turn to the accounts of Captain Ribeiro,[25] the commander of a Brazilian military post, Principe Regente, maintained at the confluence of the Alpercatas and Itapicuru rivers. A road had been pushed from Caxias around 1760 to maintain this post and protect farms and cattle ranches along the two rivers. Within several years this post had to be abandoned due to the ferocity and effectiveness of Indian attacks. Over 50 years later, Ribeiro wrote of Indian bravery in these attacks:

> In 1807 we . . . observed the audacity of a Forest [Fox] Timbira . . . who dashed from some ambush into the midst of over a hundred of our people employed with sundry tasks at the founding of the Arroyal do Principe Regente; he killed one man, attacked several others and dexterously withdrew before he could be made to suffer any injury. . . . Man to man, there seem to be few men able to vie with them in point of bravery. Even the women are not inferior in robustness and we have seen one such brought in as a captive who tried to escape by dragging along her guard under her arm and would have succeeded if he had not received aid. She was of goodly stature and so well built that our soldiers dubbed her "the big sorrel mare."[26]

Ribeiro's accounts are of skirmishes and warfare that took place while the Timbira tribes were being displaced. Brazilian settlement of the region came mostly from the state of Bahia in the southeast, but also from São Luis in the north, the capital of the state of Maranhão. These two advances of settlers came together between Caxias and Pastos Bons (See Figure 2.1). The pastoral front from the southeast was composed of cattle ranchers with cowhands to support them, who were often bandits enforcing the head rancher's power. The agricultural front from the north consisted of farming families, coming up the Itapicuru River.[27] These loosely organized peoples settled the area during the last decade of the 18th century and the first decade of the 19th century. They completed a thinly settled band of occupation across the flattest part of the area by 1810, from Pastos Bons through Riachão to Carolina, following the Parnaíba and Balsas rivers all the way to the Tocantins River. Their population pressure pushed one Timbira tribe of 3,000 to 5,000 people, the Krahô, completely from their ancestral position, just southwest of the Canela, all the way to

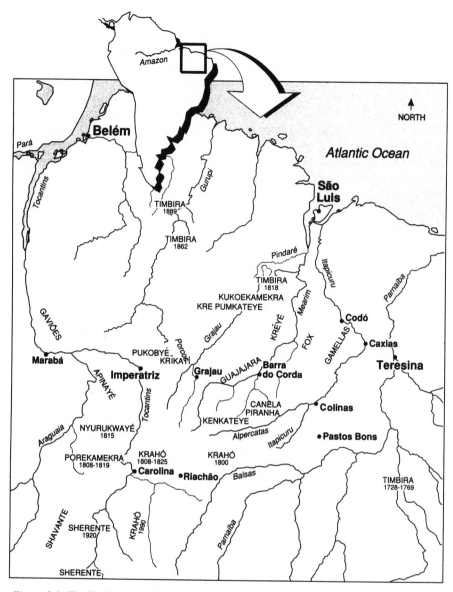

Figure 2.1 The Timbira and their neighbors, past and present

the Tocantins and then south along the river. The pioneer thrust pushed Timbira tribes
such as the Fox, Mud, Boar, Canela, Piranha, Pukobyé, and Krĩkatí into the northern
parts of their ancestral territories and into the protection of hills and forests, dimin-
ishing the lands they controlled by 70 to 90 percent.

In the typical pattern of settlement, family farmers or cattle ranchers moved west
to find and occupy new lands. Indians, objecting to such intrusions into their ancestral lands, attacked randomly, stole cattle, and killed individual settlers, but seldom
wiped out whole settlements. Settlers with such losses called on the populations of
the more established communities to the east to organize posses to kill or capture as

many Indians as possible. These posses (*bandeiras*)[28] took months to assemble and were seldom well organized. Thus, the pacification of the Timbira Indians took half a century. Smallpox, which spread to all the Timbira nations during 1816 and 1817, was a great agent of the Indian demise, as it was throughout most of the Western hemisphere.

When the settlers' communities were weak, their leaders signed treaties of peace with the most threatening Indian nations, but when these communities became stronger, or had a military post in their vicinity to assure their safety, they forgot the peace treaties and killed Indians when they could. When punitive expeditions failed, they sometimes turned instead to the destruction of already peaceful Indians. They even enticed Indians out of protected areas with promises of fair treatment in order to kill or enslave them. An important motive for fighting Indians was to capture them and sell them into slavery in the coastal cities of São Luis or Belém. Slavery was against the law of the times, but in 1808 a royal law had been enacted allowing the capture and enslavement of the Botocudo Indians, because they supposedly ate human flesh. The Timbira were held to be like the Botocudo, so they could be enslaved also. The treacherous nature of promises offered by the settlers became well known among all the Indian nations of the region during the decade of the 1810s and poisoned relations between the two groups.

North Americans recognize this treatment of Indians as all too familiar. American settlers were at least as cruel, if not crueler, to North American Indians during the 19th century. The literature on this topic is voluminous, and the record of broken treaties and genocide in North America is well documented. The parallels between Brazilian and North American treatment of Indians are obvious.

Timbira tribes of this period still fought each other, with the consequence that the losers sometimes became so weak that they surrendered voluntarily to military posts of the settlers for protection from their Indian enemies. The Fox people defeated the Ramkokamekra-Canela so badly in 1814 that these Canela surrendered the same year to the Brazilian *bandeira* based at Pastos Bons, for safety. They agreed in a treaty that they would never fight settlers again, but that they would help the Brazilians fight other Indian groups. This treaty constituted the actual pacification of the Canela. Early in 1815, the Canela helped the settlers raid a group of Fox people then at Buritizinho.

Although pacification of the Canela—their surrender and treaty with the Brazilians—had been achieved, relations between the Canela and the settlers were far from peaceful. Later in 1815, settlers lured the Canela to Caxias, ostensibly to participate in additional raids against the Fox people, but really to infect the Canela with smallpox, which had broken out in the town.[29] The Canela were left to shift for themselves around this community instead of being organized by its authorities, who were to have taken care of their economic needs. Left on their own, the hungry Canela broke into small groups and inflicted almost more damage on the settlers through theft than they had earlier through warfare. Subsequently, men who had stolen cattle and women who had pulled up manioc and other vegetables from the settlers' fields were flogged. Nursing mothers were chained apart from their babies. When Chief Têmpê and other male Canela remonstrated, the chief was flogged and several others were killed. They resolved to escape regardless of the treaty and marched off to the southwest toward the northernmost part of their homelands just south of Barra do Corda, between the Porcos and Ourives streams. A settlers' posse caught up with them 50 miles from Caxias and shot down a number of them, while smallpox killed many more.

From that time on, the Canela have remained in this northwestern part of their ancestral lands, which formerly had extended south beyond the middle Alpercatas to the Itapicuru and east to Picos. The Canela remained hidden in an inconspicuous valley of the Alpercatas hills for some time, completely away from settlers' communities (see Figure 2.2).

Movement toward Eventual Peace

Old Canela men in the late 1950s told a pitiful tale about the years when their ancestors hid from the settlers, probably from the mid-1810s to the mid-1820s. Individual Canela had to sneak daily from a valley in the Alpercatas hills to fetch water from a spring. Eventually they were seen from a distance by settlers, who reported the presence of dangerous wild savages to the military. One day, the story goes, an army major with troops sent from São Luis to tame the Indians approached the area of the hidden valley, and a group of Canela scouts fired on them with shotguns from a hill.

Forewarned by their scouts, the Canela armed themselves and left the village to set up a defensive position. One young warrior, however, whom the Elders were considering as a potential chief, said he was tired of spending his life hiding in a mountain valley. He said they should give themselves up and that he would act as the go-between with the soldiers. Thus, the young Hïï-khrô (flesh's-tail) descended alone and unarmed to the troops' encampment. The soldiers prepared to fire, but their commandant ordered them to wait. Flesh's Tail, approaching, said, "Do not kill me," but they could communicate only through hand gestures. They shook hands and embraced.

The commandant asked where the Canela were, and Flesh's Tail pointed to the hills. Since they believed him, they offered him a meal and named him Mesquite. The commandant showed Mesquite the presents brought for his people—machetes, axes, cloth, dried meat—and requested that Mesquite summon his people to come out of the valley, saying that his soldiers would not harm them. Mesquite went back to his people, where their chief, Tëmpê, assembled them. After Mesquite had spoken, Chief Tëmpê supported him and said, "Let's deliver ourselves; they will not kill us."

I vividly remember Antônio Diogo Mïï-khrô (alligator's-tail),[30] surely in his early 80s in 1958, emphasizing with his voice, weakened by age, the fear with which his grandparents descended onto the unprotected savannahs. However, by this time the attitude toward wild Indians was changing, since they were no longer a threat in the area. They were given the presents, and ten cattle were killed for them to eat.

It was hard for me to realize in the late 1950s that it was Alligator's Tail's grandparents, not his remote ancestors, who had walked down from the hills to the dangers of the savannahs, fearing the fate of other Indian peoples. Alligator's Tail heard many such stories from his grandparents, who had experienced these dangers.

Another Canela story told by old Alligator's Tail places his people south of the Alpercatas River in their former lands, already occupied by families of cattle ranchers. This is where the Canela may have gone after they left the protection of their hidden valley. The place was called Nas Pedras (on-the rocks). Ranchers' men often visited the Canela village there for trading and obtaining women in return for pieces of cloth. One rancher asked Chief Tëmpê if he could take away a young Canela

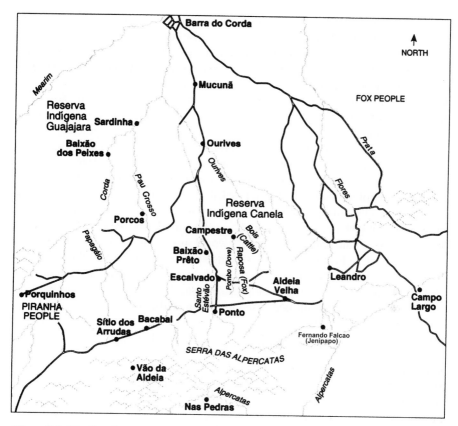

Figure 2.2 The Canela region. Canela lands were demarcated in 1971, and the borders were legalized in 1982.

woman he had seen and liked. Tëmpê allowed this, and the rancher gave a quarter of a cow for her. Many adolescent women were delivered to settlers to appease their desires, and little boys and girls were given to ranchers' families to be raised and educated as house servants. Tëmpê lost much respect among his people because of such dealings, but these were successful ways of placating an overpowering rancher and getting along with the settlers in general.

After some time, a very beautiful and spirited young Canela woman who had been sold to a rancher ran away and returned to her people, followed by her owner. Because of the rough treatment she had suffered, her father became very angry at Chief Tëmpê. Her father declared, "They will take her away again only after they have killed me." This refusal to give a rancher what he had paid for was the cause of a skirmish with the settlers some days later. The Canela Arèykooko threw a bow at the settler Barnabé, who fended it off. Barnabé sliced Arèykooko with his machete so that his guts fell out onto the ground and he soon died. The Canela Manuel Gomes Pep-tsen (war-likes) confronted Barnabé, who begged not to be killed, offering his machete, but another Canela finished him off. For fear of retaliation after this incident, the Canela left Nas Pedras and fled north across the Alpercatas River and the Alpercatas range of hills to the Papagáio area, just west of their present lands.

Another story of Alligator's Tail, probably of the late 1820s or early 1830s, tells of a rancher in the present Porcos area who had earlier taken a young Canela girl as mistress. She had learned Portuguese well in this role. Later, when she was a grown woman, her father visited her. Through him, she was able to help negotiate an agreement between the Canela and the Brazilian authorities of the region. The Canela were to settle near the unoccupied headwaters of the Santo Estévão Stream. There they built a small circular village in the savannahs according to their custom. While the Canela have moved their village to various other locations on the different streams of the region, the Santo Estévão Stream has become their principal location.

The old Alligator's Tail took me to the remains of this first village, which was only about 180 yards across, suggesting low population in the early 1840s. There he told me stories of his ancestors, which I took down roughly in speedwriting. He came to me repeatedly on other occasions, wanting me to record his stories in his language, but I could not give this particular project sufficient priority, nor did I have enough tape or batteries. I did not know then that I would spend most of my research life with the Canela. Before I could give the recording of these incomparable stories a higher priority, Alligator's Tail died. The loss of these stories and the recognition of my misplaced priorities are among my deepest field research regrets. Get first what may disappear, and leave the rest for later, I tell myself in hindsight.

A Myth Is Created to Justify Inferior Status

It is at this period that the myth of Awkhêê, as narrated at the beginning of this chapter, evolved. This primary culture hero of the Canela had merged in their imagination with the benevolent emperor of Brazil, Dom Pedro II, who had ascended to the throne in 1840. In 1845, Dom Pedro had issued a decree known as the Regimento das Missões, which regulated relationships between Brazilians and Indians throughout the empire. Indian lands were to be demarcated, warfare against them was forbidden, and they could not be enslaved.[31] Dom Pedro II also ordered that Indian women being used as mistresses by Brazilians be returned to their peoples. We can assume that Dom Pedro II achieved through this decree an almost sacred aura in the minds of a number of Indian peoples, since the myth of Awkhêê/Dom Pedro II is found throughout the region among Gê-speaking peoples.

The message of the myth for the Canela is that the backlander, since he had won the more prestigious shotgun, would become wealthy, but in return, he would have to give the Indian everything the Indian would ever want and need. This myth justifies for the Indian his dependency on the *civilizado,* and it legitimizes the Indian's begging. The Canela's insistence on his right to be taken care of became "traditional" and institutionalized through the myth.

In 1958, I carried out a study of Canela attitudes about specific backlanders of the Canela region. I asked if a certain man of a backland community was good or bad, and why. The Canela individual invariably connected a backlander's "goodness" with how much the backlander had given him or her and "badness" with the lack of such generosity. A Canela's assessment of a backlander had nothing to do with how much the backlander could afford to give. The worst backlanders were those who were poor and kept their stock of supplies for the year to themselves. Rice harvested in May had to be stored and consumed slowly, lasting until the following May; the poor backlander could not afford to buy rice. Thus, a backlander who was reserving rice for his family's consumption during the entire year was seen by the Canela as stingy. The good backlander gave the Canela rice whenever requested, but the backlander who refused to give, when rice was actually in his storage room, was thought to be evil and without compassion.

Learning Their Place among the *Civilizados*

Once the Canela had been allowed lands along the Santo Estévão Stream (a small part of their ancestral territory), and once they had accepted such a limitation, they faced an entirely new world. They had become recognized as a social entity in the world of the backland *civilizados,* though placed on the bottom rung of the social ladder as *índios* or *caboclos.* Backland merchants visited them periodically for trading, and Canela families were accepted in the traders' settlements and family houses.

During the rest of the 19th century, Canela chiefs tried with various degrees of success to get along with the Brazilian communities. There were periods of surprising acceptance of the Canela by the backlanders and townspeople. At other times renewed cattle theft by the Canela and land greed by the backlanders threatened relations. During the 1850s the prominent Arruda ranching family migrated from the east into the Canela area. The Arrudas took over the higher lands in a region known today as the Sítio, which has the most fertile soils of the area. The chief of the time, Foot's Wound, ordered his men to catch some of the cattle of the new arrivals. This planted the seed for later hostilities with the Arrudas.

By the end of the 1870s, the Canela were surrounded on all sides, whether by backlanders or by urban Brazilians. Barra do Corda, which lay about 40 miles to the north of the newly assigned Canela area on the Santo Estévão, had officially become a town (*vila*). During the late 1850s, ranchers had followed the Arrudas, and settled 20 miles southwest of the Canela's new central area. Twenty-five miles to the east, farmers had moved into the region of Leandro. For a half-century farmers and ranchers had lined both sides of the Alpercatas River, which ran 15 miles south of the new Canela base on the Santo Estévão at its nearest point.

The Canela have controlled and continue to control the central area between these streams. The area provides the Canela with about 500 square miles of closed savannahs and streams lined by gallery forests. This amount of land was insufficient for the Canela to support themselves by hunting and gathering, but especially deficient for gathering fruits, roots, and seeds in their aboriginal manner.[32] They had to turn to slash-and-burn agriculture,[33] which had sustained less than 25 percent of their former way of life. Since nothing could be planted in the sandy savannahs and since the gallery forest soils could support only one crop a year, they had to cut new fields out of the stream-side forests each year.[34] Eventually, the new fields would be so far from the village that it made sense to move the village to the fields. For this reason they moved their village up and down the Santo Estévão and to the other streams in their area, returning to the same place about 20 years later, when the gallery forests had grown tall enough to provide sufficiently fertile soils.

Since the settlers had to live on more sizable streams, they did not continue to move closer to the Canela. This distance gave the Canela considerable space in which to live in relative peace and to develop a post-pacification way of life. While one or two settlers' families may have lived within five miles of the Canela village, varying with the decade, the nearest backland communities were never closer than 15 miles.

Toward the end of the 19th century, the Canela enjoyed a period of relative prosperity under the co-chiefs Major Delfino and Colonel Tomasinho, as they were called. Colonel Tomasinho made clay pipes and mended backlanders' cauldrons and shotguns for a price. He even had a forge in which he soldered silver coins onto iron implements to repair them for Canela and backlander customers. Alligator's Tail and I found fragments of old pipes in the remains of his mud-and-wattle house, a type that was quite advanced for the Canela even in the 1970s when palm straw was still easier to use.

The junior chief, Major Delfino, had a business relationship with a firm in São Luis, which he visited several times to deliver and sell homegrown cotton. He transported his cotton on commercial launches and boats down the Mearim River to São Luis, an undertaking that required a certain degree of sophistication in the Brazilian business world. Major Delfino made enough money this way to buy and maintain between 20 to 30 head of cattle. He maintained this herd while the Canela lived in six different village locations between 1880 and 1914. Reliable information about Major Delfino's small but significant herd of cattle surprised me, because I knew that the hungry Canela of the late 1950s could not raise cattle at all. They ate a calf before it could grow up to reproduce. This information about Major Delfino's era suggested that the times were more affluent, or that game of the region was more plentiful, or that chiefs maintained far higher discipline.

When the Emperor Dom Pedro II died in 1889 and the Republic was founded, the authorities declared that Indians no longer had free passage and protection when they traveled throughout Brazil. When they heard of the loss of these rights, which had been granted to Indians by the emperor, Colonel Tomasinho and Major Delfino went to São Luis to reclaim them. They were received well and showered with gifts, including shotguns, machetes, axes, and rolls of cloth. The Republican government gave them permission and protection to travel in all parts of Brazil.

During the 1890s and the next decade, Major Delfino was honored a number of times in São Luis, where the authorities gave him his title of major and gave him a uniform and sword to wear. According to Olímpio Fialho, a historian of Barra do Corda and São Luis, when Major Delfino came to Barra do Corda with his wife, they were appropriately dressed and well behaved in social situations. The Canela were becoming more aware of their social surroundings; they were accepting them and adapting to them.

The Fox People Join the Canela

The Fox people joined the Canela in 1900, leaving their ancestral Timbira village, Mucura, 30 miles to the northeast, because their numbers had become too reduced to maintain their independence from Brazilian settlers encroaching on their lands. The Mud and Boar nations had undoubtedly joined the Ramkokamekra, the ancestors of the Canela, for similar reasons, but the current Canela have forgotten when the migrations occurred. I suggest that these two tribal mergings occurred soon after the pacification of the Ramkokamekra-Canela in 1814; if any later, they would be remembered. The Fox people were the Timbira nation that had decimated the Ramkokamekra-Canela's ancestors during the years leading up to 1814, forcing their surrender for survival to the regional Brazilian garrison. It is ironic that the Canela of the late 1950s claimed they had always been at peace with the Fox people, even when both nations had been "wild Indians."

A descendant of the Fox nation, Ka?hi, told me in the late 1950s, when he was 60, that he was carried in his mother's arms from the old Fox village to the Canela one. He said that his people and the Canela already had visiting chiefs (*tàmhàk*) in each other's tribes so that communicating with the Canela was relatively easy. According to this precontact custom, the Fox Elders chose a Canela to represent the Fox and to look after their interests and safety when the Fox came to visit. Likewise, a Fox represented the interests of the Canela when the latter came to visit.

My special group of very old Canela research assistants, while we were working on the oral history of the Canela in 1975, described for me how the joining of the two peoples came about. A group of Fox Elders took the initiative and visited the Canela in 1900. During this visit, the Fox reinstalled a Canela as their visiting chief, adorning his body with red urucu and white falcon down in the center of the plaza. Then each Fox individual placed presents on the mat on which the Canela visiting chief was standing to honor him and his people and to express their individual commitments to peace. A few months later, a group of Canela visited the Fox village and reinstalled their visiting chief among the Fox people. Still later, a Fox group visited the Canela and proposed moving to join them in the old Timbira way. They wanted to know if the Canela Elders would accept the Fox people into the Canela group of formerly independent tribes as respected equals. The Canela Elders, after consulting their extended families and after several weeks of debate during the late afternoon council meetings, decided to accept the Fox. They needed more Indians of their Timbira kind to protect them against the mounting Brazilian incursions. Subsequently, representatives of the Elders of both peoples, sitting together in the Canela plaza, planned how they would put on the ceremony for the joining of tribes in the correct traditional manner. They tried to recall how it had been done much earlier, and surely with many minds helping to remember earlier events of this sort, they largely succeeded.

During the agreed-on season, probably in June when new farms have to be started, the Fox tribe, comprised of 30 to 60 members, marched in single file to the region of the Canela village, which then consisted of 150 to 250 individuals. The Fox warriors left their weapons with their women outside the Canela village, and, entering it, walked down a radial pathway performing the Tired Deer (*poo-tùkrïn:* deer tired) act. The Fox warriors acted as if they were exhausted, shuffling their feet, breathing heavily, and hanging their heads as they walked slowly in single file to the center of the plaza. The men were representing tired deer, disillusioned by their exasperating experiences far away, returning to their preferred home pasture. The Fox warriors, having completely surrendered, were entering what they hoped would be their home tribe forever. As a part of the ceremony of unification, the Fox people formed a circular camp of beehive-shaped palm frond shelters for their extended families about 500 yards from the Canela village.

After setting up their shelters, the Fox built an especially large shelter for the family of their best female singer. This woman had been awarded a highly prized cotton sash of honor (*hahi*) for her outstanding ability to sing and for her faithful attendance and helpful attitude at the daily group singing events over a number of years. In this special shelter, her family built a platform bed on which she was to receive the Canela warriors sexually, one after the other, as they filed through the Fox camp. These men left presents in her mother's shelter after they had satisfied themselves. Similarly, the Fox warriors filed to the Canela village and had sex sequentially with the Canela woman who wore the cotton sash and who was offered for this purpose, and left presents in her mother's house.

The remnants of the Fox nation had set up their overnight camp as if they were going to make a surprise attack on the Canela village at dawn, but as prearranged, the warriors exchanged sexual favors instead. Participation in sex reduced the potentially aggressive orientation of the warriors on each side so that cooperation and friendship became more likely. (The cultural institution of sequential sex will be discussed in Chapter 5.)

It is a general female role among the Canela to stop male excesses in a number of situations. Sometimes in the course of daily events, the two relay log racing teams challenge each other to an additional race so many times that the racers become exhausted, but cannot stop challenging the other team. Then one of the two highest ceremonial girls of the tribe (a young Wè?tè) walks over to the men with a bowl of food. The moment the men see her coming with her bowl, they stop their racing activities, and the losers are relieved of their need to challenge once more to save face.

In the Ghosts' summer-long festival, when members of the male initiates' two racing teams sprint from the village out into the savannah, they might keep racing on indefinitely, it is said, each side determined to win. However, to stop the excessive enthusiasm of these young initiates, the two young ceremonial girls associated with these initiates' groups as classificatory wives suddenly appear standing stark naked in the middle of the racing path. This view of exposed female genitalia stops the racers in their tracks.

Consequently, it should not be surprising that remnants of Timbira nations, when merging, carried out the "marriage" of their tribes by their warriors having sex with an especially honored woman of the other nation.

Executing a Witch Begins Social Disorganization

In 1903, the Ramkokamekra-Canela accused a Fox-Canela and killed him in the absence of the Fox Elders. This action placed Colonel Tomasinho, a Ramkokamekra, against Major Delfino, a Ramkokamekra with Fox kin, and caused a tribal schism that lasted 10 years. In the account of this event that I collected during the late 1950s, a Ramkokamekra woman who had refused to grant her sexual favors to the alleged Fox witch, Francelino Kaawùy, subsequently became ill and died. The Ramkokamekra thought Kaawùy had taken his revenge through witchcraft, so they tried and executed him.

Three young Ramkokamekra volunteers caught Kaawùy by surprise from behind as he was log racing with his team. Just as he was turning to pass the log to his teammate, they hit him on the head with heavy clubs. This occurred near the Ponto village where I first visited the Canela in 1957. Canela research assistants proudly showed me the spot of the execution. Canela custom was to cut out the eyes of a witch who had been convicted and executed by a tribal council to deprive his ghost of sight. If a ghost could see, he could kill again. Then they made cross-shaped gashes in the executed witch's palms to immobilize them. Interment followed without further ceremony.[35] When news of the "murder" reached Barra do Corda, militia were sent to Escalvado to capture the Canela executioners, who surrendered willingly. They were tried in Barra do Corda, but after a number of months in jail were set free. The Canela complained that if they could not kill their convicted witches, their world would come to a sorry end through witches' continued murders.

Major Delfino moved with his Fox-Canela followers three streams to the east to the Cattle Stream, while Colonel Tomasinho moved one watercourse to the east to the Dove Stream. After a few years, Major Delfino proposed a ritual he hoped would reunite the tribe. Following a mock battle, each part of the tribe would install a visiting chief in the other part, so the two parts would come together to celebrate the installation and stay together. Unfortunately, because memories of the execution were too strong, the tribe did not reunite until three years later. Major Delfino's mock battle became one act in the Facsimile Warriors' festival, so the father-to-one-son descendant lines of the two visiting chieftainships still exist.

In the Facsimile Warriors' festival the Falcon society male members, 40 to 50 strong, march from the plaza and pretend to attack the platoon of Facsimile Warriors stationed on the outer edge of the boulevard. Both sides sing the rousing war song, the Apikrawkraw-re. The Formal Friends of the membership of both sides form the two front lines. With much din and drama the two sides march slowly into position opposite each other, the two "enemy" ranks holding clubs horizontally. Just at the last moment as the front ranks are about to make contact with their clubs, the two descendants of the visiting chiefs insert themselves unarmed into the gap. The high honor of their ceremonial rank obliges the two sides to withhold their attack. Just to make sure no violence breaks out, several of each chiefs' Formal Friends join them in the gap and face the two enemy ranks with clubs held horizontally, keeping the two sides apart. The opposing "hostile" ranks respect the presence of the two visiting chiefs with their Formal Friends, but they sing louder than ever, stamping their feet rhythmically, raising a cloud of dust. Finally, the singing stops, the festival act ends, and the crowd disperses. The mock ferocity of this festival act is convincing evidence of the Canela's former bellicosity. But it also shows the high value the Canela place on maintaining internal peace. The 1993 performance of this festival act can be seen in the video *Mending Ways*.[36]

Ranchers Massacre the Kenkateye-Canela

The tribal schism that started in 1903 continued until well after the death of Colonel Tomasinho in about 1911. In 1913, a drastic event caused the scattering and reuniting of both parts of the tribe under Major Delfino. Cattlemen from the ranch of the Sítio dos Arrudas wandered into the Chinello village of the Kenkateye-Canela, population 150, ostensibly to help celebrate a Kenkateye wedding. The Kenkateye were the furthest southwest of the three tribes known to backlanders by the Canela name.

When the approximately 50 cowboys from the Sítio arrived in the Chinello village, they were playing an accordion and leading a mule carrying a barrel of *cachaça* (home-distilled rum). After the bandits got most of the Kenkateye drunk, they pulled out chains from the mule pack and bound the adult Kenkateye males to each other. The *pistoleiros* then shot about 50 Kenkateye men, while the women, children, and old men ran away to the Piranha tribe, 15 miles to the northeast, or to the Krahô Timbira Indians 150 miles to the southwest. The ranchers could not tolerate the cattle stealing of the Kenkateye and were determined to reinstate their dominance.

Nimuendajú writes that[37] when the Indian inspector of Maranhão had the murderers put on trial, the jury of Barra do Corda unanimously acquitted them, and even in the 1930s, the residents proudly pointed out the members of the Arruda's troop who began the massacre.

When news of the massacre arrived at the two Canela villages, the Canela scattered and hid among the stream-lining thickets for protection, thinking their turn for death would come soon. However, when the danger had passed and with Colonel Tomasinho no longer alive as an obstacle to unifying the tribe, Major Delfino brought the Canela together from the Cattle and Dove streams to form a new village on the Fox Stream. They spent about eight years in peace there before returning to their principal stream, the Santo Estévão, in about 1921. Major Delfino died in the village on the Fox Stream, and Faustino, the older Rop-khà (jaguar's coat), took over the chieftainship in his place.

Without Warfare, Discipline Starts Breaking Down

By the 1910s, the Canela were four generations away from fighting the settlers. Canela socialization and intergenerational authority were based on military discipline. With no enemy to fight, the discipline seemed unnecessary to the young, so they began to challenge or disobey it. In the next section, we will discuss the deculturation resulting from these changes and from other outside forces coming into play throughout the 20th century.[38]

CULTURE CHANGE IN THE 20TH CENTURY

As warfare and displacement gave way to a more settled existence for the Canela, other forces from the outside threatened their way of life. Influences from the Indian Service, the backland and urban cultures of Brazil, and visiting anthropologists and missionaries challenged their beliefs. Alternating periods of sufficiency and starvation, confidence and demoralization, buffeted the Canela. A messianic movement and temporary exile brought hopes and subsequent disillusionment.

During the 17th century, Timbira tribes fought one another annually, and during the 18th century, as we have seen, they fought successive waves of settlers. The older generations of Canela enforced the discipline necessary to train the youth for military prowess. As the last incidence of warfare was as far away as the 1850s, however, the youth did not see the urgency of the discipline and the Elders lost much of their power to enforce it.

Loss of Youths Having Sex with Opposite-Sex Elders

Restrictions on diet and sex were part of the traditional training of youths. Just after reaching puberty, the time of first sex, a youth began serious discipline under the direction of a principal uncle, who chose to take on this responsibility. The youth had to avoid sex as much as possible and to have it mostly with older women when he did have it—women who were near or past menopause. In this way, he would gain the strength of these older females and avoid the weakness and "pollutants" of the girls and younger women. This style of life continued for several years for young men, after which they could have sex with available women in their 20s, but not openly and frequently with the very young girls, even their young wives.

Young women were also subject to some restrictions and discipline. Although women did not engage in combat, they had to be as mobile as the men in case of flight and strong enough to carry loads. After their first menstruation, girls underwent dietary restrictions and were required by their maternal uncles and their paternal aunts to have sex almost exclusively with men in their 40s to 60s to gain their physical and moral strength. Sex with younger men was believed to weaken young girls.

Thus, we see that husbands were supposed largely to stay away from their young brides and have sex mostly with older women in special trysts outside the village or with women their age in the plaza at night. Young brides were supposed to have sex only rarely, and when they did, mostly with much older men.[39] These customs tended to delay conception. The average age of first conception in 1970 was 15.75 years. This figure may seem surprisingly high since girls first had sex before menstruation, at ages 11 to 13, with men they liked who were about 10 years older and thereby became "married" to them. They had first sex so consistently *before* they menstruated that it was believed that the loss of virginity *caused* menstruation. The average age of first conception in earlier times was even older than 15.75 years. However, when young husbands were beginning to defy members of the older generation and starting to spend whole nights with their young wives, as sometimes was occurring during the 1910s, the young women began getting pregnant at an earlier age.

Standing Water was a member of my research assistant council in 1960, 1964, and 1966, as was his wife's mother, Pyê-?khàl (earth-striped), in 1964 at age 70. Striped Earth was clear about how she had had sex mostly with much older men when she was an early to mid-teenager (from about 1906 to 1910) and about how her maternal uncles and paternal aunts prevented her from having much sex at all during this period. Standing Water told us how he had gotten his wife, Star Woman, pregnant too early, and about how he had visited her house openly even during the daytime, long before her first childbirth. He had known he was straying from ancient practices. Nevertheless, he and his wife had wanted each other too much, he explained, for them to be apart during the daytime. Moreover, the Elders were doing little to enforce the tradition for the prenatal separation of spouses, since they were afraid they would not be obeyed. It is clear that adolescents had sex principally with older persons only because of the coercion of the older generations. When their authority began to weaken, this practice diminished. The young preferred to have sex with younger people.

Loss of the Hazing-Shaming Ceremony of Youths

An act of hazing and shaming frequently took place in the late afternoon in the plaza, when the men of the younger age classes danced in front of the wide row of singing women. The act's purpose was to instill respect/fear (*hūūpa tsà:* it-fear thing) in young men by shaming them directly before the female dance row and members of the tribe assembled around the edges of the plaza to enjoy the social sing-dance. If a young man was known to be having sex with young girls, eating polluting foods, or being generally uncooperative with the Elders, an older man who had the temperament of a fierce warrior summoned the youth to appear before him.[40]

The warrior, surprising the people, entered the plaza during a late afternoon's social sing-dance, turning it into a ceremonial occasion. He brandished a weapon (most likely a shotgun), screeched vociferously at the supposed enemy, and declared he would be the first to go out to defend his people against the attackers should they approach the village. At the appearance of the warrior, the sing-dance stopped abruptly and all conversation ceased.

One of the warrior's close male associates swiftly took the weapon from him, because no one was allowed to approach the center of the plaza—a sacred place of mediation and enjoyment—with a weapon. Somewhat more subdued, the warrior proceeded to face the center of the female line of possibly 50 women spread in a single row across the lower part of the plaza. Then, shouting in harsh, threatening terms, the warrior, acting out the role of the unfortunate young man's principal uncle with its traditional disciplinary authority, challenged the youth to emerge from his age class's troop and come before the female line. Once the youth was standing respectfully before his "uncle," this warrior ordered his "nephew" to turn around to face the women and to prepare to suffer, but not flinch or utter a sound, if he was indeed a man. (See Figure 2.3.) In earlier times, he was placed in front of the young girl he had had sex with so that she also was shamed.

The warrior might have stamped on the youth's insteps, yanked him off the ground by his sideburns, and given him a blistering lecture, describing his shameful infractions for all the women to hear. Before about 1915, research assistants said, the warrior might have scraped the youth's legs with rodents' teeth until they bled, whipped a sharp-toothed blade of grass through an armpit to draw blood, forced quantities of pepper into his mouth, and—worst of all by far—drawn back his foreskin for the assembled men and women to see the glans of his penis. Girls who had violated the norms of sexual and dietary restraint were shamed in this ceremony by having their leaf aprons torn off and their genitalia exposed.

In a world of almost complete nudity for both sexes, standards of modesty still existed. Before about 1910, when Canela women began to wear wraparound skirts, naked women kept their knees together at all times, so their labia minora could never be seen. Such exposure would be the greatest embarrassment and social disgrace. Everyone would talk about the details of what they had seen—mockingly and derisively—and about the carelessness of the offender, which was seen as social disrespect. Even husbands or "other husbands" were not to see the vulva wide open or their eyes would develop boils. Similarly for men, only their wives or long-term "other wives" might fleetingly see a glans without creating extreme embarrassment in both parties.

To this day, a man should never see the glans penis of another man. Men pull back their foreskins to wash the glans under the water of a stream in a way that must not attract attention. If a man or woman is careless, malicious gossip could spread throughout the community. Then, a little niece of 8 years could remind her uncle in a customary joking context that so-and-so had seen his glans and that it was green, purple, or some other embarrassing color or distorted shape, and he would have to laugh with her. Nephews might tease their aunts if their genitalia had been seen exposed, naming the viewer.

The shaming ceremony in the plaza effectively enforced the authority of the Elders over the youths. Its practice began to wane by 1915, and it had to be abandoned completely after 1940. The reason for the complete loss of this ceremony was

William H. Crocker

Figure 2.3 An uncle disciplines his nephew before the female dance line.

quite simple. Indian Service agents and their families came to watch the afternoon sing-dances, but because they could not tolerate the "barbarities" sometimes inflicted on youths on these occasions, their presence discouraged the practice.

Impact of Outsiders on the Canela in the 1930s and 1940s

At this time another important traditional practice was lost because of Indian Service presence. After their post-pubertal period of seclusion and restrictive practices, mid- to late-adolescent women without children slept in the plaza, enjoying sex—often sequential sex—with the men of the opposite age class moiety[41] from their husbands'. A woman's husband would be on one edge of the 50-yard wide plaza and she on the other edge, thereby avoiding sexual jealousies. However, the Service personnel of the early 1940s emerged frequently from the post building in the early morning to roam around the village, observing extramarital relationships and casting shame on the "culprits" the next day. The Canela did not want to offend individuals they liked and had to deal with, such as these Service personnel, so women without children simply stopped sleeping in the plaza.

The presence of another outsider in the tribe, the anthropologist Curt Nimuendajú, had major consequences for the Canela. Nimuendajú studied the

Canela during six summers between 1929 and 1936. His great work on the Canela, *The Eastern Timbira,* was published in English in 1946.[42] Nimuendajú's influence was generally positive; he helped the Canela to feel proud of their traditions, supporting their festivals, ceremonies, and life cycle rites. However, when he learned about their extensive extramarital practices, he left the Canela with the impression that he disapproved, thus reinforcing their stereotype of Brazilians as necessarily disapproving of extramarital sex. His presence led to their continuing to conceal such practices from outsiders. He wrote that the Canela considered adultery to be grounds for divorce,[43] which was not true.

Nimuendajú encouraged the Canela to put a monetary value on their festivals and material artifacts. They began to expect to receive a number of head of cattle for performing a festival or a high price for an artifact. The travels of Canela chiefs to large Brazilian coastal state capitals, where they sold their artifacts for high prices and were honored with expensive presents, also taught the Canela to expect and demand prices from urban visitors that were far out of line with local market values.

At the time of his final departure in 1936, Nimuendajú recommended that the Indian Service employ his principal Canela helper, the older Thunder. The Service did so in 1938 and began a trend of employing individual Canela as fully salaried Indian Service employees. By 1957, six Canela males were employed, including the two principal chiefs, Jaguar's Coat and the older Thunder. Indian Service control of the Canela was thus increased, and monetary values became greatly exaggerated in Canela expectations.

Nimuendajú's most important recommendation to the Indian Service was that the Canela not be allowed to maintain lasting schisms, like the one that sundered the tribe between 1903 and 1913. A tribal schism between his last two visits in 1935 and 1936 taught Nimuendajú how damaging they were for Canela morale and for economic self-sufficiency. The Canela scattered from the village on the Santo Estévão that they occupied in 1935 when smallpox broke out and killed the principal chief, the older Standing Water. His successors divided the tribe, taking part to the Cattle Stream and part to the Dove Stream. Nimuendajú, through his great prestige, succeeded in summoning them to put on a Fish festival in a new village on the Fox Stream, halfway between the two other streams, thus reuniting them. Later, in 1939, they moved back to the Ponto area on the Santo Estévão.

If the Canela are not together in one community to discuss and solve problems in the plaza meetings of the Elders every morning and evening, problems fester and vicious rumors fly back and forth between the two villages. I experienced this in 1957, when a farm community in the Baixão Preto area was recognized as a new village. This schism was really part of the procedure of succession to the tribal chieftainship. The last old-style chief, Doroteo Hàk-too-kot (falcon-chick-green), had died in 1951 in the Ponto village, and several potential leaders were quietly striving to take his place. In 1957, the Indian Service sent a new Indian agent to the Baixão Preto farm huts and appointed the older Thunder as the new chief of the village there. Thus, I had young Chief Jaguar's Coat, Green Falcon Chick's successor, in the Ponto village and the new Chief Thunder in the new Baixão Preto village to reckon with, both of whom were my Informal Friends. This relationship allowed me to joke with and get along with both chiefs. From my neutral position, I could see how reputations were ruined in both villages by politically and personally motivated rumors.

Further Shocks to Canela Culture in the 1950s

The year 1956 was another landmark for Canela change, due again to an Indian Service action, this time on the national rather than on the local scene, and to the economic growth in Brazil in general, which was expanding from the great coastal cities into the interior.

Anthropologists at the top federal level of the Indian Service in Rio de Janeiro changed their policy from what they called "paternalism" to "self-reliance." From 1956 onward, Indians were supposed to raise foods for themselves instead of receiving handouts each year. From 1940 to 1956, the Canela had been given considerable quantities of cloth, shotguns, shot, gunpowder, lead, salt, and even staples such as manioc flour and rice by the Indian Service. After 1956, Indians were still to receive medicines free, but were to buy other supplies with the proceeds from selling their crops. Unfortunately the Canela had come to rely on the Indian Service during the lean months of the agricultural cycle: October, November, and December. They could no longer organize and motivate themselves to put in enough crops to last the year. Because of their loss of control over the age classes, the chiefs could not dispatch them to work in the fields, as they had formerly. During my two stays between 1957 and 1960, I heard a number of complaints against the Indian Service about how the *civilizado* was no longer living up to the promise of Awkhêê, who had guaranteed the *índio* full support in return for the use of the shotgun.

The year 1956 was a landmark in regional change for another reason. This was the year the first substantial bridge was built over the Alpercatas River to the southeast, so trucks could enter Barra do Corda from the Brazilian Northeast. Previously, only mule trains, small boats coming up the Mearim River from São Luis in the north, or small airplanes reached Barra do Corda. When I arrived there for the first time in June 1957, townspeople proudly pointed out their new furniture and gas-run refrigerators and stoves, all transported by truck from the Northeast.

Before 1956, differences in material culture between the backlanders of the Canela region and the Canela themselves were not overly conspicuous. By 1959, however, new commercial items were arriving in the backland communities of the Canela area, and especially by 1960 with new, modern Brasília as the national capital, the gap in material culture between the Canela and the backlander began widening rapidly.

The Canela of Nimuendajú's time still believed in themselves and their cultural values. Nimuendajú fostered this belief, even talking to the Canela against the backlander to reinforce the Canela faith in their own traditions. Nimuendajú reports that 20 Guajajara Indians of both sexes came to visit the Canela in 1930, hoping to make friends with them. When the Guajajara men could not take off their clothes to dance and race in the daily festivities, and could not go swimming naked, the Canela realized how completely different the Guajajara were. The Canela during the 1930s were still confident in their belief in male nudity, especially in the sacred center of their plaza during a formal meeting of the Elders. During the late 1950s, I often saw old members of the Council of Elders remove, out of respect, the square of cloth hanging from their belt to cover their genitals just as they were stepping into the plaza.

During the late 1950s, however, the Canela were beginning to lose confidence in their way of life. For the first time, fathers cut trucks and airplanes out of the pulp of buriti palm stalks as toys for their sons. Mothers bought plastic dolls in Barra do Corda for their daughters instead of providing the traditional dolls of buriti stalks with tucum string girdles and breasts of beeswax. By 1959 the Canela started to dance in the couples-embraced manner of backlanders, and by 1960 Canela men were buying shirts, long pants, and shoes, and women were buying blouses, skirts, and sandals to dance properly in the backland style.

The Messianic Movement of 1963

Denied help from the *civilizado,* demoralized by seasonal endemic hunger, and diminished and overwhelmed by the Brazilian culture, the Canela were ready to listen to some good news that would redress the wrongs they were suffering. Surely, Awkhêê would not forget his people.

In late January of 1963, a woman around 40 years old called Maria Castello Khêê-khwèy (grating-woman: as in grating manioc roots) had what seems to have been a psychic experience. (See Figure 2.4.) She was working in her family field during the heat of the noonday sun when the fetus in her womb began to communicate with her. The fetus predicted what animals Maria's husband would bring home from the hunt. When the prediction turned out to be accurate, Maria began to think of her fetus as possessing supernatural powers. From this beginning, Maria began prophesying that her baby's birth would be the reappearance of the culture hero Awkhêê, who would save the Canela. This prophecy set in motion a full-fledged messianic movement among the Canela, one that held out high hopes only to dash them in the end.

Messianic movements have taken place around the world. The cargo cults of New Guinea and the Rain Dances of the Plains Indians are other well-known manifestations of this phenomenon.[44] The reasons why Maria's movement broke out when it did, along with the details of its complex growth and decline, are beyond the scope of this study. I will summarize the chronology of the movement here, however, because the tendency of the Canela to look to messianic solutions instead of self-help is one more obstacle in their adjustment to the modern world.

The heart of Maria's prophecy, which she received from her fetus, was that Awkhêê would put an end to the current world dominated by the *civilizado* and bring in a new world governed by the Canela. The índio would be living in the cities, driving the trucks, and flying the airplanes, while the civilizado would be living in the forests, hunting game with the bow and arrow. Awkhêê's original contract of the mid-1800s would be reversed because the *civilizado* had not kept up his end of the bargain; he was no longer supporting the *índio,* giving him everything he needed.

In the process of preparing the Canela for the coming of Awkhêê, Maria gradually usurped the leadership of the tribe. After bringing together the various farm and village communities, she signaled the pro-*civilizado* nature of her movement by dancing with all the males, including male babies, in the backland embraced manner. She increased her control with punishments and tests of loyalty to her "employees." These followers had to dance and feast for long hours to ensure the arrival of Awkhêê.

Eventually Maria's baby, a deformed male fetus, was stillborn. She reformulated her prophecy, but doubt had set in among the Canela, and many moved away to their farm settlements. The Canela had already enraged the backlanders, however, by their cattle theft, which had increased in order to supply the constant feasting.

William H. Crocker

Figure 2.4 Maria Castello (third from the left), the prophetess, in the late 1950s

Backlanders attacked the Canela with hired bandits from other municipalities, burning Campestre, a peripheral village of the movement, to the ground. Younger Thunder, Maria's primary supporter, sent two runners to Barra do Corda to alert the Indian Service about the disaster. He posted sentinels around the central village where the Canela had regrouped. Then Thunder led a group of young males to collect cane for arrows in the hills. They had turned over their guns to Maria, which she had sold for food to help keep the daily dancing going.[45]

While the Canela defense saved about 150 lives, Indian Service personnel raced to put down the violence. The mayor of Barra do Corda accompanied them in their Jeep, so the ranchers had to let them through their checkpoint out of respect for him. The Service employees rounded up the scattered and hiding Canela and escorted them in a march through the night to safety. The ranchers would have shot at the Canela in the dark, but they knew that the Service employees were among them and held their fire.

Once the Canela were near Barra do Corda, out of danger, the Service transported them by truck to the Guajajara Indians' reservation. Thus began the Canela's exile deep in the dry forests, away from the savannahs where they felt at home.[46]

Exile to the Forests of Sardinha

By coincidental timing, I arrived in Sardinha, the Indian Service post of the Guajajara reservation, three days after the Canela were relocated there. I have often wondered what I would have done if I had arrived among the Canela in their savannahs during, instead of after, their messianic movement. Would Maria have seen me as a threat to her movement and organized the Canela against me? Would I have foreseen the ranchers' attack and warned the Canela and the Indian Service personnel?

As it was, I arrived in Sardinha before the Canela had built any huts for protection against the climate. No rain falls there during July, so their efforts were aimed at providing protection against the noontime sun and against the cool early mornings.[47] Much to my surprise, the Canela had already cut a round plaza out of the forest near the post buildings, and they had arranged their families around this plaza according to the customary order. (See Figure 2.5.)

Maria was there in Sardinha, and some of the women had already attacked her physically, blaming her for the loss of their husbands and claiming that the story of her fetus predicting a changed world was a lie. Maria was thoroughly discredited for having claimed that Awkhêê would divert the bullets if the ranchers attacked.

Information about the messianic movement was soon given to me by Canela friends I had worked with since 1957. One of the most exciting moments in my life of field research was when I began to realize, as bits of the puzzle fell together, that the Canela had experienced a full-blown messianic movement. I had studied such movements, but to find one in the field was remarkable.

Adaptations of a Savannah People to the Forest

The five years in Sardinha appeared to be a disaster for the Canela. They were so demoralized that many of them preferred to do nothing rather than hunt and put in farm plots. The soils were harder, the thickets denser, and the trees larger, so putting in a farm took much more work. That the products of such a farm could be significantly greater, because of the richer soils, was a point that escaped most of the Canela. The benefits were too far away in time. Instead of tracking and running down game, hunting in the dry forests required knowledge of the game's habits and waiting for it to pass by. In any case, hunting and farming were seldom carried out successfully and the Canela were starving most of the time during 1963 and 1964, relying on handouts from the Indian Service. Many children died of diseases, especially dysentery, and many older people died younger than they should have, often of tuberculosis. Extramarital sex became scarce because weakened women demanded meat before they would be generous. Canela men had to wear shorts for the first time in history, because the ubiquitous Guajajara women had strong sensitivities against male nudity. Nevertheless, the greatest Canela complaint was an aesthetic one: they missed the beautiful open vistas of the savannah countryside. To the Canela, the dark dry forests were gloomy and uninspiring. They languished for their homelands.[48]

On the positive side, the young age class in its late 20s to mid-30s, led by the younger Thunder, eventually learned how to till the soil and hunt in the dry forests and therefore produced ample surpluses by 1966 and 1967. They did not want to return to the poor savannah soils in 1968. Moreover, the proximity of Barra do Corda only 15 miles away by road from Sardinha interested many of the younger Canela because there they found ready markets for some of their artifacts. The Canela were acquiring a new way of making money, fabricating artifacts by the hundreds: baskets, mats, whisk brooms, and so on, and even decorated bows and arrows for tourists.

Some of these sales could be made right in the Canela village at Sardinha, because Barra do Corda residents and tourists came to see how the Indians lived. The

William H. Crocker

Figure 2.5 Canela in exile in the dry forests of Sardinha in 1963

tourists from other cities were more respectful of the Canela than were the backlanders and Barra do Corda citizens, so the Canela began to develop a new sense of their special worth. Tourists were often good for their morale, strange as this might seem.

By mid-1966, word came from the Indian Service in Brasília that the Canela could return to their homelands in small groups. Some families did, and by late 1968 the entire remaining community was required to return. The Canela were now quite a different people from the ones I had known during the late 1950s. The most obvious difference was that no men went naked any more, unless they were old and inside their own houses. (Women continued to go topless in the village.)

The deeper difference between the late 1950s and the late 1960s, however, lay in the contrast between the messianic solution to the future and the agricultural solution. The latter was successfully demonstrated by the men of the second youngest graduated age class, led by younger Thunder, during the dry forest stay. The messianic solution relied on traditional myths and on faith in the transformations found in these myths. Awkhêê could bring about metamorphoses. In earlier times he had changed himself into a jaguar, anaconda, falling leaf, gnat, and cinder. He had created the world of horses, mules, chickens, pigs, and cattle ranches of the *civilizado*. Surely he could come again and change the Canela world once more, switching the roles of the *civilizado* and the *índio*.

The alternative demonstrated by the younger Thunder through the agricultural successes of his age class in Sardinha was a solution based more on the backland way of life than the Canela one, at least economically. From this point on the Canela would periodically move toward the agricultural solution, putting in larger farms and converting surpluses into cash. The effort required strong leadership, however, and when it was lacking, the messianic solution still had appeal. Smaller, abortive messianic movements continued to break out during the 1980s. Even at the end of 1999, younger Thunder, himself experienced in leading the Canela to put in community farms, led a large messianic movement. This time the movement was backward looking. Younger Thunder exhorted the Canela to revive the old way of life, to behave and dress in their traditional ways. If they did this Jesus (Awkhêê) would come and save them from an impending flood.[49]

Outside Influences in the 1970s

During the stay in Sardinha, low morale and hunger caused some temporary emigration from the community. Most of the emigrants eventually returned, and the knowledge of the outside world that they brought back constituted an important influence during the 1970s.

The Canela male who left as an early adolescent in 1964 and stayed away the longest, Fox's Belly (tsoo-tu: fox-belly), was living at the House of the Indian in Rio when a friend of the manager called and asked the manager if she had a young man who could serve as house helper. Fox's Belly became more than house helper; the friend, an old lady, adopted him. She sent him to grade school and then to the Brazilian Air Force high school. Since he was from my Canela family, I called him "nephew" and visited him in Rio several times, including at the house of his Brazilian "grandmother" in an old, refined section of the city.

Fox's Belly potentially had a great future in the urban world, launched from an established family and starting with a military career. But when he failed to qualify as a pilot, he dropped out of the Air Force school. His Brazilian family put him to work in their company shop, framing portraits. Not happy with this menial labor, he went back to the Canela when the Indian Service offered him the position of post teacher in 1991. This role should have been ideal for him, with his formal education and his ability to speak Portuguese. Unfortunately, he was temperamentally unable to make decisions and could not deny the Canela their many requests. The Service had to relieve him of this job and find a disability pension for him. He was too well educated to work in the fields.

Young men like Fox's Belly (no women lived away from the community during this period) brought back urban notions that changed the values of the Canela. Though even now the Canela trust their traditional curers for certain purposes, they also believe in modern medicines. While they still carry out their ancestral festivals, sometimes over a period of four months, they nevertheless enjoy embraced, paired dancing. They still like log racing, but the young also play soccer very competitively. While some like to hear stories of their ancestors, some experience deep feelings at a Catholic service (led by younger Thunder), which they have adopted from the backlanders for use on Good Friday. Others prefer singing parts of the Facsimile Warriors' festival on Good Friday to help prevent Jesus from dying at midnight. Most of them pay little attention to the customary restrictions against heavy foods and much sex that post-pubertal youths were supposed to maintain to make themselves strong runners and good hunters.

Support from the Government

Another kind of external influence during the 1970s was the increasingly strong presence of the Indian Service. Following the return from exile on the Guajajara reservation, the Service built the first brick house with red-tiled roof at the Service post. By 1974 a schoolhouse was built, by 1978 an infirmary, and by 1981 an Indian agent's house—all of the same substantial construction. By 1975 the post had a gas-run generator for electric lights and a radio station. The construction of these expensive buildings and services was convincing evidence to the Canela that the Service was committed to their protection. By 1975 the post had a trained nurse and by 1978 a dedicated schoolteacher. Between 1971 and 1983, the lands of the Canela were demarcated and became an official government reservation.

Sr. Sebastião Pereira, an excellent Indian agent with some anthropological training, was assigned to the post in 1970. He won the confidence of the Canela by going to their houses twice daily with a basket of medicines rather than requiring them to come to him, as had been the practice. Sebastião soon conquered childhood dysentery. By 1975 he had all but eradicated tuberculosis, making possible the demographic boom of the 1980s and 1990s. He trained a soccer team that soon had an undefeated season in the backlands, outperforming backland youths, some of whose fathers had attacked the Canela in 1963. Sebastião went to the evening council meetings regularly and learned to understand the language well, though he did not try to speak it. He became one of the most highly respected Indian agents. Sebastião, in effect, took over the leadership of the tribe, though he relinquished some of this power during the 1980s. Sebastião's efforts and force of character contributed immensely to the stability and growth of the Canela during the 1970s.

Rise in Literacy

A major effect of the presence of the missionary couple, Jack and Josephine Popjes of the Summer Institute of Linguistics, or Wycliffe Bible Translators, and of my presence as the Canela's primary anthropologist, has been the rise of literacy among the Canela. (See Figure 2.6.)

The Popjeses arrived in 1968 and lived among the Canela until 1990, having fulfilled their mission of translating the Bible into the Canela language and making it available to all tribal members. SIL missionaries do not initially preach or attempt to convert, preferring instead to make the word of God available through translating the Bible. The Popjeses were trained in modern linguistics. They took the rudimentary written form of the Canela language developed by Nimuendajú, along with my work on phonemes and vocabulary, and developed a consistent and linguistically sound grammar. During the long process of their translation, the Popjes couple worked with 60 to 100 Canela helpers, a collaboration that developed the Canela's reading and writing skills. This education in literacy, quite aside from the religious influence, was tremendously important for the Canela.

Likewise, I feel that the most beneficial effect of my presence among the Canela has to do with literacy. For years at a time Canela have been writing and taping

Ray Roberts Brown, 1970

Figure 2.6 Jack Popjes, SIL missionary, in 1970

diaries for me in Canela or Portuguese. I believe that the almost continuous writing of diaries—especially the translating from Canela into Portuguese for my benefit—trained the writers, teaching them to analyze in new ways. The language skills and associated analytical thinking are tools the Canela need in order to deal with Brazilian social and economic concepts.

Beginnings of Political Consciousness

Between 1977 and 1980, the Indian Service placed a powerful activist, José Porfírio Cavalho, in the agency in Barra do Corda. He established a pan-Indian newspaper in Barra do Corda through which Indians of different tribes could communicate with one another in their own languages. This forceful Indianist lectured the Canela on the worth of their culture and urged them to send delegates to national conferences. Since the Canela were already accustomed to going on trek to the great cities of Brazil, this Indianist's program of "bringing consciousness" (*conscientização*) to the Canela may not have been as extraordinary for them as for many forest-bound Indian communities in the Amazon basin. Nevertheless, his work surely contributed to Canela self-esteem and encouraged Canela chiefs to travel to great Brazilian cities, such as São Luis, Belém, and Brasília, the seats of power over Indian well-being.

The Canela were joining the pan-Indian political activism developing in Brazil during the 1980s. The Canela were not as active as the Kayapó, who in 1988 protested and defeated the building of a dam on the middle Xingu River that would have flooded part of their lands. Nor were they as active as the Guajajara who, during November of 1992, took Brazilian hostages to protest a settlement on their lands. The dispute over the Guajajara lands had cost several lives by the late 1990s. The Canela are not that confrontational. They want to agree with their "enemies" and appease them, expecting to win them over.

Every year during the late 1990s, Canela athletes have competed favorably in pan-Indian athletic competitions, including soccer, track, archery, and other sports. These meets have taken their participants by bus to Brasília, Curitiba, and other cities where they also sing, dance, and show off their "folklore," as it is called. Sports competitions seem to be a more compatible way for Canela to engage with the outside world than political activity.

In 1993, the federal government reversed direction and reduced the funding of the Indian Service considerably. After supporting its employees, the Service had little left over for the welfare of tribes like the Canela, and by 1999 the funding was reduced even further. Medical support was transferred to another federal agency, FUNASA, which trained two young Canela men in nursing. The role of funding education was given to the *município* (township) in which the Canela reservation lay. When the *município* of Fernando Falcão split off from Barra do Corda due to population growth, the Canela reservation fell within its borders, rather than those of Barra do Corda. Thirteen hundred Canela were of such significance in the new Fernando Falcão that politicians had to court their vote. Much to my consternation in 1999, I stumbled onto a gasoline generator running a television set in one of the large Canela farm communities. It had been donated by one of the candidates running to be mayor in the new *município*. By 2001, two Canela employees of the Service, younger Thunder and Whip, ran satellite television programs in the evenings on gas-run generators. (See Figure 2.7.) One time when I was watching with Canela children and teenagers, we saw Americans deployed in Afghanistan and Brazilian beauty queens arrayed in bikinis.

The Drive for Education

Again, much to my surprise in 1999, Fernando Falcão was supporting six teachers in the main Canela village's school. Two teachers from Barra do Corda were supervising four Canela teaching the first four years in Canela and Portuguese. Burnt Path, the senior Canela teacher, was euphoric about the attendance at the school. He took me to his class of about 30 students of all ages, boys and girls, and said there were three more classes in all with their respective Canela teachers to make about 120 students. (See Figure 2.8.) In his communication to me of October 2000, he spoke of the importance of education for his people:

> To know more about reading is the most important thing for them. They must have this road open so they cannot be left behind, isolated, like the animals in the forest. . . . Parents and siblings must send the children to study and come to know things so that later they can learn professions and have the capacity to work for salaries to earn things. . . . Remaining isolated like the animals in the forest without learning, without understanding, without knowing is not a correct life. It is for this reason that the federal government does not accept that the children remain isolated. . . . I have a great hope that is like a door opening that the most important thing, a matter of great joy, is ultimately useful knowledge about the Brazilian world.

Not only had Canela become teachers in their own school, but a couple of years earlier the first Canela had been appointed to be in charge of the Indian Service post.

William H. Crocker

Figure 2.7 Satellite dish in a farming village in 1999

By 2001, they had three trained Canela medical assistants. About 120 Canela were receiving funds from the three government levels, just as in Brazilian towns and farm communities. These monies were more than ample for the Canela level of subsistence, and came in the form of Service and FUNASA (government health) salaries, agricultural retirement pensions, medical disability payments, maternity assistance, and school student support. About 25 Canela students were going to the schools in Barra do Corda, attending classes from the fifth through the tenth grade.

The drive to become educated is evident in what a young woman wrote for me in April 2002:

> I am Edible Vine Canela [Kupaa-khwèy]. I am 16. . . . I am repeating the fourth grade. I am married, but for me this does not make any difference. I want to bring about my dream of studying to be my life. I have never thought of leaving studies. I just want to study and through this find a job to begin a career even if I suffer from the lack of nourishment, but I will put up with this to receive a diploma and through this become a different woman. I am not going to feel that pain [hunger] any more in my life. Who knows? I might even become chief of the tribe, the commandant of the village.
>
> It is just through education that we have the capability of freeing our future from our present for my village. We need many things in my area. I want to struggle on the side of my marvelous people.

Myles Crocker, 2001

*Figure 2.8 A Canela teacher
and students in 2001*

I have thought that I would like very much to be intelligent with a long memory which comes to one through knowledge. I am aware of the technological innovations connected to information [the Internet] which allows one to become a professional, up to date, and very successful, because solidarity with patience affirms [one's future].

I have a dream. It guarantees [success] through work. No one knows that I am hoping through my dreams.

At the end of September of 2000, representatives (*vereadores*) were elected throughout the communities of the *município* to speak for their people in the legislature of the town of Fernando Falcão. His Water ran to support the incumbent mayor, and young Anaconda-On-Fire (*Lo-ʔti-pôl:* anaconda-large it's-on-fire), age 32, competed in support of the challenger. For the first time, Canela were competing with each other for a political position in the Brazilian governmental system. Anaconda, the winner, had been appointed a decade earlier by the Council of Elders to be the commandant of a younger age class in training during a Warriors' festival, so he knew how to handle himself as a leader. He excelled in his high school in Barra do Corda, gaining an education, becoming quite familiar with the ways of urban Brazilians, and developing many friends among them. He had been one of my diarists since 1995, typing up Canela myths and translating them. He is clearly advancing rapidly onto center stage of the Canela political scene. He spoke the following to me in his diary of October 2000:

> When I take office on the first of the year of 2001, I will work with my people. I will take care of what I was elected to do as *vereador* and talk with the new mayor, Ely Cavalcante. It is for the mayor to be giving support to the Indians to end their "half hunger." First, we will be concerned about agriculture and with a machine to work with the Indians. We will form new associations [NGOs] to improve the life of the Indians, because it is through associations that we can procure projects and get our rights, since "half hunger" is going around a great deal in our village. Some have a little manioc and others have none. . . .
>
> How am I going to take care of my people, so needy and humble and yet so competent—a people who do not make confusion and do not have inclinations for kidnapping people [like the Guajajara]? Now, a person is arriving who has not graduated but at least who is studying . . . and thinking of a future . . . that lies in raising goats, chickens, and pigs with a tight hand as our *civilizado* white brothers do, maintaining control. We need a competent person to orient the Indians, because with such instructions, we can do away with "half hunger." Because I am going to be the *vereador,* various white brothers have told me that the way will be open to obtain the rightful benefits of the Indians. . . .
>
> The town of the new *município* is near our village [14 miles away, unlike the 40 miles to the city of Barra do Corda]. . . . I am going to create a Secretaria Indígena there with the new mayor, . . . because when a people work well, very well, they move ahead. Take the people of Leandro, they have everything because they have everything under control. They make things and keep them until they increase and even double. But the Indians, for example, kill a paca [a large rodent] and eat it all at once during the same day. They do not think about tomorrow. Nevertheless, the Indians have good heads to think about things, but I become very worried about the welfare of the person who has not studied.

Anaconda sounds as if he is standing in the plaza still running for *vereador.* (See Figure 2.9.) I find his speech convincing, but note that he is thinking of founding a new legal association, when the Canela already have one that could receive funds for any number of projects. This sounds political—as if he wants one of his own he could control. He counts on his people working hard in the fields to create a surplus to sell to merchants for better living, but he is still looking to the outside for financial help.

Anaconda is more of a leader and more dynamic than Chief His Water, who is an idealist. Anaconda will eventually have more of an education, graduating from high school within a few years. There is no doubt that he hopes to be the first chief some day, and if the Canela do not go back to lifetime appointments of chiefs as was their custom, Anaconda will surely have his turn at the position.

Nevertheless, the problem with Canela education is what to do with it after you have been *formado,* graduated from high school. The attitude of Brazilians of the interior, as well as of the Canela, is that "formed" people do not work in the fields to support their families. They get jobs in stores, banks, or large firms. This amounts to getting positions in the city where competition with Brazilians is fierce. A few could get jobs on the Canela reservation, but these positions are limited to nurses, teachers, drivers, technicians, Service employees, and a Service post agent, unless some small industry could be started there.[50]

More aggressive activism by other Indian tribes in Brazil has increased local prejudice against the Canela, making their employment unlikely. Locally, the Guajajara ambushed vehicles passing through their territory, kidnapping and even

Figure 2.9 Election poster for Raimundo Nonato, or Anaconda

killing whites. The Kayapó seized a gold mine in their area. One of their chiefs caused a national scandal when he raped a white woman. A Shavante was elected to the national legislature, but caused a brawl on the floor of the Assembly. These were cases of activism gone wild, bringing a backlash among Brazilians.

In spite of all the vicissitudes that the Canela have suffered, they continue to survive and increase. They cherish their culture, even though many of the traditional practices described in the following chapters have been abandoned. These changes are described further in the section, "The Demise of the Extramarital Sex System," in Chapter 5. The Canela continue to favor their circular village and the way of life it offers, however, above other possibilities. The few who have emigrated over the years tend to return.

In the following chapters, even though I use the present tense, I am describing Canela culture as it existed during the earlier years of my research. Either past or present tense tends to create the illusion that a perfect "freeze frame" of the culture is being portrayed. It is important to realize that change never stops. Much of the Canela world of Nimuendajú and of my own research has been lost. At the same time, however, new cultural adaptations and forms are being created that may ensure Canela survival.

NOTES

1. When I first arrived among the Canela in 1957, the Indians were *cabocos* (*caboclos* in Amazonia) and the non-Indians were *cristãos* (Christians) or *civilizados* (civilized people). By the 1990s, they were *índios* (Indians) and *brancos* (whites). However, these *brancos* could be dark African-Brazilians. The distinction is cultural. Nevertheless, I have been hesitant to use *brancos* or "whites" for obvious reasons, but Brazilian anthropologists use *brancos* and some American anthropologists working in Brazil have used "whites" in their publications. Thus, for simplicity I will use "whites" for the non-Indian populations.

2. See Wilbert and Simoneau (1984:102) for a similar publication of this myth.

3. For a near-exhaustive map and index of locations, names, languages, population numbers, bibliographies, and other information on South American indigenous peoples, see Lizarralde (1988).

4. For a summary of Canela culture, history, economics, ecology, social structure, and other matters, see Crocker (1994).

5. The Canela say they are *índios* (Indians: *mëhïï*) and are proud of it. While *më* means both the Timbira type of *índio* and the plural, *hïï* means meat/flesh/kind/type; I would say "our sort." They apply this term *mëhïï* only to Indians like themselves, not the Guajajara. It includes any of the Eastern Timbira peoples, but not the Western Timbira, the Apinayé (Da Matta, 1982) because they speak in a sufficiently different manner. Language is a principal distinguishing factor. I was fascinated that they allowed the missionary-linguist, Jack Popjes, to be a *mëhïï* because he spoke Canela so well.

6. Pacification (*pacificação*) is the term used by Brazilians to refer to the process of bringing a warlike tribe under the peaceful control of Brazilian authorities, local or national. By "Brazilians" I mean peoples of direct African, European, Asian, and Native American origins, including peoples of mixtures of these origins who have grown up in or who have adopted one of the Portuguese-Brazilian national or regional cultures. I use "Indian" rather than "Native American," because this is the Brazilian practice. The Canela are aware that they and their ancestors were Brazilian before the arrival of the "Brazilian" settlers. The Canela say, *"Sou brasileiro legítimo"*: I am the real Brazilian.

Thus "Indian" refers to a cultural rather than a racial distinction. The Canela see themselves as a different nation from the Brazilians, so they are the Canela and the outsiders are the Brazilians, unless they are foreigners to Brazil.

7. These surviving Timbira tribes are the Canela (also known as the Ramkokamekra), Apanyekra (*apàn:* piranha), Krahô (*kraa-hô:* paca's [a rodent's] hair), Krĩkatí (*khrĩï-kati:* tribe-large), Pukobyé (*pùkhop-yê:* yam-plural/people), Gavião (falcon), and Apinayé (no translation), the Western Timbira. (The Gavião are northwestern forest Pukobyé. For them, see Arnaud [1989].) For simplicity, we use "Timbira" to include just the "Eastern Timbira" tribes, not the Apinayé.

8. Canela research assistants use *khrĩï* (village) to talk about the unit of people who live in their principal village. This same unit is their *nação* (nation), when they talk in Portuguese. I prefer "tribe" to "community" because Timbira units were relatively isolated and self-sufficient.

9. For the Gê and other language families of South America, see Greenberg (1987) and Lizarralde (1988).

10. For a history of the pacification and settlement of a Southern Gê-speaking people, see Santos (1973).

11. For classics in the field on distant cultural cousins of the Canela, the Shavante (Central Gê), see Maybury-Lewis' amusing travel book (1965), his convincing monograph (1967), and his edited series of papers by his former students (1979). The latter are of other Gê peoples: the Kayapó (Turner), Apinayé (Da Matta), Krahô (Melatti), and Krĩkatí (Lave).

12. For a current account of a Kayapó group, the Xikrin, including external relations such as contacts with loggers, see Fisher (2000).

13. These linguistic terms are from Rumsey (MS). See Crocker (1990:57–59) for a summary account of the Gê-speaking peoples around 1990.

14. The nations that were at peace with each other traded occasionally. They sent small trading groups to each other, just when they needed to do so, to obtain the necessities for certain festivals. Thus, they traded more for ceremonial adornments such as resin, feath-

ers, chalk, and purple body paint (genipap) than for food. Their more regular intervillage (i.e., international) contacts were made through raiding their enemies annually during June through August.

15. For a detailed account of warfare among the Canela, see Crocker (2002) and for the Kayapó, the Canela's cultural second cousins, see Verswijver (1992).

16. For other styles of warfare in the Amazon, see Chagnon (1992) and Ferguson (1995). Ramos (1995), a Brazilian female anthropologist, offers quite a different view of the Yanomami than Chagnon's and presents a vivid account of one group's devastation by gold miners during the 1990s.

17. The "closed" savannahs, known to geographers as *cerrados,* are a principal vegetational type of Brazilian landscape. *Cerrados* are found in the highlands between the great tributaries south of the Amazon. In contrast to the "open" savannahs of Kenya, the closed savannahs of Brazil are grassy with short trees of 5 to 30 feet high, standing 1 to 20 yards apart. Thus vision is limited, though passage almost anywhere through closed savannahs by horse or on foot is relatively unobstructed.

18. The subject of Canela material culture is scarcely touched in this book, but Krĩkatí/Pukobyé material culture is so similar that if the interested person studies the various works of the Timbira material culture specialist Dolores Newton (1994) and goes to her collections in the Smithsonian, he or she will find, with only slight variations, what the Canela make.

19. North of Barra do Corda and Grajau are deciduous dry forests, which shed their leaves during October. The Amazonian tropical rain forests slowly begin to take shape 75 miles to the west and north, beyond the Pindaré River. Much of the rain forest that I flew over during the 1970s in the Wycliffe plane between Belém and Barra do Corda had been cut down by the 1990s. Maranhão's rain forests are the most destroyed in all of Brazil.

20. An extensive world study of blood serology and body types (Layrisse and Wilbert, 1999) suggests that the Canela are somewhat less "Asian" than the Tupian-speaking Guajajara and the classical Mongoloids such as the Japanese and Chinese.

21. Curt Nimuendajú was born a German, but became a naturalized Brazilian. He is Brazil's foremost anthropologist of the first half of the 20th century, and his great work was on the Canela, *The Eastern Timbira* (1946).

22. "Canella," which is written "Canela" and "Kanela" in modern Brazilian orthography, was applied to three separate tribes by local Brazilian authorities during the last century: the Kenkateye, Apanyekra, and Ramkokamekra (*ràm-khô-khãm-më-?khra:* tree-resin grove, in plural Indian-children: Indians of the tree-resin grove). The Kenkateye, who split off from the Apanyekra in the middle of the 19th century, were massacred and dispersed by local cattle ranchers in 1913. The Apanyekra have long been separate from the Ramkokamekra, having been traditional enemies.

23. One German charity contributing to Canela development is called Deutsche Missions Gemeinschaft.

24. See Nimuendajú (1946:29).

25. See Ribeiro (1815, 1819a, and 1819b).

26. See Nimuendajú (1946:150), translated from Ribeiro, Memoria . . . , Nos. 19 and 22.

27. Melatti (1967:21–31) presents an analysis of these pastoral and agricultural fronts, coming from the southeast and north respectively. They joined to cross southern Maranhão during the 1800s and 1810s, more as a pastoral front than an agricultural one.

28. Morse (1965) presents a history of Brazilian frontier *bandeiras.*

29. See Nimuendajú (1946:32) and Hemming (1987:185–186). Note the earlier name of the Canela's principal ancestors, spelled Capiecran by Nimuendajú and Kapiekran by Hemming.

30. Names of historical Canela, and of Antônio Diogo (Alligator's Tail) who died in 1960, are not changed. Names of most living Canela are changed to ensure individual privacy. Antônio Diogo was the living historical library to whom Canela sent me for knowledge about the tribe when I first arrived.

31. See Hemming (1987:178–180) for a famous historian's account of Dom Pedro's decrees and his book in general for the story of Brazilian-Indian relationships. See also Gomes (2000) for a Brazilian anthropologist's views and a thorough report on the history of Brazilian-Indian treaties and contacts. Darcy Ribeiro (2000), a famous Brazilian anthropologist, politician, and

educator, gives us a definitive cultural history of the Brazilian people.

32. For some understanding of a largely hunting and gathering people, the Ache of Paraguay, see Hill and Hurtado (1996).

33. For a remarkable study based on around 90 months of fieldwork in the western Amazon (Peru) with a farming people who still hunt significantly, see Kensinger (1995).

34. For various combinations of hunting, foraging, and farming in different parts of the world, see Kent (1998). A classic on the quality of soils in the Amazon is Meggers (1971).

35. See Nimuendajú (1946:240).

36. See Schecter and Crocker (1999) and Crocker (1999).

37. See Nimuendajú (1946:30).

38. For authoritative two to four page sociocultural synopses of over 100 South American indigenous peoples, including maps of their locations, their culture areas through history, and their linguistic families, as well as extensive bibliographies, see Wilbert (1994).

39. For the trend over 40 years of Canela adolescents having sex with people of much older generations, see Crocker (1984:75).

40. For descriptions of the Canela hazing and shaming act, through which Elders forced young men into general submission, see Crocker (1990:126). The Canela did not put on this mock-hazing act for me in 1975; they put it on for themselves. They enjoy staging their ancient ceremonies, though the one photographed was an "empty" (*kaprè*) one, they said, since the youth was not *really* being hazed for misbehavior during the act.

41. The term "moiety" literally means one-half (French: *moitié*) and is used frequently in anthropology to refer to customary divisions of a tribe into halves. The Canela have five moiety systems, which means they divide themselves, on different occasions, into halves in five different ways. The Canela moieties mentioned in this book are the Upper versus the Lower age class moieties and the Reds versus the Blacks.

42. Curt Nimuendajú's *The Eastern Timbira*, 1946 (357 pages, 42 plates, 16 figures, and 3 maps), written in German but translated into English by ethnologist Robert Lowie of the University of California, is one of the great ethnographic monographs of the first half of the 20th century. This monograph and similar works that are out of print but re-published online are available at www.mnh.si.edu/anthro/canela/literature.htm.

43. Nimuendajú (1946:46–47, 124) emphasizes how proud the Canela were of their nudity, though they would not offend city dwellers with it. He quotes a Canela female adolescent as saying that the visiting Guajajara Indian males should be ashamed of going into the plaza fully dressed.

44. A messianic or revitalistic movement (Mooney, 1896) occurred among the American Plains Indians during the early 1890s. Its thrust was to take the Plains Indians back to earlier forms of living, while, in contrast, the Canela movement's thrust was to move them into the future, taking the place of the Brazilians.

45. The Krahô Indians, cultural siblings of the Canela, had a similar messianic movement in 1951. See Melatti (1972).

46. For a book on the plant medicines and herbal curing practices of a tribe living in the same state of Brazil, Maranhão, as the Canela, see Balée (1994). See also Posey (2002) for relations with the environment of the Canela's cultural cousins, the Kayapó.

47. For the account of very close interpersonal relationships by a French ethnologist, who spent many years among the Yanomami and speaks their language fluently, see Lizot (1986). John Peters (1998) lived for nine years among the Yanomami with his family as missionaries, penetrating the society deeply. Later he earned his Ph.D. in sociology.

48. The ethnologist Kenneth Good spent years among the Yanomami. He married a Yanomami woman who accompanied him to the United States, but eventually returned home. Good is raising their three children in urban United States. See Good (1991).

49. For fuller accounts of the messianic movement of 1963, see Crocker (1967) and Crocker (1990:74–76). Linn and Crocker (MS) presents still fuller descriptions, analyses, and world comparisons of the several Canela messianic movements, including the most recent one of December 1999.

50. Picchi (2000) offers an interesting account of the Bakairí Indians adjusting to life in the 21st century that contrasts with the Canela situation.

3/The Web of Kinship

When the Canela first welcomed me in 1957, they needed to fill the social vacuum presented by my unrelatedness. Within two days a Canela woman, Waterfall, adopted me as her "brother" so that everyone else in the tribe would know what to call me—and how to behave toward me—through their existing relationships with her. I could almost hear a sigh of relief passing through the tribe as each person heard that it was Waterfall who had adopted me. This solved each individual's problem of how to act in my presence, because they knew how to behave with Waterfall. When I returned to the United States, relatives and friends expressed amazement that the Canela had adopted me into a family within two days. They thought that I must have been especially adept at integrating myself into the tribe. But I explained that my adoption was for the tribal members' convenience. Not all tribes adopt outsiders, but the Canela in earlier times had the custom of adopting Timbira-speaking Indians from other tribes. They had also adopted my predecessor, Curt Nimuendajú. When I was adopted as Waterfall's "brother," I thereby became part of the tribal kinship network. Each individual would know whether to call me "nephew," "son," "uncle," or even "husband," according to the appropriate rules of their system. (See Figure 3.1.)

CONSANGUINEAL AND AFFINAL KINSHIP

Kin, Affines, and "Spouses" around the Village Circle

In tribal worlds, kinship is crucially important, far more so than in most expressions of Western culture. The kinship system determines what kin (people related by genes) and affines (people related through marriage) call each other and furnishes most of the social structure of a tribe. Kinship creates expectations of behavior that are powerful guidelines even though individuals deviate from them in practice. What is different from tribe to tribe or from culture to culture throughout the world is how human beings categorize their kin and affines and how they address and refer to the people in these categories. The group of individuals whom human beings call "uncle," "father," "sister," or "granddaughter" and so on can be different genealogically from culture to culture. In the United States, for instance, people usually call

Figure 3.1 Macaw's Bone (tallest) and Waterfall with family in a 1975 census photo

their father's brother "uncle," but a Canela calls her or his father's brother "father." In U.S. reckoning, one's father's sister's son is a "cousin," but a Canela calls him "father." A Canela won't behave exactly the same way to this relatively distant "father" as she or he would behave to an actual father, but the behavior may be similar in certain ways, especially if the actual father has died.

If you are a Canela, certain of your other "fathers"[1] replace your actual father in predictable ways upon his death. Moreover, your "fathers" have similar rights and duties in relation to you. For instance, your "fathers" are supposed to provide you with meat every now and then, just as your actual father should do all the time. Also, all of your "fathers" have sexual rights to your mother, at least in theory, because they are classificatory spouses. In any case, they may act informally and joke frequently with her. Informality and joking are steps toward having sex for unrelated, opposite-sex individuals among the fun-loving Canela.

In another family,[2] my Canela brother's wife, Khop-pêê (club-greased), 52, addressed me as "husband," and therefore joked informally with me. So did my brother's wife's mother's sister's daughter, Tep-rã (fish's-blossom), 37, since she was another one of my classificatory "wives." (According to general kinship reckoning in the United States, she would be my brother's wife's first cousin.) Fish's Blossom joked boisterously with my brother and me because she did not live in our house, but Greased Club joked conservatively with us because she did live in the same house, being married to my brother, Falcon's Sight. Thus, behavior between "spouses" varies with physical and social distance as well as with genealogical distance. Behavior also varies for these reasons between "uncles" and "nephews" and between "fathers" and "sons," as well as between individuals in most other reciprocal kinship address and reference categories.

On one otherwise ordinary morning in 1975, the characteristically shy Falcon's Sight amused us all when he carried out his joking role as a "spouse." He grabbed his distant "wife" Fish's Blossom and, throwing her on a mat, proceeded to suck her breasts while she screamed playfully, struggling to push him off and get up. My kin and hers gathered around in a circle, enjoying the wrestling match, cheering on one or the other contestant, and reveling in the fun. But Falcon's Sight could only have done this with Fish's Blossom in public. If done in private without a woman's consent, this kind of behavior is considered abusive. Before pacification, such "spouses" as Falcon and Fish usually would have had sex, when most opposite-sex Canela who were unrelated did so, but such practices, though not forbidden, are almost impossible today. If a woman in Greased Club's position today became jealous and angry at her husband Falcon and her "sister" Fish for having hidden sex with each other, nobody would support her hostility toward them, especially not in the interfamily judicial hearings or in the tribal Council of Elders.

My Canela Sister's Extended Household

At the time of my adoption in 1957, my sister Waterfall was 31 and her husband Macaw's Bone was 40. Other significant individuals in our two-room house of palm straw were Waterfall's full sister Ha-pôl (on-fire), 29, Waterfall's first cousin (her "sister") Amyi-yakhop (self-searching), 22, and Waterfall's daughter Hïïpôô-tsen (lake-likes), 14. Self Searcher's husband was Khen-yawên (hill-flattened: mesa), 35. On Fire was unmarried, and Lake Lover's husband was Kuhê-?khũm (boil's-vapor), 20. However, Mesa and Boil's Vapor were not strong presences in the house, because they had married into it rather than having been born in it. Macaw's Bone had married into the house also, but since he was older than the other men and had married the oldest female born in the house, he exerted considerable authority over these other "married-in" men. (See Figure 3.2.)

The three older women of the house had about eight children living with them. (In the 1950s, approximately 60 percent of the children born to Canela women died before they were 9, mostly of dysentery and dehydration.) My niece Lake Lover had been married for two years but had not yet conceived.[3]

Macaw's Bone directed the efforts of the two other married-in men when collective work was necessary in the separate fields of all the household's adult women, though each man worked for his own wife and family most of the time. Macaw's Bone also directed the efforts of his mentally handicapped oldest son Kô?kanãl (water-endures).

By 1966 Macaw's Bone had three sons-in-law, so Self Searcher and Mesa moved out to join Khen-tapi (hill-climber), Self Searcher's "sister," a second cousin in this case. Hill Climber was not married, but had four children, and was living with her married sister one house away clockwise along the village circle.

Macaw's Bone also managed most of the household's other economic activities. He was much more demanding with his young sons-in-law, who were married to his daughters, than he was with Mesa, who was married to his wife's "sister." He never

Bonding through Kinship

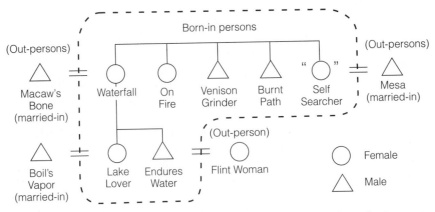

Figure 3.2 Married-in's versus born-in's in a partial representation of my adoptive household

sent Mesa on personal errands such as fetching a firebrand from the hearth to light his cigarette, but he sent Boil's Vapor and his sons-in-law on the most trivial errands such as getting used paper from me for rolling his cigarettes or matches from the post. One time he sent Mesa to the backland Brazilian community of Bacabal, 10 miles to the west, to obtain a pig for his daughter Lake Lover's belt-winning rite so that everybody in the whole household could eat and enjoy themselves.

Waterfall organized the women to carry out the domestic chores. Nevertheless, she deferred to her two brothers Poo-katwè (venison-grinder), 35, and Burnt Path, 28, when they came from their marital houses to govern their house of birth, advise its members, and settle any significant disputes. (See Figure 3.3.) These born-in male members of the house, since they did not live in it, had little to do with its day-to-day economic subsistence. But these uncles often helped their sisters discipline and socialize their children.

The underlying purposes of the leading individuals of such a Canela household are to feed its members, raise its children, and keep its morale high. Waterfall's energy and goodwill seemed inexhaustible to me as she carried out these traditional purposes: seeing that vegetables were cultivated and brought from the garden, arranging the preparation of food at the one communal hearth, and lending a hand at raising everyone's children. The principal role of Macaw's Bone was to provide meat for the household. He was one of the tribe's great hunters. He often brought venison home from the hunt or even a partridge now and then, the most difficult game to shoot. Mesa was a slow runner and his vision was poor, but he was good at digging armadillos out of their deep holes. Boil's Vapor limited himself to the Brazilian back-land hunting style of waiting in trees with a flashlight at night to transfix and shoot large rodents such as paca and agouti. Macaw's Bone's role included bargaining with visiting Brazilian backlanders for food such as beef, rice, and brown sugar, and goods such as tobacco, gunpowder, and lead shot. The return on male activities such as hunting is uncertain, unlike the steady provision of field crops by females. Since meat is relatively scarce, it is important for the status of women that it is they, not the

Figure 3.3 Women of three generations of a household prepare manioc. A typical cooking fire with three rocks can be seen behind the carrying baskets.

men, who distribute meat within the domestic unit. Moreover, the leading women reward cooperative behavior through their preferences.

The uncles Venison Grinder and Burnt Path, as well as other "uncles," represented the family judicially in the tribal council and before the chief. They also hunted to supply game for their nieces' and nephews' rites of passage through life, such as puberty, belt-winning, and the postpartum release of the contributing fathers. But with characteristic Canela flexibility, Macaw's Bone quickly stepped in to carry out the "uncles'" traditional duties if they were slow to prepare for the ceremonies of his household's children or for their judicial representation in the plaza. Similarly, if the "uncles" who were good hunters were away traveling to Brazilian cities, Macaw's Bone did not hesitate to go hunting in their place.

Otherwise Macaw's Bone deferred to the "uncles," although he was older. In February 1960, I saw him sitting quietly in a corner making a new pouch for himself, keeping his nervous fingers busy, while the "uncles" and his wife discussed his daughter's ceremonial future. They decided to allow Lake Lover to accept the role of one of the two Clown society's female associates. Macaw did not like to contemplate the fact that about 30 Clown society members would use his daughter sexually. Close opposite-sex kin are embarrassed to be made aware of their sexuality. This reluctance may seem inconsistent with the sexual freedom discussed in Chapter 5. The kinship system, however, does involve sexual inhibition. Macaw would want to ignore his daughter's sexuality in order to maintain his proper kin relationship with her. In contrast, her "uncles," being more removed emotionally, were not as sensitive, and thought it would be best for the Clowns to bring Lake Lover down a bit in ceremonial rank. No men's society had touched her when she was winning her belt earlier, because she was one of the two ceremonially high Wè?tè girls.

Lake Lover's husband, Boil's Vapor, had trouble with the male members of my Canela family since he was only a married-in man and a new one to us in 1957. The two uncles Venison Grinder and Burnt Path and Lake Lover's brothers, as born-in men, interrupted Boil in conversations. They also helped themselves to items from the thatch where Boil kept things wedged near his wife's platform bed, such as tobacco and razor blades.

Avoidance Relationships

Boil referred to his wife's male kin as *i-pree*, which I will translate as "in-brother," while they in turn referred to Boil using *piyōyê* (out-brother). Boil remained silent in our presence most of the time. In fact, he *never* spoke to my sister Waterfall, his mother-in-law (*pān:* avoidance mother). Boil will have an avoidance-woman as well, when he and Lake eventually have a grown and married son. Then Boil will also refer to his son's wife as *pān* (avoidance-daughter). He won't be able to speak to her or to her sisters and her many "sisters." Similarly, Boil could not speak to Waterfall's sister, On Fire, her same household's full sister; nor could Boil speak to Self Searcher, Waterfall's "sister" in the neighboring house. Similarly, Boil could not speak to Waterfall's many other "sisters" (her more distant cousins) along the village circle of houses in both directions. In the same way, Waterfall could not speak to Boil but could refer to him as her *wawè* (her avoidance-son), and Boil's future daughter-in-law will not speak to him but will refer to him as her *khrā?tūmyê* (her avoidance-father).

Full avoidance relationships are common in tribal life throughout the world. I first became impressed by the compelling force of this relationship among the Canela when Hanging Fish, 45, who was a "son" to me, though I was 33, invited himself into the room I worked and slept in while I was studying one morning in 1957. He explained, apologetically, that he just wanted to sit there out of the hot sun without disturbing me, but I questioned him. Hanging Fish finally admitted that he could not stay in his own house that morning because everybody had left except his primary avoidance-mother, making them both very uncomfortable.

Hanging Fish told me that he never looked directly at his avoidance-mother's face. He would walk off the trail if she were coming, and he would delay bathing whenever she was near the water hole. Hanging Fish and his avoidance-mother would never exchange the same cigarette as the Canela commonly did. When it was necessary to communicate with her, he would speak to his wife and let the older woman overhear.

I received the full avoidance treatment when my wife, Roma, came by missionary plane to join me in the village in the mid-1970s, and we lived together in a room in her adopted Canela kin's house. Before she had actually arrived, I had to remain in my sister Waterfall's house or in my brother Falcon Sight's house. Roma's kin would not let me move into our room to spend the night in their house without her. Since poor regional communications prevented my knowing exactly which day Roma would arrive, I carried all our things over to our room on several consecutive days, only to have to carry them back in the afternoon when she had not arrived.[4]

On the first occasion of this sort, Roma's mother, my primary avoidance-mother, Star Woman, had to speak to me, because she thought I was going to spend the night alone in Roma's room. So Star Woman gave one of her unmarried daughters a lecture about how husbands stayed in their sisters' or mothers' houses when their wives were away unless they had children, so that I would overhear and leave. I was so absorbed in my work that I did not overhear her at first, and when I did, I assumed she was lecturing her daughter. She raised her voice louder and louder, always speaking to her daughter, until I caught on and started to pack up our things. To offend your avoidance-mother is embarrassing.

Other Kinship Terms and Their Roles

In our house, Boil's Vapor got along best with his wife's sisters and "sisters" (On Fire's and Self Searcher's daughters), with whom he could joke sexually. Boil addressed and referred to each of them as "wife," which at their unmarried age consisted of calling them by their personal names. These girls were his "other-wives" (*prō-?nō:* wife-other). They in return called him by his personal name, Boil, since he was their "other-husband" (*pyê-?nō:* husband-other).

Spouses and relatively close "spouses" use teknonymy when full grown, whether they have children or not. Teknonymy is the practice of two related people speaking to each other by referring to their children. Thus, Waterfall called her husband, Macaw's Bone, "Kō?kanāl-më-hūm" (Kô?kanāl-his-father), or "Endures Water's father." And Macaw's Bone called Waterfall "Kô?kanāl-më-ntsii" (Endures Water-his-mother), or "Endures Water's mother." Couples who have occasional quick extramarital trysts use each others' personal names, but couples who are carrying on long-term affairs use the other "spouse's" oldest child's personal name (of either sex), just as if they were married.

During my research assistant group meetings in 1964, my special helper, the younger Thunder, 32, repeatedly called an old research assistant, Pyê-?khàl (earth-striped), 71, by her personal name. This intrigued me. I thought Thunder was being too familiar with his avoidance-mother's mother (his actual wife's mother's mother), whom I thought should be an "avoidance-woman" to him. But Thunder told me that in earlier times calling a woman "avoidance-mother" applied only to persons one generation above yourself, and that this custom was gradually being lost. (The sophisticated Thunder was well aware of many of these changes.) The loss of this personal name usage paralleled the disappearance during the 1930s and 1940s of the practice of adolescents having sex with far older men and postmenopausal women. I deduced that if adolescents would not have sex with these older people anymore, they also would no longer call them by their personal names. So I accepted that old Striped Earth was Thunder's "wife" according to earlier usage. My young helper Thunder could behave familiarly with her even though the sexual basis for the familiarity had died out.

While my Canela research assistants could find no current examples for the corresponding male pattern, they assured me that an adolescent girl could call her avoidance-father's father (her father-in-law's father) by his personal name. Research assistants also said that the age span between sons and fathers is usually greater than that between daughters and mothers, which would make this practice unlikely. More probably, the girl would call her avoidance-father's father "uncle" (*kêt*), as younger people call almost all men in their late 60s and 70s. In the same way, they call almost all old women "aunt" (tùy).

A wife, whether young or aged, refers to each of her husband's female kin as *i-pree* (my in-person), except for her husband's mother, her sisters, and her "sisters," whom she calls *i-pree-kêy* (my in-person senior). In return, she is their *i-tswèyyê* ("out-sister"/"out-daughter"), depending on generational differences. "In-" and "out-" for women-in-law refer to those born in the house and to those married in but living *out* of the house (see Flint Woman in Figure 3.2). A bride continues to reside in her mother's house and does not move permanently to her husband's and mother-in-law's house even when old. The behavior of this reciprocal relationship was harder for me to observe than most others, because my Canela sister Waterfall's sisters- and daughters-in-law lived in other houses. Occasionally, her sons brought their wives to work in our house, and I observed that the females of our house treated them well. Moreover, both my regular female and male research assistants spoke well of the female in-/out- relationship when we had group discussions about it. They said it is epitomized by collective work, goodwill, and cooperation, unlike its male counterpart described above for Boil's Vapor and his in-brothers (his wife's brothers and uncles). This male relationship, as we saw, is marked by petty harassment.

In contrast to the close relationship between uterine sisters, uterine brothers are more distant when grown. They live apart in their wives' houses and call each other by terms of address meaning "older brother" and "younger brother," instead of using personal names as uterine sisters do. The male world is more hierarchical than the female one.

For several years, Waterfall's mentally handicapped son Endures Water and his older and more capable wife Khrùt-khwèy (flint-woman), 28, came to live with us, disregarding the generally well-kept rule of matrilocality, so that Endure's parents could give him moral support in his marriage. Flint worked well with the other women of the household and was treated substantially as if she were their kin instead of their out-sister or out-daughter. The Canela kinship system allows adaptations for special living arrangements. By the 1990s, Endures had matured sufficiently to live with Flint in her house with her sisters and mother.

One of the rites I liked most to record is the making of the bride's social maturity belt, one of the Canela's many steps into marriage. Canela research assistants said the belt represents the bond between the two sets of female kin—its makers (the bride's kin) and its painters (the groom's kin). To make the cord for the belt, each one of the bride's female kin "rolls" tucum fibers on her thigh, forming many three-foot sections. Then the sections are twisted together, forming an approximately 100-foot-long cord, which is sent over to the in-mothers and in-sisters. The bride's husband's kin paints the cord red, each woman running it through her urucu-coated hands. Then they play out the cord as the standing bride rotates her body, thus winding the cord in many loops (about 80) around her upper hips. (See Figure 3.4.) They tie the loops together in front, forming a knot, and the wedding belt is removed over her shoulders.

In former times, when a girl lowered her belt past her shoulders down to her hips each day, she tucked two large leaves under the belt's knot. The leaves extended well below to cover her genitals. By the 1950s, she wore the belt only for certain ceremonial appearances. More recently, girls have been wearing the belt more frequently, even on social occasions, over brief panties.

William H. Crocker

Figure 3.4 A bride's female in-laws hold the cord of tucum fibers while she rotates, wrapping the long cord around her hips, forming the wedding belt.

Another close bond exists between a naming-uncle and his named-nephew, usually his sister's son or his "sister's" son. (A similar but weaker bond exists between a naming-aunt and her named-niece.) A naming-uncle gives his little named-nephew a small set of bow and arrows. He teaches his named-nephew all his ceremonial roles and takes the youth to perform beside him during the transition period of several years. Then the uncle retires and lets his nephew carry on. The paired naming-uncle and named-nephew used to be so close that they had sexual access to each others' wives, and today they still address each others' wives as "spouses," though sex between them is rare.

I still wonder why my naming-uncle, Deer's Nest, actually my sister's "brother" (a second cousin), called my first wife "wife" and referred to my second wife as his "avoidance-woman." Whatever his reasons, his choices demonstrate the existence of customary alternatives. Canela women and men have many "other-spouses." Some couples of this sort are "spouses," as reckoned through a particular series of kin linkages, and others are "avoidance-people" to each other even though the series of linkages is identical. The choice can be made. Deer's Nest considered both my first and second wives his named-nephew's wives. If he felt he could joke with such a category of person, she was a "spouse." If he did not want to joke (and in earlier times have sex), she was an "avoidance-daughter." I found many examples among the Canela of individuals who had made such choices, consciously or unconsciously.

Committing "incest" (incest being a culturally defined concept) with distant kin or affines is one of the ways many Canela obtain their actual spouses, though they more often marry individuals to whom they believe they are not related. Pairs of individuals can think they are unrelated in a society of this size (1,300 in 2001), because people are likely to forget certain sets of kinship linkages by the third generation. In the Canela case, if the linkages are through males, people may not remember them by the second generation down. That is, a man and his father's father's brother's son's son *probably* do not know they are related, though they would be second cousins in most kinship systems of the United States. In contrast, a Canela woman and her mother's mother's mother's sister's daughter's daughter's daughter *usually* know they are "sisters," though they would be third cousins in most parts of the United States. For the Canela, Crow kinship patterns, matrilocal residence, and stress on the continuity of matrilines in longhouses are factors that place more emphasis on kin links among women than on those among men.

The closest bonding among the Canela, however, exists between siblings, especially between sisters. Siblings are believed to grow off one and the same umbilicus. Consequently, all siblings have "blood" (*kaprôô*) that is "similar" or "equivalent" (*ipipën*). Brothers tend to drift apart because they live with their wives in different houses at widely separate locations on the village circle, while sisters live in the same house or in adjacent houses along the village circle. Sisters are so close that respect between them does not have to be built up and maintained through the use of special terms of address and reference. Thus, sisters can call each other by their personal names, although senior and junior terms of address and reference are used when a serious difference arises. In contrast, brothers always use senior (*i-hà*) and junior (*iyõ?hêw-re*) terms of address, as determined by relative age.

Opposite-sex uterine siblings, those born of the same mother, may call each other by their personal names when they are young and still close. If they have drifted apart, however, they practice teknonymy, though a different kind than spouses use. It is traditional for a sister and brother, whether uterine or classificatory, to give a name to one child of the other sibling, a child that is the same sex as the name-giver. Some opposite-sex siblings (and "siblings") may have exchanged names and others not. In any case, they all use the following terms of address: The sister calls her brother "my name-receiver's father" (*i túware-më hüm*), and the brother calls his sister "my name-receiver's mother" (*i túware-më ntsii*).

Name-exchanging takes place three times more frequently between non-uterine opposite-sex "siblings," to strengthen the "siblingship," than between uterine siblings, whose "blood" similarity keeps up their relationship. The Canela male has an alternative to name-exchanging with a distant "sister": He can make her his "spouse" through sex, if she is willing. He either exchanges names with her to maintain the extensiveness of his kin ties, or he has sex with her to increase his number of "other spouses," who can be politically helpful to him later through their brothers.

When Thunder's "nieces" chose to have fun with him, they teased him mercilessly, sometimes saying he had few female kin because he had turned most of them into "spouses." His "nieces" proceeded to name most of the kin he had committed "incest" with, one after another, describing the occasions—common knowledge in the village anyway. Thunder was both embarrassed and pleased because being liked by a large number of "spouses," and keeping them all happy, was something to be proud of in the Canela world. Women with many "husbands" were also prestigious.

Because I was adopted by Waterfall, I was considered her name-exchange "brother." In 1960, I gave a name that I invented to her newly born son. Instead of giving the child one of my unused names, I chose "Strong Locust" (Ku?tàà- tèy: locust-strong), because locust trees are believed to furnish strength. Each person, male or female, carries a set of names and can give each one to a different nephew or niece. Instead, I invented a name. They have two customs. In return, in 1970, Waterfall put her name on my stepdaughter Tara, calling her Little Waterfall. As name-exchange siblings, Waterfall and I have great respect for each other. We talk to each other only when we have to, and we never joke. We have to talk quite often, however, since I live in her house when in the tribe. As any Canela woman does for her male kin or husbands, Waterfall sees that my domestic necessities are taken care of: the food preparation, the small amount of laundry, and the occasional cleaning of my living space. Her abilities as female head of household win my highest respect. However, by the late 1990s, with the earlier authority of uncles, aunts, and grandparents lost and the balance of power descended to the younger generations, Waterfall fills in where she is wanted, not running the household anymore.

One morning in 1959, an accident occurred that might have been a disaster for me. My three "nieces" from next door had playfully attacked me. We were throwing empty orange skins at each other, sneaking around from house to house to the amusement of all present. Trying to hit a "niece" by surprise, I threw a whole, mushy orange skin around a corner at her only to hit my sister Waterfall squarely on the side of the face. Silence filled the house, and I grew red with mortification. I had insulted my principal ally in the tribe and broken one of the strongest Canela taboos, joking with a sister. But Waterfall, great lady that she is, saved the situation after a pause by continuing to talk with one of her sisters as if nothing had happened. Soon I retired to my room, aghast at how she might have taken my mistake. I also realized how deeply I had absorbed at least two Canela values: respect for a sister and shame (pahàm) if that respect were violated.

Changes in the Balance between the Sexes

In accordance with a general shift from male power to female power, which has been occurring in several cultural sectors over the last few decades, the visits and influences from the male kin of a Canela household are lessening. In theory, as we have seen, the sons, brothers, and mother's brothers of these closely related women, though living with their wives and children, come home to where they were born and grew up to govern the women, their children, their grandchildren, and their husbands. In modern times, however, they seldom do so, and consequently the control of the household is left to the older and more dominant females of the domestic group. This modern lessening of visits and influences from the male kin constitutes a very important change in the balance between the sexes, a change that conveys more power and responsibility to women.

Bonding around the Village Circle of Houses

The network of kinship *around* the circle of houses bonds sectors of adjacent houses into "longhouses," while the network of kinship *across* the circle bonds pairs of "longhouses" for several generations, as discussed in the next section.

The Canela kinship system is called "Crow," because it is similar to the system of the Crow Indians of the North American Plains. In Crow systems, which are found throughout the world, siblings of the same sex are often addressed similarly. As we have seen above, Falcon's Sight calls Fish's Blossom, his wife's "sister," "wife." Similarly, a woman calls her husband's brother, or his "brother," "husband."

Each society chooses which pathways of kinship linkages it wants to maintain. Maintaining these pathways often depends on the support of certain institutions. These institutions serve to keep the persons at the opposite ends of the pathways in contact with each other. The number of kin linkages, which all together constitute a pathway, between the speaker and the addressed person, may be as many as 10 in some well-supported Canela relationships.

For the Canela, the village circle of houses is one of the institutions that supports the significant pathways of kin linkages, bonding the society together. Another institution is the arrangement of the female kin living in these houses. By the word "arrangement" I mean the particular pattern of kin linkages that unite the female kin. These patterns are consistent with Crow kinship patterns. Kin linkages passing through males are not supported by the arrangement of females in the houses around the village, as will be shown later.

In theory, the principle that siblings are equal to each other—are called by the same kin term by certain other related people—is extended to a Canela individual's cousins of the same generation, if the reckoning of the cousinships is carried out through all-female linkages. The pattern of cousins being "siblings" is maintained for several generations down. Thus, an individual's mother's sister's daughter is this same individual's "sister" (a first cousin in most systems of the United States). An individual's mother's mother's sister's daughter's daughter is this same individual's "sister" (a second cousin). An individual's mother's mother's mother's sister's daughter's daughter's daughter is this same individual's "sister" (a third cousin), and so on.

In one extended family (see houses *aa* through *nn* in Figure 3.5), everybody was descended from one female ancestor, Amyiyakhop, an Apanyekra (a Piranha woman). Here I found "siblings" during the 1970 census, who were fifth cousins and still called each other "sister"—Thorn Woman, 23, in house *bb,* and Village Plaza, 28, in house *nn.* These women were teaching certain of their children to call each other "sibling" (sixth cousins in this case). The women of this great family extended over 14 houses, a segment of the village circle that contained 27 percent of the 52 houses. The village had 13 segments or longhouses of this sort, the smallest of which was composed of one house.

Within her longhouse (*ikhre-rùù:* house-long), Thorn called many, though not all, of her "sisters'" mothers "mother" and her "sisters'" fathers "father." She called each of her "sisters'" children "child" and her "sisters'" grandparents "aunt" and "uncle," since no special terms exists for "grandmother" and "grandfather" in Canela. Thirteen such longhouses—each bonded internally through the same pattern of kinship reckoning (that is, through all-female linkages)—comprise the units found around the village circle. These unnamed longhouses, with known and traceable

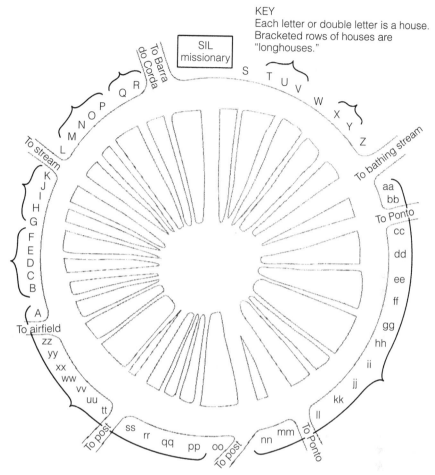

KEY
Each letter or double letter is a house.
Bracketed rows of houses are
"longhouses."

Figure 3.5 Village circle of longhouses (approximation, 1970)

ancestors, are bound to certain longhouses *across* the village circle through another pattern of kinship reckoning.

To summarize, bonding *around* the village circle of houses starts with *same*-sex siblings—with two or more uterine sisters. Then the bonding around the village circle is continued with mother-to-daughter-to-daughter lines (called "matrilines") descending from each of the founding sisters down through the generations and spreading out from each of the founding sisters to form a longhouse. At each generation below the original sisters, the women are "sisters" to each other. On the first generation below, the "sisters" are first cousins to each other by our usual reckoning, on the second generation they are second cousins, and so on, as long as the matrilines last.

This mother-to-daughter-to-granddaughter structure is what holds a longhouse[5] together internally through the generations. (See Figure 3.6.) Marriage should not take place between members of a longhouse; in other words, a longhouse is "exogamous," so marriages internal to a longhouse are considered incestuous and forbidden.

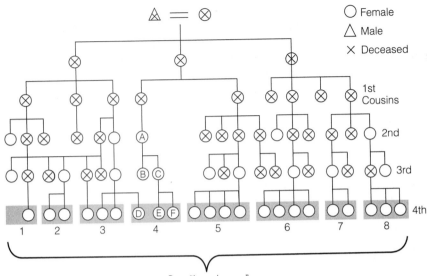

Figure 3.6 Matrilines in a longhouse (model)

When marriages do take place within a longhouse between distant kin, these marriages begin to terminate the longhouse. Longhouses also become weakened and shrink in size if few daughters are born to continue their matrilines. My special helper Thunder sometimes points with nostalgia to a location on the village circle where his natal longhouse had stood before the lack of female descendants terminated it completely.

Bonding across *the Village Circle of Houses*

In contrast to the bonds *around* the circle, bonding *across* the village circle begins with *opposite*-sex siblings instead of *same*-sex ones. The pattern starts with a young man leaving his mother's and sisters' house to go across the plaza to marry somewhere on the other side of the village circle.[6] There the young man procreates the first daughters of the mother-to-daughter-to-granddaughter lines that parallel through the generations the mother-to-daughter-to-granddaughter lines descending from the sister he left behind in his mother's house. The first-generation female descendants of this young man and his sister (normally first cousins in the United States) are not Canela "sisters" this time, because they are not descended from *same*-sex siblings, who are called "parallel-cousins" in anthropology. They are descended from *opposite*-sex siblings, who are called "cross-cousins." In Crow and many other kinship systems, parallel-cousins and cross-cousins address and refer to each other using quite different terms.

Let's apply the different pattern for cross-cousins to the situation created by a young man, Whip, who crossed the village plaza to marry on the other side of the village. Whip's sister, Bat Woman, and all her female descendants call all Whip's female descendants "niece" (*hapaltswèy:* niece/granddaughter/female descendant), and all Whip's female descendants in return call all Bat's female descendants "aunt" (tùy: aunt/grandmother/female ancestor). The "niece" in the first descending generation below Whip refers to her "aunt's" sons as i-päm (my "father"), and the "nieces" in the still lower generations below Whip refer to their "aunt's" sons as kêt (uncle/grandfather/male-ancestor).

The across-the-village bonding described above joins two longhouses for about three generations, down to the second cousin level, rarely to the third and never to the fourth. Thus, a pair of across-the-village longhouses, which are united by a marriage on the first generation, should be exogamous for the next two generations.

The bonding *within* longhouses may continue for more generations than the bonding *between* longhouses. Actually, when longhouses become sufficiently long—when they consist of more than about two to four houses—they break informally into extended household units for the purposes of their youths' marrying across the village circle. Thus, every marriage creates a bonding between two longhouses, or between two extended households, which are said to be "across" the village circle from each other even though they may be next door to each other, as were Lake Lover and Boil's Vapor, temporarily, in 1957. This "across-the-village" bonding is massive. Figure 3.7 is a partial representation of most of these marital bonds in 1970.

In summary, the Canela tribe is integrated by matrilines of parallel-cousins descending from one female ancestor. These generation-to-generation structures hold the longhouses together internally. The longhouses exist end-on-end around the village circle and consisted of from 1 to 14 houses in 1970. With husbands coming from other longhouses, marriages continue the matrilines within the longhouses down through the generations. Marriages also tie different longhouses together across the village circle.

The principal integrative building blocks for the kinship level of Canela social structure are the village circle of houses (which operates in space) and the matrilines based on Crow kinship (which operate through time).

Life on Farms away from the Village

The Canela work on their farms, living in their farm settlement huts intermittently, about half the year. All women above the age of about 18—whether married, single, with children, or childless—must maintain their own farms, producing bitter and sweet manioc, rice, corn, beans, yams, sweet potatoes, peanuts, squash, and other garden crops. Like houses, farm gardens belong to women only. The women's gardens are generally clustered geographically according to the same grouping of nuclear families that composes the domestic hearth units back in the village. Thus, the same nuclear families that live together in the village according to female kinship usually farm together in the same region of the tribal reservation. Many exceptions occur, however, because husbands can exert their preferences more effectively when on their wives' farms. Husbands are politically stronger on the farming scene because the ecology of the region requires the farms to be scattered. They are located sufficiently far apart so that sisters of a village domestic unit are often parted by distance when living on their farms, having to spend their nights in nuclear family huts by their separate farm gardens. Consequently, a village unit with one hearth is often split into several farm hearths. Since husbands carry out the heavy work to prepare farms and like to work in male groups, a firm husband may sometimes convince his wife

The circle represents the village circle.

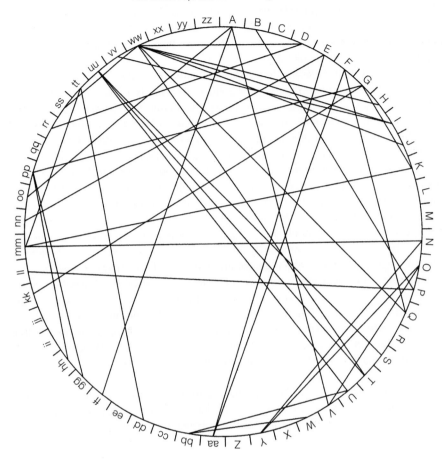

Letters and double letters represent Escalvado village houses.
Lines between the letters represent some of the marital connections.

Figure 3.7 Marital bonds across the village circle (actual, 1970)

to go with their children to farm a garden near his male relative's wife's farm, or near his male friend's wife's farm. His justification to his wife might be that the male friend is a hard worker, that the soil is better there, or that the political alliance there could be advantageous.[7]

Joking Behavior between Aunts, Uncles, Nieces, and Nephews

Youths especially enjoy their "aunts" and "uncles" who live across the village plaza. They can be very informal with these "aunts" and "uncles" because of their social distance and because these relatives rarely assume responsibility for them. While same-sex practical joking and teasing is common among such relatives, opposite-sex joking offers better opportunities for expressing the fun and sport the Canela seem to need so much of the time.

Belt Pulled Off, 62 in 1975, besides being my great kinship specialist, was my sister Waterfall's father's sister's daughter, our "aunt." I called her three sons "father" and behaved respectfully to them, though they were younger than I. On the other hand, I joked moderately with Belt and excessively with her three daughters, Single, 41, Alligator Woman, 30, and Silent, 27.

During June of 1975, while the husbands of these four "aunts" were clearing their fields, Aunt Belt invited me out to their field hut to spend Sunday. I brought my hammock along for an afternoon nap. However, my three "aunties" may have thought I was sleeping too long. They quietly untied one end of my hammock and retied it to another tree so that my feet hung over a low fire. Fortunately, their unintentional jostling of the hammock woke me before the heat of the fire did. Then I had to get out of the double-sized, deep matrimonial hammock (my size required a large one) without falling or stepping into the fire. My mock antics and verbal threats kept them laughing for some time.

An extreme example of "uncle" to "niece" sex-joking occurred one morning in 1979. Slippery Forest, 35, ordinarily a responsible and serious age class leader, caught his "niece" Long Woman, 10, and threw her on her back in the sand of the circular boulevard just outside my brother Falcon Sight's house. He spread her struggling little legs, lowered himself between them, and jerked his hips as if he were copulating. He had on long pants, however, which was unusual dress even for 1979, and she had on the usual wraparound cloth and panties. The young Long screamed with joy and continued wriggling to pretend to get away until Slippery Forest got up. The crowd was amused by the performance. At age 10, Long had learned enough about sex to mimic screams of delight rather than of fear or anger.

While the principal joking roles among the Canela are between the sexes—between "aunts" and "nephews," "uncles" and "nieces," and between "spouses"—a same-sex joking role also exists between males who have chosen to enter the traditional relationship of Informal Friends to each other, as discussed below.

OTHER FORMS OF "KINSHIP"

Besides the two relationship systems, the consanguineal and affinal, the Canela have several other interpersonal relationship systems of significance.

Informal Friendship

Boys and young men become Informal Friends by participating in a ceremonial performance. Early one morning during the four-month initiation festival-pageants, the Khêêtúwayê (Ghosts) and the Pepyê (Warriors) boys and youths establish Informal Friendships with each other. They enter a swimming hole in pairs, side-by-side, and submerge themselves completely. (See Figure 3.8.) When they emerge, still as pairs, they look at each other steadily. In the 1970s, most of them held hands when they emerged from the water, but some of them shook hands, a Western adaptation.

The male pairs choose each other for their closeness and their desire to remain Informal Friends for the rest of their lives, unless a new relationship of higher priority, such as an affinal role, requires a change. Informal Friends call each other i-khwè-?nõ (my-group-one: a person of my group, or my age class).

William H. Crocker

Figure 3.8 Youths emerge from the water as Informal Friends. The Canela use such spots in the stream for bathing as well.

Informal Friends formerly exchanged each other's wives for sexual purposes and still refer to each other's wives and children as "our wife" and "our child," using a special dual form, the personal pronoun *pa*. Extensions of this Informal Friendship system of address and reference sometimes spread through the Informal Friends' children, wives, and wives' parents to still further-linked kin and affines, thereby changing the usual pattern of the terms otherwise used in a longhouse and breaking up the mother-to-daughter-to-granddaughter lines.

Informal Friends take each other's possessions freely, without asking. They are constant companions and confidants. A war story tells of a youth who was shamed and disrespected by a sister. She did not consider him important enough to reserve and keep meat for regularly. He told his Informal Friend that he was going out of the tribal area and into the region controlled by an enemy tribe. Of course, the enemy warriors would kill him on sight, so this was an honorable way of committing suicide. The youth preferred death to living with his shame. The youth's Informal Friend felt obligated to accompany him, so they both were killed.

While the intensity of Informal Friendship behavior was considerably reduced by the late 1950s, evidence of the institution's continued existence surfaced almost every day in practical jokes. If a youth dumped a calabash of orange buriti palm juice on another youth's head, I thought they must be Informal Friends, but sought verification from research assistants when necessary. If a young man shoved another one into a young woman, who then screamed and moved quickly away, embarrassed, I suspected that the young man had pushed his Informal Friend into one of the latter's avoidance-women.

In a farm hut during the heat of the afternoon on the Wild Boar extramarital exchange day in 1958, Fox's Belly, 17, saw an opportunity to play a joke on his

Informal Friend, Jaguar Head, 16. Fox's Belly was also playing up to his entire age class for their favor while they were lying around and resting with little to do but tell stories. No women were present.

Jaguar Head was lying on his back and snoring so loudly that he was disrupting the story telling. Something had to be done to stop the noisy distraction. The offending person's Informal Friend often helps his age class in such delicate situations. Jaguar must also have been dreaming about some appealing woman because he was sporting a partial erection to everyone's amusement. In those days, some youths still went naked, especially out in the farms.

Fox approached Jaguar slowly, trying not to wake him, with the whole age class watching silently. Fox rolled back Jaguar's foreskin carefully and caught the noose of a light cord under Jaguar's glans. Then he dusted the glans with sand and rolled up the foreskin gently, stopping to wait each time the snoring lessened. Jaguar kept waving his hand in his sleep at what he may have dreamed was a fly settling on his penis, and the men had difficulty restraining their laughter. Finally, Fox, still holding the far end of the cord, positioned himself just outside the hut—and yanked. Jaguar sat up quickly to hear his age class roaring at him, and he searched the hut with his eyes for his Informal Friend, whom he assumed had played this trick on him, but could not see Fox. Jaguar would have to wait for some appropriate occasion to return the intimate compliment to their friendship, made in full confidence of its acceptance. However, he felt great shame that others had seen his glans, an exposure that was the principal violation of male modesty in a formerly naked world.

The practical joke between Informal Friends that I remember best, however, took place repeatedly between the older Thunder and my out-brother Macaw's Bone. I first saw it happen during the informal meetings of an age class in the late 1950s and again during the formal meetings of the Elders in the late 1970s. It was usually the irrepressible Macaw's Bone who reenacted the joke by tossing the first handful of sand in the more prestige-conscious Thunder's face. Then Thunder characteristically acted as if nothing had occurred, but later raised a hand to brush the sand out of his eyes, nose, and mouth. Maybe a half-hour later, when Macaw's Bone had become less watchful, Thunder caught him in the face with a return fistful of sand. I was always surprised at the accuracy and success of such assaults and amazed that otherwise dignified members of the Elders would play such jokes on each other while the Council was meeting.

Formal Friendship

The institution of Formal Friendship is extensive and very evolved among the Canela, so it can only be summarized here. Pairs of Formal Friends behave toward each other as avoidance affines. Full avoidance takes place between some pairs ("primary" ones: -*mpey*) and moderate avoidance occurs between other pairs ("secondary" ones: -*kahàk*). Avoidance behavior proscribes speaking and looking, but not other behaviors and rites. As a Canela, your primary Formal Friend decorates your body for ceremonial occasions and paints your corpse when you die, while your secondary Formal Friends have no prescribed ceremonial roles in relation to you, though they have many general ones. Your primary Formal Friends are considered "primary" because you carried out a special rite to originate this special status. The rite (*ntêê*) is performed before the house of a pregnant woman—chanting a song and giving food—to indicate that you would accept her offspring of either sex as your primary Formal Friend. Secondary Formal Friends are name-linked or ceremonially role-linked in origin. Such Formal Friendships may also be made during the swimming hole rite, like Informal Friendships, except that the pair enters and emerges from the water facing away from each other in shame and respect.

As a Canela, your secondary Formal Friends always support you when you are in serious trouble. Unlike your kin, however, your Formal Friends expect compensation for special services. They also withdraw from any competitive situation you are in. When I observed during log races that the individual log-carriers of both teams had slowed down, so that one was not attempting to pass the other, I knew that the two runners were Formal Friends.

When I was first with the Canela in 1957, Painted Leg was my primary Formal Friend. We never spoke or looked each other in the face. Nevertheless, in 1959 during a trading day, Painted Leg spoke to me directly and looked up into my face, much to my surprise. She saw I was confused, so she quickly reassured me that a little talking was all right for us now, though joking still was not acceptable. She told me they had transferred the primary Formal Friendship between us to her newly born daughter, pointing to the infant in her arms. Now we were secondary Formal Friends. The helpful and flexible Macaw's Bone had performed the transference rite for me, but had forgotten to tell me.

During the Facsimile Warriors (Pepkahàk) festival-pageant, a wasp's nest is crushed with sticks to let wasps emerge near the hut in which the Facsimile Warrior troops are secluded. It is believed that because of the festival internment and its restrictions against food and sex, the Facsimile Warrior membership had entered into a ritually vulnerable state of being, so that wasp stings would harm them far more than persons in the ordinary state. To prevent the freed wasps from reaching the Facsimile Warriors' hut, their secondary Formal Friends station themselves around the hut and swat wasps that come by with large whisk brooms. The Facsimile Warrior members' Formal Friends always succeed in protecting the Facsimile Warriors by killing all the wasps, but usually some of the Formal Friends are stung.

In 1958, I was interned with the Facsimile Warriors, but was allowed to leave their hut just outside the village to conduct my fieldwork activities and sleep in my usual place in my sister's house. I had read about the crushing of the wasps' nest and the swatting of escaping wasps in Nimuendajú's volume, so I was determined to witness and photograph the act. I hung my equipment on my shoulders and charged out toward the Facsimile Warriors' hut only to hear my sister calling me back and to find others running to stand in my way. They reminded me that as a Facsimile Warrior and a ceremonial Chief-of-the-whole-tribe, which they had recently made me, I must not be stung by wasps, because I was ceremonially vulnerable. My Formal Friend, Pàl-khô (bed's stick) was especially vehement, saying that he would have to swat every wasp coming my way without fail, which he could not be sure of doing.

Personal Name-Set Transmission

Each Canela baby, whether female or male, receives a set of personal names from a name-giver, as described earlier, who is usually a female baby's father's sister (or her father's "sister") and a male baby's mother's brother (or his mother's "brother"). A personal set of names may contain anywhere from 1 to 15 names, depending on the donor's memory and interest in conserving ancestral customs. In any case, the name-giver designates only one name in the set for the name-receiver to be known by. The name-receiver, however, passes the entire set on to each of his or her name-receivers, so the name-set goes down the generations "forever" (nō?nù?ti-mā). This transmission of names occurs each time a name-giver exchanges names with a uterine or a classificatory sibling of the opposite sex.

A name-giver can either create a name on the spot when it is required for exchange with an opposite-sex sibling, or a name-giver can rely on one of the names already in her or his name-set. An example of name creation is the following: A woman who was angry with her husband ripped apart his half of the tied-together rods of their platform bed, leaving no room for him to join her at night. Later, remembering her great anger for her husband, she named her brother's daughter "Platform-bed thrown-down" (pàl-rë), possibly shaming her husband "forever." If Platform Down passes this name on to an eventual named-niece and this named-niece passes it on in turn, the name would be considered "ancestral" (mäm mënkêtyê mënkaakaa tsà khôt: early uncles' breath thing following: according to the breathing of the ancestors).

Contributing Fathers

The Canela believe that once a woman is pregnant, any semen added to her womb during her pregnancy becomes a biological part of the fetus. Thus, children usually have one mother but several "contributing" fathers, or "co-fathers." The Canela expression is "other fathers" (më hŭm nō: pl. father other). Recently, ethnologists have been comparing the forms of "partiple paternity," the current term for multiple paternity, practiced by many Amazonian groups.[8] While a child's father's brother and her or his father's sister's son are "fathers," among the other classificatory fathers, the child's contributing fathers are closer to the child in certain ways. Like a "social" father, the one married to the mother, a contributing father observes restrictions against food and sex when his contributed-to children are sick, unlike the classificatory fathers. His contribute-to children, in return, have to observe food restrictions when he is ill, to help him conserve his strength so that his condition does not worsen.

When a person is seriously ill, her or his immediate kin and spouse send messengers (usually able runners) to the sick person's absent one-link-away kin (parents, siblings, and children) to inform them that they must observe restrictions against certain "polluting" foods and against sexual relations that can also "pollute." Since contributing fathers are included in this close group of one-link-away kin, messengers are sent to them also. In contrast, messages are not sent to the sick person's father's brother (two biological links away) and her or his father's sister's son (three links away), though they are classificatory fathers.

A pregnant woman usually seeks handsome men she likes, who are also good hunters or good providers of food, as the contributing fathers of her fetus, since she believes such characteristics are inherited. However, she limits her choices to the men who promise to maintain a high level of postpartum restrictions against polluting foods and sex, so the baby will survive and grow strong.

At the time of birth, only women cluster around the laboring mother, who sits on mats, leans back onto the abdomen of a sister, and pulls on a rope slung from an overhead beam. When the baby "falls" (i?-pèm: it-falls: is born), its father's mother usually "catches" it. This woman then asks the new mother, her "out-daughter" (her daughter-in-law), to designate the baby's contributing fathers for the sake of its health and survival. The new mother names the men who had sex with her during her pregnancy, and a child is sent to walk around the village circle to announce at pertinent doors the name of the designated contributing father.

These contributing fathers, pleased or compromised, have to go into a state of seclusion that is called "couvade" in anthropology. They have to live alone in a darkened compartment for some time, just as the social father does. Since the social father and the contributing fathers are all considered "biological" fathers in their relation to the recently born infant, they have to observe extensive food and sex restrictions against potential pollutants. This is done because these "fathers" believe their blood to be continuous with the baby's blood, so that if they allow their blood to become contaminated, they could also be poisoning the baby. By eating certain foods or by having sex, these one-link-away "biological" kin could even cause the baby to die in its newly born and therefore very weak condition. The concept of pollution will be discussed further in the next chapter.

A man may be embarrassed by his public designation as a contributing father, because he probably is living with his wife and his wife's sisters and their mother. These sisters may give him a hard time for not having been "faithful" to their sister, his wife. (Fortunately for him, his wife's mother and his wife's mother's sisters cannot even speak to him, being avoidance-women to him.) For these reasons, a contributing father may move at this time to the house of his own sister and mother to pass the period of the couvade's seclusion and to practice its requirements in a more sympathetic and supportive environment.

I do not use the anthropological expressions "genitor" and "pater" (the mother's husband) for the Canela, generally, because no one knows who the genitor is in the sense of the one whose sperm fertilized the mother's egg.[9] A Canela social father may be the genitor or just the pater. And any one of the contributing fathers, who may have been lovers of the mother before she conceived as well as after, may be the genitor or just a contributing father. A particular case involving a male homosexual illustrates this point as well as the Canela quantitative concept of procreation.

While three homosexual men were living in the tribe in 1971, only one of them was married. This man and his wife were taking a long time to produce a baby. Talk was going around that the young homosexual man could not maintain an erection, but no one really knew whether this was the case because he refused to take part in the activities of the extramarital sex-exchange days. During these group occasions, the sexual abilities of both sexes were experienced by a member of the opposite sex, who subsequently discussed them so that any unusual sexual characteristics became common knowledge. However, in 1971 the young homosexual man's wife became pregnant and gave birth to a baby girl, even though he had not allowed her to go out on the extramarital sex days.

In Canela thinking, the young homosexual, the social father in this case, was not considered at first to be one of the contributing fathers, even though he had the best opportunity to impregnate his wife. Later, however, people began to think the designated contributing fathers might not have contributed enough semen to be significant "biological" fathers, since the young man had not allowed his wife to go out and about in the usual manner, collecting a sufficient amount of semen from each lover to make them biological fathers. The people began to think the young homosexual man might have been the only biological father after all. Nevertheless, to follow custom and to play it safe, all the men declared by the new mother as having had sex with her during her pregnancy were considered contributing fathers—so that no significant pollutants could possibly reach the baby. Thus, Canela contributing fatherhood is an arbitrary quantitative concept, which makes the term "genitor" meaningless.

Although the social father has to continue to maintain his restrictions against certain foods and sex for about 6 to 12 months, the Canela terminate the couvade restrictions of the contributing fathers after about 40 days. At this time, the mother's female kin put on a special rite, the *më hà?-khrël* (they it-eat), to dismiss the contributing fathers. The mother, painted red, walks around the village circle to summon some of her "husbands," those that are her baby's designated contributing fathers. The social father and all the contributing fathers squat on their heels in her house around a large meat pie, holding 8-inch scratching sticks. At a signal, they dip the thin sticks into the pie and raise any morsels adhering to the sticks to their lips, but do not eat them. (For making a meat pie, see Figure 3.9.)

This act signifies abstention and thereby the concept of restrictions against certain foods and sex at critical times. As the biological fathers continue to sit, an "uncle" of the mother gives a formal lecture to these fathers, saying that they must never forget their responsibilities to their contributed-to child. They must provide their child with meat every now and then, and they must observe food and sex restrictions for their child when it is sick. Through this rite, contributing fatherhood is made a lifelong responsibility. Most villagers are looking on to witness the contributing fathers' dedication to their child. These villagers are certainly going to remember who the contributing fathers are and will make occasional remarks later if the fathers are not living up to the responsibilities of their important roles.

Contributing father-child relationships extend beyond the two individuals involved, altering significantly the mother-to-daughter-to-granddaughter pattern of terms in long-houses. Through merely a contributing father relationship, individuals who may not be genealogically related at all in the Western sense call each other "sister," and their "siblingship" may continue down for several generations—matrilines in parallel with each other—changing the usual patterns in their different longhouses.

KEEPING THE PEACE THROUGH ALTERNATIVE SYSTEMS

The various relationship systems that change longhouse patterns—Informal Friendship, Formal Friendship, female name transmission, and contributing fatherhood—mix with the consanguineal kinship system, breaking up the mother-to-daughter-to-granddaughter matrilines. Nevertheless, this mixing of the various relationship systems adds to the overall social integration of the tribe. The various systems provide alternative pathways between two individuals, helping to preserve communication and peace between them and their families. Thus, the various systems help maintain the high level of social cohesion that is so characteristic of the Canela. An episode that took place in my sister Waterfall's household in 1960 illustrates that interpersonal problems are often solved through the use of two different systems (or pathways) of terms at the same time.

William H. Crocker

Figure 3.9 Women prepare a meat pie. They place meat cubes in a layer of a manioc mush. After they fold the wild banana leaves over the mush and meat, they tie them with cords of buriti and bake the pies by placing them on hot rocks and covering them with earth.

Lake Lover and her husband Boil's Vapor were not getting along. Boil had left Lake and had moved all his possessions over to the house of his mother, Sweet Potato's Wisdom. Besides the problems between Lake and Boil, an interfamilial problem was contributing mutual hostility to their relationship. Someone had seen Lake "talking" (flirting) alone with a man, Hard Bed (*pàl-tèy:* bed-hard), down at the swimming hole in the middle of the afternoon, when most people are sleeping or resting. Since the incident had become public knowledge and had therefore "passed shame onto Boil's face," he wanted a payment from our family to "erase this shame."

Waterfall and her brothers pointed out that Lake Lover had not gone off in the bushes to have sex with Hard Bed, so that her behavior did not warrant a significant complaint. Nevertheless, Boil and his family were adamant about receiving a compensatory payment. Burnt Path, who was Waterfall's brother and our spokesman (and my research assistant), promised Boil's people that we would cooperate in holding a legal hearing between our two extended families. In return, Burnt Path asked Boil to move back with his belongings as soon as possible to begin living with Lake once again for the sake of their two children, who were crying and missing their father. However, Boil refused to cooperate. Boil said he was carrying too much shame (*pahàm*) on his face to appear in our house before being compensated through a public hearing. This exaggerated pride showed the influence of the backlanders' machismo.

Waterfall and her brothers knew it would take several days before all the appropriate persons could assemble to hold a proper legal hearing, and they did not want the hostile feelings to continue even for this short period. So we agreed to send one of Lake's two immediate uncles, Burnt Path, over to talk with Boil.

By coincidence, Burnt Path and Boil had been Informal Friends, but their joking relationship had been weakened by their later having become in-laws. Boil generally referred to Path as an "in-person," his wife's mother's brother, to whom he had to show considerable respect because Path partly controlled his wife. But when Path approached Boil in the plaza, he called him "Informal Friend" and referred to the days of their roaming the savannahs together with their age class members, as they were undergoing initiation. With Informal Friendship invoked, Boil could listen in a friendly manner. Path expressed his sympathies for his Informal Friend Boil and agreed man-to-man that his niece, Lake, was not the easiest person to get along with. Thus, out of respect for their earlier Informal Friendship, and in keeping with their continuing membership in the same age class, which requires mutual cooperation "forever," Boil gave in. He "came home to his children," as the Canela always put it; they do not talk about leaving or "coming home to a wife."

In the trial that was held a few days later, Alligator's Tail, 82, presided. After listening to witnesses from both sides and especially to Boil's "uncle" Standing Water, 71, who was representing him, Alligator's Tail rendered his nonbinding opinion. He maintained that while we, Lake's kin, were in the right according to custom, we nevertheless must pay Boil's kin reparations to keep the peace between the two extended families. Lake had not done anything offensive in merely talking to Hard Bed, or even if she had had sex with him. Nevertheless, since she had been so indiscreet as to flirt in a public place where she was likely to be seen by one of Boil's female kin, we owed Boil a "payment" to ease his shame. We (Lake's kin) would have to pay for Lake's lack of concern and respect for her husband.

Alligator's Tail pointed out that we, as a highly prestigious family, should give in to a family of low prestige—to keep them happy and to maintain peace in the tribe. Our Lake had been a Wè?tè girl, one of the highest ceremonial honors in the tribe. With our high honor keeping us feeling well (*amyi-?kïn:* euphoria), we had to give in to less fortunate families in the tribe to spread the state of personal and familial satisfaction to them.

SUMMARY

The Canela kinship system is the most obvious and the most all-inclusive of the major sources of bonding. Kinship is the main organizing structure in aboriginal groups of less than two or three thousand people. The Canela are not unlike other similarly sized groups in this regard. Where members live and how they behave toward each other in such groups is strongly influenced by kinship. Among the Canela, almost everybody above about 12 years of age knows everybody else. Any individual's identity can be rapidly established by a brief conversation about his or her relatives. The kinship system, with its likely behaviors, prevents the growth of privacy and the harboring of secrets. This kind of intimate knowledge about everyone in the tribe is often supplemented by shamans' communications with ghosts and by extramarital sex practices, as will be discussed in the chapters to come. Unless Canela emigrate, they cannot detach themselves from their family or have a secret sex life. The Canela do not go off on tangents; the circle is the paradigm for village life. With around-the-circle as well as across-the-circle bonds, the kinship system constructs an intricate web that allows some flexibility, but which weaves many connections holding the tribe together.

NOTES

1. Quotation marks around a kinship term indicate that it is to be taken in a classificatory sense, which means in the case of a father that he is a distant rather than an immediate person called "father." Also, quotes around a kinship term are used to distinguish my Canela from my American relatives the first time they appear in a chapter. Later, no quotes are used for my immediate Canela kin and affines.

2. Since the Canela were living in two villages at the time of my arrival in 1957, they adopted me into a separate kinship network in each village. Thus, when the tribal schism ended in 1968, I had two primary families in one village.

3. Greene and Crocker (1994) furnishes a demographic study of the Canela from which the reader can glean quantitative data on living arrangements, the incidence of disease, and the ages of certain demographic thresholds.

4. During the early to mid-1970s, the Wycliffe missionaries flew my wife Roma from their base in Belém, Brazil, to a small field by the Canela village in a single-motor plane in about 3.5 hours. When the missionaries were not in the village to receive radio messages, communication between home in Washington, DC, and the village was by ordinary airmail. Thus, I knew the week when Roma hoped to arrive in the village, but not the day. She had to arrive by noon or the plane could not return to Belém before dusk.

5. Lea's theory (2001) of the importance of the "House" among the Kayapó may be compared to the Canela longhouse.

6. The Canela do not have exogamous moieties, as is erroneously stated in Nimuendajú's monograph (1946:79).

7. The aboriginal Canela relationship to their ecology was lost some time during the 19th century, probably between their surrender (1814) and their resettlement (around 1840). Their current relation to their ecology is similar to that of their Brazilian backland neighbors, so I have not studied it extensively. For an excellent monograph showing an ongoing relationship between an Amazonian people and their ecology, see Descola's (1996) analysis of the worlds of the Ecuadorian Achuar.

8. Partible/multiple paternity (Crocker 2002) occurs among many indigenous peoples throughout lowland South America including the Amazon, Orinoco, and Guyana watersheds and also just west of Lake Maracaibo in Venezuela, though more frequently in the eastern than the western parts of these areas.

9. The Canela have no concept of the human egg or the sperm. The male ejaculate (*hiràà*) accumulates in the womb to form a fetus, if enough ejaculate is contributed by one or more men.

4/Affirmation through Ritual

One morning, when light had arrived but the sun was not yet up, I left my hammock earlier than usual. Instead of listening to taped recordings in Canela to help train my ear, as I usually did in the early morning, I put the strap of my super-8 camera over one shoulder and hung my 35 mm still camera from my other shoulder. Then, I put the strap of a Canela basket over my head and neck so that it hung down in front. The basket, a large flat pouch, held a hand-sized tape recorder, tape cassettes, extra film, and a clipboard with carbons to make on-the-spot duplicates of my notes in speedwriting.

Heavily armed, I walked rapidly over to the house where I had been told a male ear-piercing rite was to take place. As I was arriving, Khrèy-tep (parrot-red) joined me. The night before, Red Parrot had agreed to help me cover the ear-piercing rite.

Slippery Forest greeted us with an expected *Ka apu më mõ* (you along plural go), and I returned with a *Ka tsa* (you stand), the usual greetings referring to the other person's activity. Slippery Forest explained that his son, Ka-?hàl (it-enter) was old enough (about 10 years) to have his ears pierced. The ear-piercer, Tsùù-khè (decoration-smelly), was preparing his equipment on a mat in a spot behind the house that would be out of the sun's rays. I could identify Enter It, because his mother, Wakhõõ-khwèy (coati-woman), was cutting away the hair around his ears with scissors. Enter It's mother's brother's first cousin, Enter It's classificatory "uncle," Mesa, was in charge of the occasion, because he was Enter It's naming-uncle. The rest of Enter It's nuclear family, and the ubiquitous little boys from other families, completed the cast of characters for the performance.

LIFE CYCLE RITES

The ear-piercing rite that I was about to witness socialized boys of 9 or 10 into obedience to the Elders. This prepubertal rite was one of many that marked transitions in life, as such rituals do among all peoples. Birth, puberty, marriage, and death are usually marked by ceremony, as are adolescent induction into religious responsibility, assumption of legal adulthood, and retirement. Many life cycle rites mark moments in the lives of individuals that are as much cultural as biological in both timing and meaning.

I will describe two Canela life cycle rites in detail: the ear-piercing rite and the cluster of rites associated with death and mourning. At both of these life passages, the individual's relationship to the tribe is defined. In very small tribes, life cycle rites are usually handled by the individual's extended family. In a large tribe, such as the Canela in the past, from 1,000 to 1,500 members, some life cycle rites are handled by the whole tribe. Festivals represent the tribal level of celebration for the Canela. The Ghosts' festival, for instance, forms boys into an age class that will last their lifetime. Young adolescent women earn their social acceptance belts through service in a men's society during a great "summer" festival. The rites surrounding the birth of a baby, on the other hand, are carried out within the extended family. The reader will recognize that many of the events described elsewhere in the book are in fact life cycle rites, such as those involved in socialization for sex, the various steps into marriage, and establishing other relationships such as Informal Friendship, Formal Friendship, and contributing fatherhood.

Ear-Piercing Rite: "Opening" Boys to Knowledge and Compliance[1]

When Coati Woman had finished cutting Enter It's hair, she had him sit on his ankles on a mat behind their house, as the sun was beginning to appear on the other side. Smelly Decoration approached Enter It and fingered both of his earlobes, massaging them as if to soften them. Then he squatted by him, and with cotton on a small stick carefully dabbed a dot of red urucu paint onto the center of each of his earlobes. Mesa squatted by his nephew to inspect the location of the red dots. I remember thinking that Mesa would never let the dots' placements stand, because he would have to maintain his authority. A discussion between the two men followed, and Smelly slightly altered the position of one of the dots.

The objective was to pierce a well-centered hole through each lobe. The holes were to be stretched first by inserting wooden pins, then by increasingly larger round wooden plugs, and years later by larger wheels of wood or even chalk stone up to three inches in diameter. The resulting loops of flesh and skin, like wide elastic bands, hold the dangling wheels in place. Whenever the wheels are not worn, the loops are hung over the top of the ear.

With the locations of the dots on the earlobes approved, each character in the performance assumed his or her position. Enter It remained patiently on the mat, looking impassive and resigned. He knew he must remain motionless throughout the operation, showing no reaction of any sort, or great shame would be part of his people's memory of this occasion. Those witnessing the operation would tell others of his behavior, constructing his persona, bonding him further to his people for better or worse. Enter It's mother, Coati Woman, knelt behind his back, holding his shoulders to remind him instantly with a word or finger pressure should he wince. (See Figure 4.1.) Smelly edged closer to Enter and drew the mat holding his equipment to his side. Two of Enter's sisters, squatting on either side of him, smeared red urucu paint from his nose across his cheeks under his eyes, almost to his ears. When finished, they moved away to join the encircling crowd.

I had created an artificial situation by requesting that one-quarter of the circle of people around Enter It be left open for my filming. Red Parrot, my assistant, was con-

William H. Crocker

Figure 4.1 A mother supports a youth during the ear-piercing rite. The youth's earlobe holes will gradually be stretched to accommodate plugs.

tinuously clearing little boys out of this area, where I had placed the mat with my equipment covered with a towel to protect it from the low-blown sand. I had already taken a number of high ASA still shots of the scene, and especially of the placement of the dots and the relocation of one of them, but I was careful not to hamper Smelly and Mesa's movements, staying outside their area of activity and relying on telephoto shots. Now that there was enough light I could begin the super-8 sound filming. Every now and then I retreated to my mat to make observations on my tape recorder or to draw spatial relationships on my clipboard.

Mesa stood beside the squatting Smelly and bent over to look along the wooden awl in Smelly's right hand. This was the signal that the performance could begin. The awl was made of a red hardwood (*pau brasil*), which had been filed to a sharp point. Together with its grip, it was close to one foot in length. Smelly firmly secured Enter's left earlobe with his thumb in front just below the dot and his first two fingers behind the earlobe. He placed the point of the awl on the dot and waited for a moment. Then he thrust hard and rotated the awl clockwise and counterclockwise until I could see two inches of the point showing on the further side of Enter's earlobe. I was watching Enter's face through the camera lens, and saw no tensing on his part. Burning told me that the pain began later. With one earlobe successfully pierced, the quiet that had descended on the family group during the moment of anticipation was broken and everybody began to talk. The tension was over; young Enter It had behaved like a man. (The Canela ear-piercing procedure can be seen in the video *Mending Ways,* Schecter and Crocker 1999.)

Smelly withdrew the awl from the left earlobe and put red urucu paint into the wound with a cotton swab. Then he inserted into the new hole its first wooden pin, Enter's "child." A half-hour later, Smelly pierced the other ear and inserted Enter's other "child." Coati Woman put a sheet of fine white cloth over her son's head, and then she and her "brother," Mesa, lead Enter to his cell of confinement in a corner of her house. The cell was made of old mats held erect by tall stakes thrust into the ground.

Mesa lectured his nephew to remain in the cell until "his children" had "grown" sufficiently, which was for about two weeks. Before then he was to emerge from his cell only in the evening or during the night, if possible, and only to relieve himself. If he had to go out during the day, he must cover his head with a white cloth to protect himself from the sun, and he must avoid stepping on leaves or small sticks that might injure him. He was now in a sensitive state so that he was vulnerable to injuries from a number of sources. In this ceremonially special state, he and "his children" would grow more rapidly. His mother, Coati, would feed him foods that were low in pollutants, so that they would not hinder his growth and the growth of his "children."

Mesa gave Enter a little bag of unshaped wooden pins and a knife. He told his named-nephew to fashion earlobe pins of graduated sizes. Mesa would come around each day for the insertion of the new, larger pins and the cleansing of the wounds with fresh urucu paint. Mesa would take advantage of Enter's confinement to tell him stories about the ancestors that would teach him to grow up into a fine Canela. Large boys Enter's age spent much of their time with their age class, playing or carrying out communal activities, so his seclusion provided Mesa with an excellent opportunity for personal instruction. His "captivity" reminded me of driving my son to visit colleges. Sitting in the front seat as I drove, he could not get away, so we had long talks.

Canela males had told me that the adornment in their earlobes enhances male beauty and attracts women. They said gleefully that women give themselves more readily to men with large, painted ear wheels, showing what they meant by thrusting their right forefinger through a circle made by their left thumb and forefinger. Nevertheless, while accepting this generalization, I knew that deeper reasons for male earlobe piercing must exist.

From a study of key Canela words and phrases, I know that the verb *khãm hapak* (in ear) means to hear/listen/understand/obey/perform. The suggestion is that in earlier times when a young Canela heard an order, he performed it automatically: that in their quasi-military society, hearing was doing. Taken alone, this observation would prove very little. However, I know also that *to hapak-khre* (make ear-hole) means to "advise," that *ha-?khre pey* (its-hole good) means to "know," and that *i?-kuni* (it's-whole) means "it is whole/complete/virginal." The imagery here—and my Canela research assistants confirmed this—is that information (advice) enters through the ear holes into the head; that good, large, well-opened ear holes lead to building up knowledge and compliance; and that unopened ear holes (virginal ones) lead to stupidity and lack of obedience. (Similarly, a virginal girl is a useless one, for the Canela.)

Understanding this semantic context, and knowing the Canela as a quasi-military society, I see the male ear-piercing rite as a symbolic opening up of these older boys to receive information from their Elders and to become obedient to them. It is a socialization rite that takes place not long before puberty, introducing the boys into the adolescent world of obedience while they are withdrawn temporarily from the activities of their age class. To my Canela research assistants, such an interpretation was food for thought and not denied, but they could not express this interpretation themselves.

It is important to examine what each member of the cast of characters in the performance represents. Usually, the rite takes place in the boy's maternal home, but it is run by the boy's naming-uncle who is the representative of the boy's home to the rest of the community, especially for ceremonial purposes. The uncle calls in an ear-piercer, who is a nonrelative and who represents the greater society. Thus, the ear-piercing rite and its subsequent seclusion keep the boy at home, while calling on the greater society for a service. Other Canela rites take the boy and girl out of the home, creating the separation from their families that bonds them to the larger community. The tribe as a whole is more important than the individual and his or her family.

Death and Mourning as a Cluster of Rites[2]

Of all the deaths I have witnessed among the Canela, the death of Kuwrè (Slippery One) was the most moving. Slippery One was a lovely young woman of 16, married to Katut-khà (straight-body), a good runner and hunter. She had been a girl associate in the Warriors' Festival, and thus a person of high honor. Late one afternoon she went alone to fetch water from the stream, and when she returned, it was dusk. Soon thereafter she joined the sing-dance line of women in the plaza. She began to feel pains and turned toward home, only to fall as she made her way up the pathway. Onlookers carried her to her house, where she lay gravely ill. Both Jack Popjes, the missionary, and I tried to help; Jack gave her injections of penicillin. He thought that she suffered an ectopic pregnancy. Canela stated that ghosts had hit her in the back when she was getting water. She should not have gone out alone at dusk. Neither shaman's efforts nor medicine helped, however, and Slippery One died around 2:00 in the morning.

Slippery One's family continued to hope that her soul might return to her body, but all hope was lost when the first rays of the sun hit the house. This is when the rites of death and mourning begin. The adult women over 30 among Slippery One's close kin began the traditional wailing, a high-pitched yodeling with words expressing longing. Once the wailing begins, the soul will not return. Then group after group of more distant kin walked across the village to join in the mourning, squatting on their ankles around the corpse. Slippery One's immediate kin closed her eyes and cut her hair in the traditional style. According to Canela standards of beauty, they plucked out her eyelashes and eyebrows. Then her Formal Friend and the Friend's relatives decorated her body with urucu and falcon down, indicating her high honor.

When the decorating was finished, Slippery One's husband was allowed to approach her body and mourn. (See Figure 4.2.) Although I was shaken by Slippery One's death, I did record this moment with my camera. At the first Canela death I witnessed, I had left my camera behind out of respect, but the Canela urged me to photograph the rite. After that I had no more inhibitions about recording these sad occasions. When all the kin had mourned, the young Warriors lifted the body of their girl associate and held it upright between them. They locked their arms around hers and danced one last time with her in the sideways-stepping dance style for a few yards, as they had years before around the village circle in the Warriors' Festival.

Figure 4.2 Slippery One's husband and other close kin mourn her death.

The associates of Slippery One's Formal Friend dug and prepared the grave in the cemetery about a half-kilometer outside the village. They returned quickly to Slippery One's house, wrapped the corpse in palm frond mats, tied it with ropes, and slung it from a pole horizontally. As they carried the body out of the house, the wailing of the mourners reached a dramatic crescendo. When the pallbearers returned about an hour and a half later from the cemetery, having buried the corpse, the wailing broke out again. The associates of the Formal Friend tore out some of the walls of the palm thatch house and swept its floor, so cleansing breezes could pass through.

The Canela rites of mourning reinforce the Canela belief of living in the present. The ritualized wailing is the concentrated and sanctioned outlet for grief. The most severely bereaved, such as a father for his small son, have been known to attempt suicide by somersaulting onto the backs of their heads, breaking their necks. It is the role of the Formal Friend's associates to watch and intervene to prevent these acts. Mourning of this intensity is the most frenzied emotion I have witnessed among the usually self-controlled Canela.

The deceased's Formal Friend's associates usually have to pull the close kin away from the decorated corpse. While the wailing mourners are oblivious to what is going on around them, people from other houses help themselves to the possessions of the bereaved family. When a death occurred in my Canela family's house, my sister Waterfall used to stuff a few family valuables for safekeeping in my private room before the wailing started. The material loss seems to be a corollary to the personal loss. The loss of property may also be another of the social leveling mechanisms that keep the Canela society relatively egalitarian.

Though often very intense, expressions of grief are tightly channeled so that the attention of the living returns to their responsibilities in ongoing Canela life.

Usually none of the normal activities of the tribe stops when a person dies. Because Slippery One was so highly esteemed, the Facsimile Warriors' Festival was suspended for one day.

During the days following a burial, before the gravediggers are paid for their services, the bereaved individuals may break out wailing as the sun appears in the morning and as it sets in the evening. Wailing may also break out as kin return to the village from farms or from travel and come to the house of the bereaved. The very severely bereaved, such as the mother of a favorite child or the wife of a lifelong spouse, wail with every person who returns to the village after missing the death and burial. Almost every time I returned to the Canela, my Canela sister and mother used to wail over me, pushing me down to kneel on a mat, my head bowed. If they did not do this, I knew that no close relative had died during my year's absence.

A few days after a Canela burial, depending on how long it takes to gather the necessary items of payment, the bereaved family pays the deceased's principal Formal Friend, the gravedigger, for his services and for the help of his associates. At sunset, members of the extended family of the deceased sit on the edge of the boulevard just in front of their house. One of their leading mothers' brothers summons the gravedigger by chanting out in a formal manner for him to appear. Soon the gravedigger walks solemnly along the village boulevard and arrives before the assembled family with several associates following him. The principal spokesman of the deceased's family tells the gravedigger in formal language of exhortation to take the items laid on a mat, which might include any combination of axes, machetes, cast-iron cauldrons, shotguns, cuts of cloth, or sections of tobacco wound into the form of a rope.

As the gravedigger and helpers walk casually away with the items, the kin of the deceased break out wailing again; the most severely bereaved sustain the wailing for about 10 minutes. Then their principal uncle calms the last mourners and lectures the group. The living must forget the deceased and live for their surviving relatives, especially their children. It is dangerous to brood over the dead, for if the mourners remember the loved one too intensely, she or he might return as a ghost to claim their lives.

If strong memories of a husband still persist in the thoughts and feelings of a widow, for instance, a female Formal Friend goes with her to all the locations in and around the village where her memories are strongest. The widow may vividly remember where she went bathing and had sex with her husband, or where she pulled up weeds with him on their farm. The Formal Friend listens to the widow's memories and joins her in wailing. By prolonging the wailing, the Formal Friend helps her exorcize her memories and live in the present for the sake of her surviving family.

One time in the late 1950s, a Brazilian backland farm woman complained to me that when she had lost her small son, the women of one Canela family came to her and compulsively wailed by her side, expecting to be paid for their wailing. The backland woman had failed to understand that the wailing Canela women were trying to help her forget her loss and that this was a service as well as an expression of care and bonding. These Canela women had stayed with the backland woman's family many times, working there for food, and they remembered her lost son. They were carrying out the role of Formal Friends to the backland woman, helping her wail and cry so she would forget her loss—a service that was always paid for in the Canela village. Of course, it also might be true that the Canela women were hungry and had thought of a legitimate way, from their point of view, of obligating the backland woman to feed them.[3]

FESTIVALS

In their festivals, the Canela reinforce cultural norms for behavior, though they sometimes do this paradoxically by acting out the opposite of the norms. Teaching the mores of Canela life and associating them with the pleasures of feasting, singing, joking, and sex, the festivals are both didactic and celebratory. At times these dramas present symbolism that is so deeply held that my Canela research assistants cannot provide interpretations. These had to be left to the ethnologist who, after years of study, might be able to offer valid ones.

The Nature of Festivals

Canela festivals are really pageants that are acted out in the "same" way every year or every time they are put on. The Canela believe they do not make changes, though, of course, they occasionally do. Festivals go on for a day or several months.[4] The composition of almost all festival groups is the following: Two girls, or two young women, are assigned as female associates to the festival group, each group consisting of 30 to 40 men. Three of these pairs become ceremonial honor women for the rest of their lives, a significant advantage. Other roles assigned to the female associates are middle or low level in prestige. Any female roles assigned by the Council of Elders can be refused by the women in the candidate's extended family, aided by their uncles or brothers, but appointment to festival roles cannot be initiated at the extended family level. Thus, in the arrangement of festivals, the male-female balance is strikingly in favor of men. The girls or young women appointed to the most prestigious festival positions are chosen to reward their "good" social behavior, as judged by the male councilors.

The two female associates of each large male festival group are considered ceremonial "wives" to the men of the group, except for one pair of females who are considered "sisters," the Wè?tè girls. The ceremonial wives engage in sex with the members of the male groups. In Chapter 5, we will see how certain days of these three-to-four-month-long festivals involve a pair of women performing sex sequentially with a number of men.

It is hard for the Canela to remember every event of these complex and lengthy pageants, but the members of the Council of Elders try to do so by holding meetings before each festival phase and each evening during the festival to plan the next day. The councilors often summon the actors to appear before them to assign them roles. More than one role may be carried out by the same person, who has the right to do so either through matrilineal inheritance, through personal name connectedness, or through assignment in an earlier performance of the same festival. In any case, most performers need to receive the order to carry out their customary role or they do not do so when they are supposed to. For instance, the owner of the Hardwood Log ritual, Paa-pôl (our-fire), knows that only he or his younger brother through matrilineal inheritance can go out and cut the pair of hardwood logs (*pàlrà*) required for this race, but he has to be summoned to the plaza and ordered to do so by the Council of Elders. Our Fire judges the propitiousness of the day of the ritual by noticing, for instance, whether chips fly near his eyes or whether wasps buzz around when he chops the log. If they do, he may judge the time is not right to put on the ritual and may report this to the Council in the plaza in the evening.

Festivals Reinforce Roles and Values

The Warriors' Festival (*pep-yê:* warrior-plural) and its internments for adolescents—a youth undergoes two and sometimes three Warriors' festivals—are crucial to the maturation of the youths. The middle section of the Warriors' festival stresses the importance of maintaining restrictions against pollutants in order to gain personal strength. The youths are interned in beehive-shaped cells (like wombs) in their maternal homes and fed carefully by their families. At first they are fed small amounts of nonpolluting foods (never meat) until they have grown lean and strong. Then they are fed large amounts of relatively unpolluting foods until they put on weight and presumably strength.

Near the end of their seclusion, their naming-uncle's men's society calls upon each individual "nephew" in turn. An uncle harshly summons the youth out of his cell and demands to know if he is ready to go out into the savannahs to fight the enemy. The youth, knowing his role at this moment of the pageantry, answers no, and returns to his cell for more preparation.

Later, the youths, when considered strong enough to race with large logs, are let out of their cells together as a troop. They are exposed to the effects of being out of doors and among people only in stages. It is believed that from the beginning of their long internment they had become very sensitive and therefore vulnerable to all sorts of "injurious things" (*kurê tsà*), such as sunlight, twigs, the odor of sex from women, and the evil eye of witches. Thus, they must be shaded from the sun, supplied fresh leaves to sleep on, and kept away from young women. The youths must also be shielded with mats from the eyes of villagers as they pass around the village for their food. Each day that they are out of internment, their vulnerability diminishes, and they are shielded less until the mats are finally omitted. They are out of the ceremonially dangerous condition that helped them to grow rapidly.

Canela research assistants explain that the adolescent initiates learn through their internment how to maintain high restriction against pollutants, which they supposedly carry out during the rest of their lives. They also learn about their coming adult roles. In one dramatization of future duties, the initiates march around the village boulevard attached to their mothers-in-law by strings around their waists or heads. (See Figure 4.3.)

Adult men repeat the restrictions of their adolescent internments in the Facsimile Warriors' festival. This festival also teaches important roles through drama. In the Firebrand act, young girl associates of the men's societies are given firebrands by the sing-dance master. The girls throw these burning sticks at the young men who are circling around in the center of the plaza carrying pots, machetes, shotguns, or other common objects. A girl's mother chooses the item her family needs and her daughter throws the stick according to the manner of her ceremonial rank: Low-ranked girls throw viciously to hit and hurt, while high-ranked girls throw to hit the ground near the youth carrying the item her mother wants. The differences among ceremonial ranks are thus demonstrated for the young, and they are expected to carry over these behaviors into daily life. The ceremonially high-ranked Wè?tè girl in my family took care to

William H. Crocker

Figure 4.3 Women hold strings of palm straw tied to the necks or waists of their sons-in-law as they march around the boulevard.

behave with forbearance, and if she did not, she was reminded of her status. Another part of the Firebrand act is that whether or not a young man is hit, one of his sisters rushes out of the crowd to throw water from a gourd onto his shoulders, exemplifying the role of sisters to brothers—one of administering to them when they may be hurt.

In the Fish festival, the Clowns demonstrate the right way of doing things by acting out the wrong way. The troop of Clowns govern the festival proceedings instead of the Council of Elders. The Clowns represent individuality in contrast to conformity. While the Clowns sing the songs of the dignified and proper Facsimile Warriors, they sing out lewdly worded statements between each song. They end each session in disharmony by walking separately back to their houses and by singing out of tune and time with each other. The establishment-oriented Facsimile Warriors, who accept the governance of the Council of Elders, are too dignified to act this way. The superior Facsimile Warriors even stop singing—they withdraw disdainfully—when mild opposition presents itself in the form of a barking dog or a loudly crying baby. The Clowns are demonstrating the opposite of the Facsimile Warriors' dignity.

The most hilarious act of any of the Canela festivals may be the special performance by the two female associates of the Clown male troop, who are chosen partly for their willingness to please men in extramarital sex. During the middle section of the Fish festival, on one late afternoon on the edge of the plaza by the Clowns' improperly constructed hut, the Clown women do everything the wrong way. (See Figure 4.4.) They have a pulp doll to represent one of their babies. Its mother drops it and lets it cry instead of picking it up. One Clown woman pretends incest with her brother, in an exaggerated demonstration that makes the crowd roar in laughter. She initiates it and then resists.

In the terminal phase of the Fish festival, the Clowns compete against several kinds of Fish societies and water animal societies, such as turtles, stingrays, ana-

William H. Crocker

Figure 4.4 One of the Clown society's two female associates. By doing everything wrong (the crooked house, the mishandled doll), the Clown associate implies what is right.

conda snakes, and river otters, but the Clowns *always* win (eat) their opponents. In the other festival-pageants, the competition is mediated before the end of the festival, but the Clowns, as individuals, must win; their victory is not mediated.

The victory of the Clowns is portrayed during the last night of the terminal phase of the Fish festival. The men and the female associates of the Fish society are in a weir (a circle of vertical palm fronds) in the center of the plaza. The Clowns start to enter the weir to catch and "eat" the Fish, but the Fish choose to escape instead. Each Fish is carrying a meat pie of manioc meal on his or her shoulder. The meat pie is wrapped in wild banana leaves and tied in a frame of supple sticks shaped like a fish. What follows is like a game of Prisoners' Base in which each Fish tries to escape by racing from the weir to a house, a safe base, before a Clown snatches the meat pie off his shoulder. When a Clown is not looking, a Fish streaks from one house to another, or even back to the weir. (See Figure 4.5.)

This act is not really a contest, because all know that the Clowns will catch all the Fish in the end. The Clowns pile the fish-shaped meat pies high in their spot at the edge of the plaza and sing a triumphal song. Competition and winning are anathema to the Canela, except in log racing and other sports. Problem solving and mediation are the true Canela way. The Clowns epitomize Canela values by acting out what is held to be wrong—the smashing of social bonds—by winning outrageously and gloating at the demise of other Canela social groups. In the Fish festival, a Canela is allowed what is not permitted in life—winning totally.

The Festival of Masks

The one festival I will describe in detail here is one that is no longer performed. It may have been abandoned because its dramatization of "begging" now embarrasses the Canela. Or it may have been abandoned because the manufacture of the masks may seem too burdensome for the older men, while the younger men no longer know

Figure 4.5 Men of the Fish societies run from the weir with fish-shaped meat pies on their shoulders, trying to escape from the men of the Clown society.

William H. Crocker

how to make them. These days, the festivals that are still put on are those in which the time-consuming roles can be passed down for the adolescents or boys to perform.

During an initial phase of a few days, male members of the Mask society induct their girl associates and other members. During a middle section of about six weeks, the men weave their life-size masks in a lean-to several kilometers from the village. Then, to open the terminal phase, Mask society members march in single file inside the large masks, entering the village in the early afternoon. A mask ranges from five to six feet tall and is about three feet wide. Its height depends on the size of the wearer and the size of the "doughnut" of palm straw he wears on his head. This doughnut supports the horizontal bar holding up the mask, which covers the bearer completely. The upper part of a mask is woven like a palm straw mat. From the waist down, loose lengths of shredded palm straw reach the ground to form a skirt. A slit in front of the wearer's face allows him to peer out, and he can manipulate this opening by pulling the attached strings, mimicking facial expressions. Spear-like poles of hardwood about seven feet long are tied onto the back of the mask and extend diagonally upward to represent horns.

As the festival's terminal phase opens, the 30 to 40 Masks march in single file through the savannahs along a trail from their lean-to toward the village, raising a small cloud of dust as their feet shuffle through the sand. These feet are the only human parts the villagers can see, except for an occasional glimpse of an eye or nose as the man inside the mask parts the opening to see what is going on. The Masks' two female associates, in their slightly smaller masks, follow the leading Khen-pey (mountain-beautiful) Masks. (See Figure 4.6.)

The masks' "faces" are painted to depict their character, and each one of the dozen kinds behaves in a slightly different way. The Beautiful Mountain Masks are the leaders, so they move sedately and slowly. Their faces are minimally painted, with only a large black horizontal stripe just below the transverse supporting bar.

Figure 4.6 The Masks march toward the village from their lean-to in the savannah.

The Tôkaywêw-re (no translation) Masks have eyes formed from three concentric circles, and the Espora (spur in Portuguese) Masks have eyes circled with points to look like spurs. These two Masks run around in the boulevard, playing jokes on each other and having a great time. The Little Bad Mask (*i?-hô-?khên:* its-straw-bad) is made irregularly by the Clowns, and it runs about trying to steal things from villagers.

As the Masks file into the village, women approach them, wanting to be their "mothers." If the man in a mask sees a female relative approaching him, he avoids her, knowing that sexual relations should be a possibility with the approaching "mother." If a nonrelative approaches, the Mask does not avoid her, but allows her to tie a short chain of beads to one of his "horns." Then he goes off, running and playing around the boulevard, dodging other Masks. Occasionally, two pairs of feet are seen sticking out from under the skirt of a mask, the smaller of the pair being the feet of one of the "mothers." At night such a pair drift off behind the houses into the darkness for mutual pleasure.

On the second evening of the terminal phase of the festival, just after dark, each family lights a small bonfire in the boulevard in front of the family house. The Masks dash water on their skirts and file past the fires, trying to put out each fire by a swish of the skirt. If it succeeds completely, the fire must remain out. However, a partly extinguished bonfire can be nursed back by family members between assaults. The Masks play a number of other crowd-amusing games.

The Little Bad Mask plays a special role. Made by Clowns, this mask is painted irregularly; its skirt may be hitched up on one side, and its horns may be crooked and small. The Clowns make this mask somewhat differently each time the festival is put on.[5] As Clowns, they must do the job unevenly and improperly. While most villagers are watching a performance in the boulevard or the plaza, the Little Bad Mask sneaks into a house from the side or the back and steals something, such as a small pot or a machete. According to custom, the Little Bad Mask really wants to be caught in the act. If a woman of a house is not sufficiently watchful to catch him, he may do something "careless" to attract her attention, such as knocking over a water gourd. Once the woman sees him, she gives chase, screaming at the Little Bad Mask, who tries repeatedly to attempt a theft and to receive a scolding, much to the amusement of the villagers.

The Masks try to perfect the feat of entering a house door sideways, one horn after the other, without spearing the doorpost or the thatch around the door with a horn. They try to accomplish this feat faster and faster and vie with each other in the eyes of the watching villagers for the most skilled performance. Running across the boulevard up to the house chosen for the contest, they dip the leading horn in time to enter the door, then lower the rear horn in time to avoid tearing the thatch. Considering the weight and unwieldiness of the masks, and the wearers' obstructed vision, this feat requires dexterity and practice. The spectacle continues all morning as the villagers watch and voice approval or disapproval. (See Figure 4.7.)

As the demonstration is about to terminate, the Little Bad Mask enters the game, but never succeeds, of course. He must do everything incorrectly. After several Masks have demonstrated their perfected art of house entry, the Little Bad Mask takes his turn. However, his horn pierces the thatch on one side of the door, not letting him enter the house at all, but pinning him to the thatch. His ridiculous efforts to extricate himself amuse the crowd.

After failing to enter the house several times, the Little Bad Mask, pawing the ground, charges madly at the house like a bull blinded with rage. If he succeeds in doing what is expected, he breaks his leading horn on the doorpost, while the villagers collapse in delirious laughter. In a final attempt at entry, the Little Bad Mask trots up to the door, drops his entire mask onto the boulevard, and walks through the door as a man, standing proudly upright. This breaks up the crowd into convulsions of laughter, approval, and delight. This independent Clown, doing it his own way, will make the entrance with dignity.

All Masks except the Beautiful Mountain ones spend much of the time begging from the villagers, though less outrageously and shamelessly than the Little Bad Mask. All Masks can put on several facial "expressions," such as entreaty, joy, and shame, by manipulating the facial slits with internal strings. They rub the facial slits together for impatience and thrust their horns up threateningly for anger. When they want food, they manipulate their faces in the begging style, thrusting up the lower facial edges and grunting. When a piece of food is put on the stick extended through the slit, they bring it inside the mask and grunt and dance around with glee. When they beg but are refused, they appear to wilt as they twirl around and down to the ground, bowing their faces and horns to the sand, grunting piteously. It was impossible for me to refuse these endearing creatures.[6]

Food Distribution Enhanced

The Festival of Masks illustrates the combination of activity, food, humor, and sex, which brings the greatest delight to the Canela. On a more serious level, I see the festival as a cultural justification for begging, as an acting out of the message of the

William H. Crocker

Figure 4.7 A Mask deftly maneuvers to pass through a doorway.

myth of Awkhêê: Begging from the backlander and the urban *civilizado* is the way for the Canela to compensate for their disadvantaged position. Begging from each other is simply the other side of sharing. Thus, the festival reinforces the food distribution system and the social subordination of the Canela. Aggressive "begging" without embarrassment, as some categories of Masks portray, was consistent with the economic necessities of Canela life.

Hunters do not kill game and produce meat every day for their families. Those families in mourning, or with members who are very ill, often lose most of their crops and have to rely on the compassion of others. Sharing food occurs automatically among members of the same household and is expected to occur among extended family members, as is true of most Amazonian peoples. Melatti states the Krahô Indians distinguish between kin and non-kin by whether food is exchanged freely. Among the Canela, however, this sharing was extended even to non-kin when they were hungry and when they came and *asked* for food. Giving food to those in need provided occasions for the givers to express compassion (*kaprï: ter pena*), the value that underlied Canela bonding for survival as a largely food-collecting tribe living in a single village-community.[7]

BELIEF SYSTEMS

When I was with the Canela in 1991, I witnessed the distressing death of a 14-year-old youth. The Canela's explanation of his death illustrates their belief in ghosts and the role of shamans. Word went around the village circle one day that the young man was very ill but refused to go to the hospital in Barra do Corda, even though the truck was available to take him there. Evidently he had a stomach ulcer and dysentery and was becoming severely dehydrated. I was told that he refused to go to the hospital because he wanted to die. How could such a young man, a couple of days earlier healthy and vigorous, want to die? The Canela explained it in terms of his soul's journey to the ghosts' village.

The young man's family believed that his soul had left his body and was traveling on the path to the ghosts' village. They summoned a shaman to persuade his soul
to return to its body. The shaman caused his own soul to go out into the ghostly
world, following the youth. The shaman's soul found the young man's soul in the
company of the ghost of the shaman's aunt. The shaman's soul tried to bring the
young man's soul back to the living Canela village, but the young man's soul physically knocked down the shaman's soul twice in rapid succession. Nevertheless, the
shaman's soul kept working with the youth's soul, urging it to return, until the
shaman's aunt's ghost told her nephew's soul to go home, saying that the youth's soul
wanted to stay in the ghostly world. The shaman's soul returned to the Canela village
empty-handed, the young man died, and his soul stayed in the ghostly world, becoming a ghost. My research assistants said that the youth just wanted to die and that this
was why his soul would not come back.

For the English words "ghost," "soul," and "spirit," the Canela use only one
word, karõ. "Ghosts" are recently dead ancestors in the human form. I use "soul" to
mean out-of-body living human forms that leave temporarily and return later to their
living Canela human bodies. "Spirits" are out-of-object forms of zoological, botani-
cal, and even mineral materials—animistic representations. Ghosts, souls, and spirits are invisible to ordinary Canela, but visible to Canela shamans. All are inhabitants
of the Canela other-world.

The Canela world of ghosts and spirits is only one of the Canela other-worlds.
Except for the ghosts' world, the other-worlds exist almost entirely in the past. The
other Canela other-worlds are inhabited by culture heroes, who are portrayed best in
creation myths, war stories, and tales about the origins of festivals. See Appendix A
for some of these stories.

The Other-World of Ghosts

Ghosts, who have left their this-worldly bodies (i?-khre-?khà: its hollow's/space's
cover/structure) forever, inhabit a village to the west of the living Canela world, but
return to it to wander about, observing the activities of the living Canela. Thus,
everything a Canela does is seen by some ghost. Ghosts carry out almost all the same
activities that living (hĩĩá) Canela undertake, but they experience less pleasure in
each activity. For instance, the water ghosts drink in their other-world's village is
warm instead of cool, their meat is relatively tasteless, their sex is less invigorating,
and festive activities are less fun.

Ghosts eventually turn themselves into animals, which turn themselves into still
smaller animals and even small plants, so that they eventually cease to exist as living entities. Thus, ghosts are not immortal; their life spans are finite. I maintain that
the lack of a concept of immortality coincides with the Canela preference for their
this-world of the living over their other-world of ghosts. Today, however, most bap-
tized Canela believe they go up to the folk-Catholic heaven upon death.

The advantages ghosts have over living Canela are that they can travel simultaneously throughout all of time and space and that they know instantaneously what
any one ghost has seen while moving around among the living Canela. Thus, ghosts
serve as a source of information for shamans (kay), with whom they can converse.
Ordinary Canela do not have access to this other-worldly source; contacts between
ghosts and ordinary Canela cause them to die, so they become ghosts in turn.

Shamans can summon ghosts when they need to know who stole a machete and where it is, and when they need to know what sex or dietary restriction was broken by a Canela individual, and where in the body of this individual the resulting pollutant is. Shamans can also summon ghosts when they need to know whether a certain witch (also a *kay*) cast a spell (*hūūtsùù*) of illness on a victim (the shaman's client), and what sort of a spell it was. In former times, shamans could "see" arriving enemy warriors or approaching plagues days in advance on their own initiative—a this-worldly ability—though ghosts might warn them well in advance—an other-worldly intervention.

A strong opposition exists in Canela thought between this-world and the ghostly other-world. If a ghost appears to an ordinary Canela as an apparition in human form, the Canela has not long to live. This means that the ghost desires the Canela and that the Canela desires the ghost, which most often occurs between spouses parted by death. The Canela other-world of ghosts is a hostile one to the ordinary Canela, whose mourning practices are intended to lessen feelings for the deceased, especially for a spouse or child. The Canela live for the life of *this* world and feel sorry for relatives who have had to move on early to the less gratifying other-world of ghosts.

Ordinary Canela are not only sorry for ghosts, they are afraid of them. If a Canela goes down to the stream at dusk to fetch water, ghosts may injure that person fatally. If a messenger runs 40 miles to the city of Barra do Corda alone at night, he carries a protective device that ghosts do not like, such as a tail feather of a macaw parrot. Taken collectively, these harassing activities of ghosts tend to make Canela want to move around in groups for safety.

With their specially developed powers of communication, shamans bridge the living Canela world and the world of ghosts. Nevertheless, an old shaman who understood the earlier shamanic practices, the older Deer's Nest, astonished me by stating firmly that he looked down on the ghosts he dealt with and that he was their master—they were serving him.

Becoming a Shaman

Ordinary Canela become shamans through two distinctly different ways. First, a youth who wants to become a shaman carries out extremely careful restrictions against foods that are believed to have a high level of pollutants. Meat juices, not solid meat alone, carry this degree of pollution. Once an individual has ingested pollutants, he or she can transmit them to his or her sexual partners through sexual fluids. The aspiring shaman therefore avoids the more highly polluting foods and sexual intercourse with the individuals who have sex most frequently, those in their teens and twenties. The concept of pollution is quantitative, and, therefore, relative.

Ghosts are attracted to relatively unpolluted, that is, to relatively "pure," individuals. Ghosts will choose their time to visit such an individual in a dream or in the wakeful state. A youth may be very pure from carrying out long, careful, and extensive restrictions, but a ghost, nevertheless, may or may not choose to visit him. The initiative is up to the ghostly world rather than the prospective shaman, no matter how hard he tries to attract ghosts.

Women seldom become shamans, although one of my best female research assistants was one. It is believed they rarely have the strength and persistence to maintain sufficiently high restrictions against pollutants to attract ghosts. Nevertheless, at least two women were shamans in the ancient war stories and myths. One female shaman was able to "see" enemy warriors at a distance and tell that they would arrive at dawn. Consequently, she had time to flee with her family from the village to their farm, where they were not found by the enemy. Many tribal members were killed during the dawn attack because they had not believed her revelation, made before the all-male meeting of the Elders the evening before.

If a ghost decides to make the aspiring youth a shaman, the ghost visits him in animal or human form. The ghosts issue instructions, which, if followed, enable further visits. The instructions have to do with keeping out more and more pollutants, increasingly purifying the body. If the youth carries out the instructions well enough, the ghost eventually gives him "powers" (*hũũtsùù*), which the youth carries in his body, usually in the left armpit. Thereafter, the youth as a shaman uses these powers on his own. He does not have to summon a ghost to empower himself, though he may summon a ghost to obtain needed information.

The second way of becoming a shaman occurs when an individual is very sick and possibly dying. Then ghosts may choose to visit the sick person to cure him or her. If a shaman thinks that such a visitation is likely to occur, he orders Canela families to vacate the part of the village in which the sick person lives and to leave him entirely alone in his house for a night. Dogs may have to be tied up or taken to a farm, because their barking would scare away the visiting ghosts. If the village is sufficiently quiet, the ghosts might choose to come during the night. If they do, and if they choose to cure the sick person, the cured individual has become a shaman and will possess powers to make certain kinds of cures.

The distinction between the living Canela world and the ghosts' world is an artificial one. They really are one continuous world of existence to the Canela, even though its beings are antagonistic. The Canela living world and their ghosts' world are one world, though they can make the distinction between "my" two worlds through their choice of verbal expressions. The importance to me of this distinction, nevertheless, lies in the fact that as the Canela adopt Brazilian backland and urban ideas and practices, they are giving up the this-worldly self-reliance of their pre-pacification state for the other-worldly reliance of backland folk Catholicism. This backland attitude is best expressed in the ubiquitous expression *Se Deus quiser, . . .* (If God should wish it, . . .), which constitutes a surrender to other-worldly forces. The Canela individual is little by little giving up a self-reliant approach to life's problems for the fatalism of the regional backland Brazilian.

Social Use of Shamanic Powers: Curing

When shamans first receive their powers from ghosts, these powers serve to cure very specific illnesses, most of which are believed to be "intrusions" into the body. Some shamans are snakebite masters, others cure problems from broken restrictions, and others try to cure pains of internal organs or even tuberculosis. In any case, they lay hands on the patient's sore area, blow smoke on it, and suck out the intrusion.

One morning during the late 1950s when I was working alone on my research materials in the house of my brother, Falcon's Sight, two messengers burst in and started talking urgently. My brother Burnt Path, in my other family, had been bitten in the right hand by a rattlesnake and was in a farm hut on the next stream to the east, the Dove Stream, about four miles away. I put generic anti-snake serum ampoules, syringes, needles, alcohol, matches, and the metal box for boiling everything into my carrying bag and started running off with the messengers, soon slowing down to a jogging pace. I wondered if I would get there on time. Burnt Path was one of the uterine brothers of my sister, Waterfall. I could not fail this test; I must save him.

Arriving at the farm hut out of breath and exhausted, I was relieved to see that my help would not be needed immediately. Burnt Path was sitting up, and Khlúwa-tsù (arrow-decorated), the old snake master, was already attending him. I greeted Decorated Arrow, Fish's Plant, and others, and was pleased to realize that Decorated Arrow had actually welcomed me. We were on generally good terms, but in this context he could feel that I might disapprove of his medicine. Apparently, this was not the case. (See Figure 4.8.)

Decorated Arrow had applied a tourniquet of string on the lower arm well above the wound on the patient's finger and was sucking on the wound, spitting out the blood. Then he went out of the hut and over to a small tree, on the back side of which he placed something he had just taken out of his mouth. I assumed that this was the intrusion he had just sucked out. Then he returned to Burnt Path, applied a poultice to the wound, and tied it onto the hand with string. He talked to Burnt Path very quietly for a while and then turned to me, saying it was my turn to use my medicine. I remember feeling deeply relieved, but my medicine was not ready, since I had been watching Decorated Arrow's treatment so closely—always the ethnologist.

I set up the metal box that served as burner and water container, alcohol in the lid and water in the box itself, elevated above the lid on supports. All the equipment for sterilizing the needles and syringe was now set up. Trying to light the alcohol to boil the water, I found I had to shield the flame from the breezes to keep it from going out, but finally the water came to a full boil. I let it boil for five minutes before withdrawing the equipment.

The Canela were watching the preparation of my medicine with interest, though they had seen similar activities carried out at the Indian Service post. They believed that injections were more powerful medicine than pills. Nevertheless, I almost always gave pills, since I was not an M.D., though I had been a pre-med student. During the late 1950s, backlanders and Indians expected urban-educated people to give injections, so I had to learn to comply, but gave shots only in the large muscles of the arm or leg. Disposable needles and syringes did not exist; but neither did the threat of HIV.

Burnt Path's lower arm was somewhat swollen, so I injected the nonspecific antisnake venom serum into his upper arm—and waited and waited. Presumably, the venom would spread up Burnt Path's arm and I would have to give three or four more shots, as the instructions indicated. After two hours the venom had not spread, Burnt Path's eyes were clear, and the swelling had subsided.

I asked why they thought the bite was made by a rattlesnake, so they showed me the rattles. Then I casually wandered out of the hut and meandered indirectly over to the far side of the tree where I had seen Decorated Arrow place the intrusion, the illness he had sucked out of Burnt Path's hand. Wedged into the bark of the tree was a small piece of paper folded several times. It was a piece of my notepaper, which the Canela "borrowed" for making cigarettes. I felt conspicuous while walking out to the tree, as if I were defiling something sacred, questioning the efficacy of Decorated Arrow's medicine. I felt very guilty, but decided the gain in research was worth the risk of offending the shaman. Although people watched me, no one said anything. I was taking the situation more seriously than they were.

Myles Crocker, 2001

Figure 4.8 A shaman works on his patient.

What had happened? I had administered only one of the several injections that should have been needed, since my serum was not rattlesnake specific. Was it really Decorated Arrow who had cured Burnt Path by sucking out most of the venom, or removing the "intrusion" by shamanic methods? If so, what use had he made of my piece of paper? Did Decorated Arrow believe he had to have something foreign in his hand that people could glimpse for them to be convinced of the cure? I knew this was a question I could not ask Decorated Arrow or any other Canela shaman, or I would get a meaningless answer. Even today I do not know the answers to these questions.

Antisocial Use of Shamanic Powers: Witches' Spells

In contrast to these curative powers, shamans also have the power to cause harm. Most Canela shamans are "good" and are known as *curadores* (curers) in Portuguese. But a few turn antisocial and throw spells (*hũũtsùù*), it is believed, and are known as *feiticeiros* (witches). I will use "witches" only in this negative sense.

Nobody knows for certain who is a witch, and no one would admit to being one. When carrying out my censuses of the Canela in 1975 and 2001, I asked all male adolescents and adult men whether they were *kay,* or psychic. This was not an embarrassing question to ask. To become a curer was considered a great service to the community, and having a reputation for having cured a number of people was very prestigious. About 20 percent of the men claimed they had *kay* abilities, but they usually modified their claims, saying that they had more powers when younger, or that they needed to undertake thorough restrictions to bring back their currently reduced powers.

My Canela research assistants were hesitant to say that any particular man was a witch. (Women seldom were curers, and I have never heard of a female Canela witch.) To actually say that so-and-so throws negative spells is a terrible accusation. Nevertheless, my research assistants indicated quietly to me that a certain man was generally considered a witch. He had caused certain individuals to become sick and several had died. My research assistants gave me the victims' names in hushed tones. Nimuendajú[8] describes this same man as probably being a witch, so I was surprised to find him still alive during the late 1950s, and he died by the late 1960s. People avoided him, but gave him everything he asked for, being afraid of his powers. I found his eyes wandering when I talked with him, as my research assistants said was characteristic of a witch.

Fortunately, when I first arrived, I had not identified this man as a witch. By coincidence my first serious curing experience was carried out on one of his daughters, an adolescent. The first chief, Jaguar's Coat, had summoned me to cure her. I decided that she had a beginning case of pneumonia and knew that Terramycin pills would probably cure her. I gave her one and left the rest of the day's supply for her to take with meals, only to find the next day that she had taken none of them and that she was worse. Her father objected to the color of the yellow pills, saying that they would be bad for her. If I had known he was a witch, it would have been wiser to have slipped out of the case. He might have wanted to discredit me. I went to the chief for support, and he marched me back to the sick woman and spoke harshly to her father. He told me to continue with my treatment. I was in a dilemma, caught between an uncooperative family and the chief. Thinking about it now, my medicine was on trial. I had to go over to her house four times a day for at least a week to see that she took the pills, waiting around until she did so. She recovered, and the chief was pleased. After that, I was obliged to spend a lot of time on patients, but it surely built up my rapport with the Canela.

A witch "throws" a spell of illness into another person, where it is lodged in a certain place as an intrusion, making the victim sicker and sicker. Witches are said to throw spells when they do not get their way. The victim's kin call in a curer who, if he has strong *kay* abilities, will know who the witch is. The curer will see exactly where the intrusion is and what it is, such as a lizard or a beetle. If he's not powerful enough, the curer may have to consult ghosts to find out such information. To the extent that the curer has the power to cure the victim, the illness reverts back to the witch who threw it, making him sick. But the witch cannot go to a curer for help, because a curer sees a witch as being evil. This is why I was surprised that the witch mentioned by Nimuendajú was still alive more than 20 years later.

When I returned to the Canela in 1978, I was sad to learn that my naming-uncle, the older Deer's Nest, had died. He had been a good research assistant and privately had taught me much about shamanism. I was shocked when I learned how he had died. Canela reported that one of his eyes had become infected and swollen so that little *bichos* (animals) crawled in and out. They confided that he had died of an illness he had thrown into a victim. The illness had returned to him, making him very sick. I knew my naming-uncle had been a good man, always beaming with goodwill and high self-esteem. To me he epitomized the highly favored Canela expression *amyi-?khïn* (self-liking: joy, euphoria). I knew he was a powerful shaman, a good curer, but how could he have turned evil? Did the manner of his death prove he was a witch? An ordinary Canela would be able to give me only gossip, but a shaman could definitely declare what had happened. A shaman's pronouncement becomes accepted as social fact. But would the declaration necessarily be the "truth"?

Tobacco-Induced Journeys

At least some shamans' insights are obtained through smoking tobacco. In earlier times, the Canela had no tobacco, intoxicants, or hallucinogens. His Water told me that the mythical shaman Yawè "journeyed" without the use of any stimulant or percussion instrument. Later, the Canela learned to use tobacco for personal consumption and for shamanic purposes. In 2001, while in their village, I saw Pedro, the shaman of the video *Mending Ways,* use his powers to "see" which Canela in Barra do Corda were ill in the hospital. He predicted that a certain one of them would die, as indeed the indicated man did. To go on this journey, Pedro had smoked tobacco in a traditional pipe (*hàt hô*), which he had made of a catolé palm frond for this occasion.[9] Standing before us, he drew in tobacco smoke vigorously many times, circulating it through his nasal passages and out his nose, but not drawing it into his lungs. Doing this for about 10 minutes, he became intoxicated, finding it hard to keep his balance and almost vomiting. After he had recovered, maybe 30 minutes later, he made his several predictions and put his hands on assembled babies and youths to cure them.

Power of Shamans' Pronouncements

Powerful shamans live a life that is quite independent of chiefs of the tribe, though they have little political power. They are not leaders of the community, or of any group, except when they are conducting a village-wide curing ceremony to ward off the arrival of a plague. Their power and respect come from their special knowledge, from successful cures, and from the threat that they could become, some day, antisocial witches.

When someone falls ill, shamans are usually expected to know something about what has happened. The person may have broken certain food and sex restrictions, been injured by a ghost while wandering alone, or be ill in the urban sense and need urban medicine, which a shaman cannot furnish but may indicate.

While carrying out the Brazilian national census of 1970 for the Canela, I had to ask a number of intimate questions of every third adult Canela woman. I had to find out about their miscarriages, abortions, and causes of their babies' deaths. Sometimes, I spent over an hour patiently questioning one woman with the help of a special research assistant to determine her reproductive history. One time, when I asked a woman why one of her babies had died, she was clearly evasive. My research assistant, trying to be helpful, shocked me when he said abruptly, in the presence of the woman, that she had killed this baby. Knowing that the Canela do not have infanticide of any sort these days, I tried to remain calm, hoping I had not uncovered a murderer. The woman was impassive, apparently accepting the statement, so I summoned my courage and asked my research assistant what he could possibly mean. He said simply that she had broken her sex restrictions while the baby was only a few months old, so the baby had grown sick and died. He said that the older Deer's Nest had revealed this, so that everyone was sure what had actually happened.

I knew that it would be futile to ask the woman if this were true, because the reason for the death of this baby had become a social fact—part of the tribe's history. More than likely, if she had not believed the accusation before the shaman's pronouncement, she had come to believe soon after the pronouncement that she had "in fact" committed the lapse. Nothing she could say would alter what her people accepted and believed. There had been no trial, because a shaman's pronouncement is always right. Either the older Deer's Nest had "seen" what had happened on his own or a ghost had told him what had occurred. No possibility existed for her to deny information backed up by this other-worldly source. Her uncles had no opportunity to come to her defense. On the other hand, there was no punishment for losing a baby in this way. People just remembered her as a not very responsible woman.

Shamanism as the Ultimate Social Control

When the authorities in Barra do Corda intervened in the execution of a witch in 1903, the Canela knew they could no longer carry out these executions. Nimuendajú reports that after that time, they were afraid witches would take over the tribe and do much damage, but this did not occur. Among a people who do not have a police force and do not have agents to carry out the decisions made at hearings between extended families or by the chief of the tribe, the fear of sorcery takes the place of such agents. When a young man, Hard-headed, defied the decision of a hearing in 1960 and would not return to his wife or make the payments specified at a hearing, and when he also defied the orders of Chief Jaguar's Coat, people said that eventually a witch would get him and he would die a horrible death. Fear of sorcery was the final law enforcement agency. By the 1990s, however, the fear of sorcery had almost disappeared. While many men believed they had *kay* abilities, people were little concerned about their becoming witches. Although accusations of witchcraft were made every now and then, they were quickly denied at hastily called meetings. I believe that a limited trust in curing, however, is one of the last of the ancient beliefs the Canela will lose.[10]

Pollution Control by Food and Sex Restrictions

The Canela believe that many pollutants are out there in the world they live in, though their pollutants take quite different forms from Western ones. Instead of smoggy air, leaded gas and paint, and carcinogenic foods, the Canela believe that all meat juices are polluting to some extent, some meats more than others (*hïï kakô ?-khên:* meat's liquid it-bad). Generally, gamier meats are more highly polluting than domesticated meat products, male meats more than female ones, and internal organs more than long muscles. Meat juices of the male forest deer are very polluting, while those of a domesticated female chicken are not. Chicken soup is almost harmless. Canela also find pollutants in some vegetables and fruits, but only to a small extent.

Canela pollutants enter the body through food consumption and through sexual intercourse with an already polluted person. The system of a healthy, strong individual can endure a considerable degree of pollution, but when that same person becomes ill or very old, his or her system handles already internalized pollutants less well. Babies, also, are especially vulnerable to pollutants. These vulnerable individuals should eat only relatively pollution-free foods, or the body becomes weaker and the person could eventually die. Once a person is weak, he or she should not have sex, because pollutants that may be in the sexual fluids of the partner may be transmitted, making the sick person weaker.

The problems of pollution are shared by the nuclear family, because the Canela believe that all kin who are just *one* blood-link apart share most of the same blood (*kaprôô*). (The Canela explain kin ties in terms of blood distance just as we do in colloquial speech.) Canela parents and children share the "same" blood as do siblings, being *one* link away from each other. Thus, they are in the same blood "pool." Long-term spouses, or even long-term lovers, have come to be part of the same blood pool. Sharing perspiration, body heat, and sexual fluids transforms blood differences between spouses into similarities. When any person becomes sick, the members of the same blood pool must take measures to prevent new pollutants from entering their bodies. These protective measures are called "restrictions" (*më ipiyakri tsà:* Canela's restrictive device; Portuguese: *resguardos:* protections), which are similar to, though somewhat different from, taboos.

When Lake Lover, 14, the daughter of my Canela sister, Waterfall, fell ill of severe dysentery and dehydration, her parents and siblings became cautious, avoiding sexual intercourse and foods that carry pollutants. Lake Lover's one-link-away relatives knew that by ingesting pollutants, they would be causing them to spread through the blood shared in common to the blood of Lake Lover, making her sicker, possibly eventually killing her. However, her grandparents, uncles, aunts, nephews, and nieces, being two blood-links away from Lake Lover, did not change their practices. They did not have sufficient blood equivalence with Lake Lover, though they shared some blood with her, as all kin do.

Macaw's Bone, her father, paid a machete to a runner to find her brother Pèp-re (electric-eel little), to tell him about the illness of his little sister, and insist that he must carry out careful restrictions to save her. The messenger ran four miles to Electric Eel's wife's farm, but was told there that he and his family were staying at a backlander's house in Bacabal. There they were working on a backlander's farm to have manioc products to eat during the coming months of scarcity, since their supply had run out. The messenger then jogged the eight miles to Bacabal, where Electric Eel's wife told the messenger that her husband had gone off into the world, who knows where. She said he was falsely jealous of her attentions to another man.

The messenger knew he had come to the end of his search. Electric Eel could be moving through any number of cities in greater Brazil. If Electric Eel ate "heavy" foods or slept with prostitutes who happened to have eaten polluting foods, he could be weakening or killing Lake Lover back at home. His distance away from the tribe made no difference. Thus, Canela individuals traveling away from their people's area were usually careful about what they ate and with whom they slept.

This concept of blood's relative similarity—of shared blood, or of blood equivalence (*kaprôô pipën:* blood weighed-similarly)—among one-link-away kin is supported by the following belief. The Canela hold that a woman has only one umbilicus through her lifetime, and that all siblings come off of this umbilicus at birth. Research assistants drew a woman's belly in the sand for me. It had a protruding umbilicus, like a horizontal branch of a tree, from which many siblings were hanging like pieces of fruit. They drew this picture to convince me of the correctness of their belief. Thus, siblings, though born in the usual way, must have the same blood, though life's experiences, especially sex, will cause their blood equivalence to diverge later. As described in Chapter 3, contributing fathers, men who have introduced sufficient semen into a pregnant woman they are not married to, are considered one-link kin to her fetus. Thus, they too have to maintain restrictions when the child they contributed to forming is sick. In return, such children hold restrictions for their contributing fathers until either one's death.

The need to maintain restrictions for one's siblings, parents, or children serves as a constant reminder of the existence of such one-link relationships, as they are defined "biologically" by the Canela. While parents and children, or sisters, do not need to be reminded of such reciprocal responsibilities, contributing fathers and contributed-to children, as well as married brothers, need to have these bonds reinforced, since they live in different houses according to the village plan.

Bonding through "blood" is extended through a person's grandparents, uncles, aunts, nephews, nieces, and grandchildren, and through to these relatives' ancestors and descendants. Maintaining restrictions for these two- and further-link-away relatives, however, is not necessary. The blood held in common among these relatives has become diluted enough by other blood entering the blood pools through marriages that few pollutants will be transferred among them. Nevertheless, the recognition that some blood is held in common among such relatives bonds them together in the same longhouse and across the village plaza.

Self-Empowerment through Maintaining "Restrictions"

At almost every transition stage of their lives, Canela men and women maintain careful restrictions against the entry of pollutants in order to attain the new state. Restrictions grant the individual power over his or her own development, contrary to the powerlessness they may feel when threatened by witches or ghosts. At puberty, boys and girls are secluded for a number of days to help them learn how to maintain such restrictions. In the Warriors' festival, as described earlier, boys are interned in cells in their maternal houses for as long as three months, where relatively nonpolluted foods are provided by their families. During this period they are supposed to grow physically and morally strong, and to learn the practice of restrictions to help them develop in other transitional stages of their lives. When a young woman wins her social acceptance belt, she is secluded for four or five days during which time both she and her "child," her belt, gain strength through maintaining restrictions in preparation for one of her most important marriage rites, when the belt and woman are painted red by her female in-laws to indicate their greater acceptance of her. When a young man wants his recently pierced earlobe holes to heal, and to grow in size as larger wooden pins are inserted, he is secluded in his maternal house with his "children," the holes and pins, to maintain careful restrictions for about two weeks to ensure his and their growth.

The most important practice of restrictions takes place outside of formal rites, especially for men. Not long after puberty, a male adolescent is supposed to maintain thorough restrictions for one to three years, depending on how determined he is to become an enduring runner and skilled hunter, or, formerly, a great shaman. During this period he smears charcoal indiscriminately on his body to indicate his condition and to make himself unattractive to young girls and women. This maintaining of thorough and extensive restrictions is an act of self-empowerment. I believe that self-control developed in this way generalizes to most other activities in Canela living. When my Canela research assistants spoke with great respect of a strong, tough, middle-aged man and his accomplishments, they invariably added that he maintained a high level of restrictions for a long time when he was an adolescent.

The effects of maintaining strict adolescent restrictions are described in the story of Pàà-tsêt (forest-clearing burnt). For some unknown reason, Burnt Forest Clearing lived with his grandmother alone in an isolated valley far away from his people through the years of his puberty. Since he had no sexual contact with women and since his grandmother fed him largely pollutant-free foods, he grew remarkably strong. When Burnt Forest Clearing and his grandmother moved back to live with their people, he won all the foot and log races easily. No one could keep up with him. His traits of endurance and strength attracted young women, however, who flocked around him wanting sex. After much sex with them, he lost his special abilities and began to lose some races. He became a regular Canela young man, though an especially strong one.

SUMMARY

"Ritual" as Contrasted with "Religion"

Although folk Catholicism pervades Canela thinking these days, along with the influence of Protestant missionaries, the Canela formerly had no god, did not worship or pray to any supernatural being, and did not try to influence supernatural entities to bring about improvements in their harvests and living conditions. (I exempt their messianic movements, which have occurred since 1963, as being products of their modern circumstances.) Thus, it is easy to identify numerous rituals in Canela life, but difficult to find "religion." If one looks far enough into the social system of any culture, however, one will find some form of religion. The Canela "religion" is hard to recognize because it is so this-worldly.[11]

Instead of defining "religion," I am here using the simple concept of a belief security system. This chapter has described some aspects of the Canela belief system, one that met their needs as a large hunting and gathering society with some agriculture.[12] In a relatively benign environment without floods, earthquakes, volcanic eruptions, droughts, or famines, the Canela evidently did not need a more complex religion to explain and protect against catastrophe. At least in pre-pacification times, when the belief system took shape, snake bites, foraging uncertainties, and seasonal warfare constituted the worst insecurities.

A religion provides not only a sense of security, but also a sense of community. A common history is contained in myths. Emotional needs of the individual as well as general bonding is supported by Canela festivals and rites. Festivals as sources for role models provide one dimension of most religions.

A religion usually furnishes sufficient challenges to infuse direction and meaning into individuals' lives, as found in the Canela initiation festivals and in the system of restrictions against pollution. Pollutants are internal "enemies" to be overcome. Restrictions enable individuals who are strongly motivated to discipline themselves; the threat of pollution bonds the nuclear family into a cooperative unit that must work closely together.

A religion usually supplies rituals that provide for the expression of human emotions such as joy, as well as controlling them for the safety of the society. Canela rituals are outstanding here. Only a small sampling of life cycle rites and festivals has been discussed, but they are numerous and provide scope for ample recreation in the form of athletics, social sing-dances, and extramarital sex. Through extensive recreation, hostilities are reduced and gratification is acquired. Among the Canela, religion takes on very this-worldly forms.

NOTES

1. For interpretations of ear-piercing and other body perforations and adornments among other Gê-speaking peoples, see Seeger (1975) and Turner (1969).

2. Conklin (2001) takes the reader into the lives of an Amazonian people, who consume the cooked flesh of their recently deceased affines out of respect, honor, and compassion. It is a way of lessening the sorrow of the bereaved.

3. For a contrasting study, a structural one, of a similar Gê-speaking people, the Suyá, for a different, though parallel, set of life cycle rites, see Seeger (1981:147–179).

4. Melatti (1978) provides an extensive presentation and an interesting analysis of the festival-pageants of the Krahô Indians, cultural siblings of the Canela.

5. In contrast to the relatively egalitarian Canela with minimal material resources and ceremonial hierarchy, see Chernela's (1993) socially stratified Wanano Indians of the Amazonian Northwest.

6. See Crocker (1990:457–58) for plates of Canela masks in action.

7. For a more comprehensive understanding of the Canela festivals, see Crocker (1982), Crocker (1990:269–289), and Nimuendajú (1946:163–23).

8. See Nimueudajú (1946:238) for an account of the witch and snake shamans.

9. See Crocker (1990:144, No. 59).

10. For an account of shamanism from the native point of view in South America, see Langdon and Baer (1992). Crocker (1995) gives an analysis of Canela shamanism, especially from the this-worldly versus other-worldly view.

11. While the Canela are relatively this-worldly, the Araweté are comparatively other-worldly, including the practice of cannibalism. See Castro (1992).

12. A popularly written, but scientifically sound book (Diamond, 1999: 104–113) discusses the momentous significance of the great leap from food-collecting to food processing. The Canela are still hunter-gatherers psychologically, which makes likely their emphasis on sharing.

5/The Extramarital
Sex System

When I first started living with the Canela, I was already aware of the festivals that separated spouses for extramarital sex, because Nimuendajú wrote about them but with few details. On certain ceremonial days, spouses go with different tribal moieties for feasting and log racing as well as sex. By nightfall, a person knows that her or his spouse probably has had sex with someone else, or with several other persons. Feelings are not hurt, however, because a spouse's partners are not identified and because the arrangement is sanctioned by custom. Nimuendajú's monograph describes the Warriors' festival's Wild Boar day,[1] when wives of men of the Upper age class log racing teams amble out to a Canela garden hut with men of the Lower age class log racing teams for feasting and sex, while wives of men of the Lower teams stay in the village for dancing and sex with men of the Upper teams. Nimuendajú wrote that extramarital sex practiced apart from such ceremonial occasions was "adultery" and cause for divorce.[2] As my research eventually found, Nimuendajú's view of the Canela extramarital sex system was partly erroneous, so I had some surprises coming as my field research deepened.

On my first trip to the Canela, I asked questions about extramarital sex only to be countered by denials. Canela research assistants, who were otherwise helpful, assured me that Nimuendajú was wrong in saying that extramarital sex was practiced away from the village at a garden hut on the Wild Boar day. Were the Canela lying to me? A more plausible explanation was that they were being protective about their extramarital sex practices.

The Canela knew that others disapproved of these activities. Indian Service agents had talked to me depreciatingly about Canela practices. "Women sleep in the village plaza with men who are not their husbands," an agent warned me privately. He had observed this activity while wandering in the village after midnight. Later, a backlander took me aside and complained that Canela couples, when they lived by his house, sometimes crept under their large mats, moving them in sex, not caring about what was heard. *Bichos do mato,* "beasts of the forest," backlanders often called the Canela. It had become clear to me that I needed to prove to the Canela that I did not condemn their sex practices.

After several months, I brought out from my field trunk two large medical volumes, which I had brought with me to consult in case of illness. These volumes had colored plates showing all parts of the body, internal and external, female and male. I had concluded that talking about sex with outsiders embarrassed the Canela and that I needed to make them, and myself, more comfortable about this subject. I hoped that my use of the medical volumes' explicit pictures would convince them I was neither critical nor prudish.

I sat on a mat by the door of my sister Waterfall's house to provide better light for the pictures, a few Canela kneeling around me in the sand. Although I had intended to show the medical books first to men, women crowded around eagerly, pointing out and naming the sexual parts in the anatomical drawings. I remember my anxiety as I started asking them the names of various parts of the body, repeating their answers several times to get the pronunciation right: head (*?-khrā:* its [body's] ball), arm (*?-pa:* its branch), leg (*?-te:* its limb), penis (*?-hù:* its seeder), testicles (*n-kre:* its eggs), foreskin (*?-hù ?khrā ?khà:* its seeder's head's hide), vulva (*?-hê:* its [vertical] cleft),[3] pubic hair (*?-hê ?hô:* its cleft's pendants), clitoris (*?-hê ?khrùt-re:* its cleft's beak little). As well as learning the Canela terms, I was ridding myself of the inhibitions characteristic of my upbringing.

The Canela were interested in the photographs and diagrams, and groups frequently came by to look through the volumes on their own. Soon, by joining these groups, I became at ease describing and joking about the color and shape of sexual parts. Such talk was easier in Canela than English, as I discovered when I tried to describe such joking back in the United States. After several episodes of fun with the volumes, I had convinced the Canela that I was not embarrassed by a discussion of sex and that I did not hold their sexual practices against them. Subsequently, Canela research assistants willingly furnished the intricacies and intimacies of their unusually extensive extramarital sex system. As I learned its patterns, I realized that Nimuendajú had been largely mistaken about one of the principal Canela concepts. His belief that they considered casual adultery untraditional had contributed to the Canela's need to hide most of the details of their extramarital practices from him.

PUBLIC AND PRIVATE ASPECTS OF THE SYSTEM

Public Extramarital Practices

During my first year, the Warrior's festival's Wild Boar day feast was held in a hut on a garden clearing several miles from the Canela village of Baixão Preto. From the hut I watched small groups of young women disappear into the woods followed by groups of young men. An hour later these groups returned separately, the bodies of all individuals haphazardly decorated in charcoal stuck on with white latex sap. Such groups vanished into the bushes and emerged all afternoon, some individuals joining them more than once. Canela assistants denied sexual activity was occurring out there, but I did not believe them.

The next year, on the same festival occasion, Canela assistants confirmed that the groups in the woods away from the garden hut were indeed having sex. Informants added that since each group had more men than women, some women satisfied several men. They said that the women of a group found separate bedding-down spots for each man who came to them in sequence.

I quietly savored the field victory that this new information brought me, but tried not to appear too interested or curious. I tried to strike a balance between being appreciative of the Canela fun derived from such practices and being matter-of-fact about the special knowledge Nimuendajú had missed. My training had taught me that if I appeared too eager to hear about their sex practices, they might bring an inflated number of examples to please me.

The black charcoal, stuck firmly but haphazardly on the bodies of individuals emerging from the woods, proclaimed the occurrence of an episode of extramarital sex. Most styles of body painting signal meaning. Charcoal rubbed on loosely, for instance, without latex as a binder, announces that the individual is undergoing strict dietary and sex restrictions.

On another ceremonial occasion, a Red versus Black moiety day during my second year, adolescent women and adult men assembled at a point about 500 yards along a road leading out of the village around 7:00 in the morning. Because it was the beginning of a formal occasion, the participants were painted in carefully applied solid black charcoal on latex, horizontal lines for the Reds and vertical ones for the Blacks. The precise traditional designs represented the two moieties involved.

By the time I arrived, a fence 4 feet high had been erected across the road so that no one lying or sitting on the village side could see anyone on the savannah side. Red women and men were sitting or lying on the village side of the fence in separate groups, while Black women and men lay or sat apart quietly on the farther side. Besides several Canela elderly observers and myself, only two male performers were standing, one painted in each pattern. The Red man asked several Red women in low tones which men they favored to go hunting with. Then, he went beyond the fence to the Black side and tapped each chosen Black man with a stick. At the same time, the Black messenger walked in from behind the fence to tap certain Red men so that they would know they were a Black woman's choice.

Later, the Reds and Blacks filed separately along a wooded trail, and women caught the eyes of the men they had chosen. The men were waiting for such meaningful glances. Later, small groups of individuals ambled off into the bushes eventually to pair off with their chosen partners. Individuals tried not to let their spouses see whom they were joining. Attempting not to be conspicuous myself, I kept watching women and men I knew to be married to see how careful they were being. Their care was minimal, but they did cooperate by averting eyes from the location of their lovers.

Canela research assistants said that once deep in the small woods scattered in the savannah, the man hunted, while the woman waited under a tree. If she was sufficiently pleased with the game he brought her, she might give him sex. That evening back in the village, sex or no sex, the woman gave the meat to her mother-in-law who, knowing that the meat was supplied by her daughter-in-law's lover, made it into a small meat pie for herself. The older woman had accepted the pie and thus her son's wife's free sexuality. Then, the mother-in-law in turn gave a bowl of meat and manioc to the men's group to which her daughter-in-law's lover belonged, when it was assembled in the plaza that evening—a return for the lover's meat.

This meat pie rite represents the mother-in-law's acceptance of her daughter-in-law's right to be involved in extramarital sex on public occasions and in private trysts. Before this rite, the older woman might have taken her son's side if he were complaining about his wife's extramarital trysts and his consequent embarrassment. And before this rite, the younger woman would not have gone on public ceremonial occasions, such as the Wild Boar day, for fear of the vicious talk any of her female in-laws might spread against her. Now they could say nothing. They had accepted the marriage more completely, including the couple's customary full participation in extramarital sex.

A Ceremonial Chief sing-dance day[4] could occur many times a year to install a singing chief, a town crier, or a visiting chief of another Timbira tribe. Such sing-dance days were also put on to honor the visit of a high-ranking government official or to extract goods from the tribal anthropologist or missionary, who had to contribute an outrageous amount when so honored. I felt exploited when they did this for me, but decided they felt they were exacting a fair exchange for my future books and photographs. Otherwise I would be getting a "free ride on their backs." The Canela feel they lose something, dignity or self-respect, when they are used without a proper return.

During every Ceremonial Chief day, the honored person, female or male, is painted red and with white falcon down applied onto a resin base. This installation into a ceremonial position of respect takes place in the plaza, while the tribe spends most of the day performing sing-dances in separate male age class units. These male groups dance sideways around the village boulevard in single files, facing out toward the houses. An Upper age class group dances slowly clockwise, arms around shoulders. They invite wives of men of a Lower age class to come out from their houses and dance with them, interspersed in the male row. A Lower age class of men dances counterclockwise and inserts wives of Upper age class men into their row.

During an hour of this sing-dancing, approximately 50 men collect about 10 women into their age class's sideways-moving rows. (See Figure 5.1.) Then the men, perspiring and elated, take the women away for sex. The age classes of one moiety dance into the house of a Wè?tè (ceremonial) girl's family, enlarged and equipped with a special room, and the age classes of the other moiety drift to a secluded area along the village stream. Spouses are thus well separated.

My assistants said that the dances of these sing-dance Ceremonial Chief days arouse sexual feelings in participants, and I occasionally saw dancing males in the line brushing their hands casually over the women's breasts. In any case, this hopping and sidestepping around the boulevard just inside the circle of houses, the rear foot crossing behind and ahead of the forward one, require considerable stamina. After I turned 40, I could not complete the long journey, about 1,000 yards, around the village circle even once, while Canela up to 50 years old completed it many times.

In the ceremonial house, members of the host family erect enclosures of light mats in their special room to screen each woman. Some sets of mats are placed around existing platform beds and some are strung up around piles of mats on the floor. By the stream, the women are separated by bushes so that any of the men who want sex can go, one at a time, to a woman who is not a relative, in-law, or Formal Friend without their activity being seen.

A similar arrangement is set up on tribal work days, when the Council of Elders decides most of the men will perform services together. They might cut open vistas through the savannahs and woods along the tribal boundaries, work on the roads so vehicles will not stall in the sands, or harvest a family's field of rice. On such occasions, each age class moiety files out swiftly to different sectors of the work area.

Figure 5.1 On Ceremonial Chief day, men and women dance together, sideways along the main street, facing the houses.

Three to five women are assigned by the chief to each moiety for the day. They flirt with the men while they work and chat with them while they eat light lunches in the early afternoon. Then, the women walk out about 30 yards in different directions from their moiety's central location to prepare comfortable nests in the low bushes. There they will please a number of men in turn. A man picks a woman he is not related to and walks out to her. He swiftly completes the sex act and stands up. Then the next man, seeing the first one stand, walks out to the woman's nest. She moves the nest slightly for each man so that his feet will not come into contact with any sexual fluids left on the grass from the earlier trysts. These liquids weaken a man's legs, and consequently his prized running ability.

This traditional placing of women so that men can go to them sequentially for sex also occurs at the end of a two-week hunting encampment away from the village. Such hunting trips provide enough meat so that the whole tribe can eat well during a 10-day festival without leaving the village. Again, the men are divided in two large groups by age class moiety, and the half-dozen women assigned to each moiety are spouses of men of the other moiety. The women cook and prepare the meat throughout the hunting period but have sex with the men only after the last sing-dance, during the night before their return to the village. To have had sex earlier might pollute and weaken the hunters and spoil their rapport with the game. Assistants say that game animals like hunters who are unpolluted by recently eaten "heavy" meat or by sex with women who are thus polluted. Animals like to approach hunters who are in such a state of relative "purity," and then the hunters can easily kill them.

This arrangement for sequential sex also takes place informally on any day the men in their age class moiety units work close enough so that they can join each other to race back to the village in the mid-afternoon, each moiety team carrying a log. While such races, preceded by group sequential sex, do not occur every day, they are a potential element of the daily cycle of events when the members of the tribe are living in their central village and not generally dispersed to their gardens or to the houses of backlanders. These events are thus daily in nature, not ceremonial. While it is relatively easy to recruit women for ceremonial events, it is often difficult to obtain them for daily work occasions. These daily work sessions therefore have usually lacked women in more recent times.

While the sequential extramarital sex arrangements described above place many men with a few unrelated women, the Festival of Oranges places about half a dozen men with 40 to 50 women for about 10 days. The Festival of Oranges is an occasion for men and women to reverse roles. A woman, instead of male leaders, is in charge of the arrangements, and the women get to enjoy male privileges. Women generally enjoy discussing among themselves how a certain man performs sexually, so the capabilities of most men are well known, just as the characteristics of most women are known to the men. Thus, the women can choose the young men with the greatest sexual abilities to accompany them in their quest for oranges and other foods for the festival. Several of the women, maybe six, seclude each man separately, and have sex sequentially with them. The women sit erect on top of the men, mimicking the male position. After the women have satisfied themselves, while the man has restrained himself, the man is allowed finally to reach climax, squatting between the legs of the last woman.

When I was away from the village for several days on a mapping trip during my second stay with the Canela, my assistant asked me the first evening if he could send for women from the village to help my work party members enjoy the night. Of course I said yes, hoping to witness activities usually hidden from me, since I could not participate in them. (Aside from my personal and professional ethics, Brazilian law was clear on this restriction; Indian Service personnel would have reported infractions quickly and canceled my authorization to work with the Canela.)

Later that evening I remember feeling delighted at this opportunity for observation when four laughing young women arrived. After one of them, my assistant's long-term lover, had satisfied several men in the bushes, not quite out of my hearing, she climbed into my assistant's hammock that was hung on one of the same posts as mine. Between about midnight and five I was awakened six times by a rhythmic shaking that the common post transferred to my hammock. Six times I confined myself to listening, afraid to be caught peeking to collect field data, even though the night was dark. After what I heard and felt that night, I was no longer surprised that the women usually sought my mapping assistant as one of their Festival of Oranges male companions each year.

One time when I asked about whether women were ever sexually aggressive with men, assistants told me a story of earlier times. Young Hole Grater was said to revel in having sex with as many women as possible. The young women decided to teach this boastful youth a lesson. Ten of them climbed a tree and one called down to him for sex as he was passing beneath. He spat on his hands and climbed the tree, grabbing at one then another, but each one said it was another who had called him. Finally, near the top, he cornered one girl, stretched her out on a branch, and had sex with her there, publicly and perilously, to the others' consternation. Further action was needed to humble this man.

Several days later, the same group of young women, hoping to teach Hole Grater a lesson and wanting to take advantage of his superior attributes, invited him into the woods. There they made a bed to lie in, and each one came to him in turn, lying down for him. Nobody can say these days just how many sex acts Hole Grater's erection survived, but he finally got tired, saying he was hungry and asking for something to eat to bring back his strength. However, the next woman in line insisted on her turn and would not let him rest. So she lay down and started pulling on his penis until it became erect (a totally uncustomary manipulation). Then she inserted it and they had sex one more time.

After this last attempt to humble him, they had pity on him and took him home to his wife. The news of his lesson had reached the village and his wife's ears before he did, so she teased him when he came in the door. Nevertheless, Hole Grater rested a moment and ate something, and then demonstrated that he could perform one more time with her. He had not quite been tamed.

Private Extramarital Practices

Besides the festival-sanctioned and work-group occasions for extramarital sex described above, personally arranged trysts are also traditional and more frequently practiced. If a man feels a strong sexual desire for a woman, and if she is neither kin, affine, nor Formal Friend, he gives her a certain look as they pass, or he says, possibly, that he would like to rub his hand on her (*i-mã a-kuupên prãm:* me-in you-touch need). She responds in kind if she feels the same way. Later, when the opportunity arises, he sends her a spoken message through a neutral person, usually a child of either sex who would have inconspicuous access to her, suggesting a location and time: for instance, down behind the locust tree that juts into the wet meadow left of the main stream when the sun is low.

A frequent cause of fun, when I was moving around with male companions, was the discovery of a trysting place. The discoverer would gleefully summon his friends to the spot, and the group, thoroughly enthralled, debated what each mark in the sand indicated: her buttocks were here, his feet were there, his buttocks swung low here, and her head relaxed there afterward; the couple were in a hurry and did it quickly because there was only one set of relatively unblurred markings.

While I saw many tryst spots in the sands, I seldom was close by when sequential sex was taking place. However, I once found myself conversing with the men going to and from such an episode. In the Canela village of Sardinha in the dry forests, the soil was sufficiently fertile within the village circle, unlike the soil in a savannah village, so that corn could be planted between the radial pathways leading from the village plaza to the houses on the circular boulevard.

Ràm (tree resin) emerged from the corn stalks. I overheard him talking to younger Thunder and gathered that a woman was hidden there, available for sex. Thunder then disappeared into the standing corn. When he emerged two minutes later and was alone with me, I teased him for just having had sex, which he denied at first, as was the custom, and then admitted privately to me, as my helper and friend. Electric Eel Girl was there, only 10 to 20 yards from the plaza, a woman in her late teens. Thunder said she had been lying there first with Macaw's Bone (age 45) and was desirable because of her large vagina. He said that Resin (age 30) had spotted them, and so had joined them for sex in turn, and that he had done the same after Resin. When Macaw's Bone emerged from the corn, I teased him that I would tell his wife, my "sister," which he knew from experience I would not do. Although he said nothing, he smiled.

I found the constant interest in sex remarkable. With sex so easily available, I wondered why the interest was so keen. At the beginning of my fieldwork, young men discussed the arrival of panties as a threat to their easy access to women. (Women previously wore nothing under their wrap-around skirts.) Perhaps such lively interest reflected concern that sexual availability was waning. Possibly extramarital sex was the principal joy in a society that offered few other excitements and many overwhelming social and economic discouragements. The principal societal sources of satisfaction other than extramarital sex are team racing with logs, sing-dancing in the plaza, performing festivals, hunting animals for food and sport, and providing for children, kin, and spouses. Nevertheless, except for the last one, all these sources of gratification among the Canela are accompanied by sexual activities.

Canela assistants assure me that women take the initiative as often as men. My best evidence for this occurred in May 1959 on the evening of my third return to the tribe. I had been paying my respects to the Indian Service personnel by having dinner at the post. After dinner, while slowly climbing the sandy hill back up to Ponto village, I heard the beating of a drum, a sound I had never heard in the village before. The rhythm reminded me of the several backlanders' dancing festivals I had attended during the two previous years, and I knew from the sound that someone was beating an empty metal gasoline barrel.

Easing through the crowd in the larger of the two Ceremonial Girl's houses, I found Canela women and men paired and dancing bare-topped in the embraced manner of the backlanders, shuffling their feet to the monotonous rhythm of a metal drum. No instrument or singing provided a melody. I realized that this was an historic event: a first occurrence of dancing borrowed from the backlander, but only partly reproduced. After waiting in the crowded room for the pattern to repeat itself several times, I noticed that when the beating ceased for an interval, couples parted according to the backland custom. However, contrary to the custom, when the dancing resumed, it was the women who chose the men they wanted as their next partners. A year later, Canela couples were dancing fully clothed, often with shoes, to the music of an accordion. Only men were standing and choosing seated women after each break in the dancing. Now the adoption of the backland pattern was nearly complete. But before this happened, it had seemed appropriate to the Canela to have the women do the choosing.

LEARNING ABOUT SEX

Children Are Exposed to Sex as a Joyful Activity

Canela children learn about sex in a casual, natural way by witnessing the scarcely hidden sexual activities and public sex games engaged in by the adults around them.

Several nights after I was taken into Canela life, assigned an adoptive family, and given a corner in their house, I was awakened by soft noises coming from the rafters. Although it was dark, I knew there was a platform bed high up in the area the sounds were coming from and surmised the moderate creaking was from sexual activity. I wondered how the children of the house interpreted these sounds and whether the parents of the girl up there found the sounds appropriate.

Nimuendajú wrote that unmarried women received lovers on such rafter platforms at night. Lake Lover was recently married, however, and about 14, so I wondered if

William H. Crocker

Figure 5.2 Civilizado-*style dancing*

what was going on was appropriate for her whole family to overhear. Waterfall, her mother and my sister, rose to stir the fire, appearing not to hear the noises. Single Girl, 4, was returning from relieving herself just outside with her mother's sister, Self Searcher, following her. However, except for one slight turn of her head, Single Girl paid no attention to the noises. I concluded that little girls and boys grew up hearing their older sisters having sex, but I thought that I had better check this point with my research assistants in the morning. In this case, I thought (though could not see) that the young man who had climbed the notched pole to the high platform was Boil's Vapor, Lake Lover's new husband. Family members confirmed this the next day. Boil's Vapor had departed quietly before dawn. Assistants said later that young couples seldom have sex in their platform beds, but only when overcome by great desire and only when they think every one else is sound asleep.

During my second stay among the Canela, in my adoptive sister's house, two pre-adolescent boys, Electric Eel and Fast Pig, were teasing Flint Woman, the new wife of their older brother, Endures Water. The boys were trying to pull off her wrap-around skirt. She resisted, screaming with fun, while they persisted unsuccessfully. The smaller children watched the sex-oriented fun with delight.

William H. Crocker

Figure 5.3 A woman sits on a platform bed. Mats woven of palm fronds provide privacy. Beds for younger women would be even higher. Possessions are stored under the rafters of the house.

A month later, again in my sister's house in front of all the children, the younger Thunder, an "uncle" to the children, called me to join him in having fun with our adolescent "niece," Kô-rên (water-spilt). We both caught her, and he tried unsuccessfully to suck one of her breasts while I tried to hold her. Spilt Water was strong, however, and managed to evade Thunder by ducking and wiggling. This traditional "uncle"-"niece" game was broken up when her wraparound skirt began to come off, turning the game into a serious embarrassment for her. Spilt Water had screamed in delight earlier, but with her skirt slipping, she began to scream in fear and anger, so we released her. Thunder accused her of being angry, *a-khrùk* (you-angry), a social offense that Spilt Water heartily denied, resuming her social good nature, at least in appearance. Younger Thunder initiated such fun and games only in a limiting familial setting.

I had qualms about becoming involved in such customary games, even to the extent of just holding by the shoulders a "niece" whom I already knew very well. What if a backlander or an Indian Service agent saw what I was doing? What if a Canela innocently told a backlander or an Indian Service agent that they liked me because I was participating in the fun of Canela life in this way? Fortunately, this did not happen.

One day during the summer of my second year, while I was eating lunch in my sister's house, a sex game occurred between Macaw's Bone, my sister's husband, and one of his "other wives," Three Forests Woman. Macaw's Bone had severely hurt his leg in the log race the day before, so he was spending the day in his hammock, hung in the open part of the house so he could observe all that was going on. Suddenly, Three Forests dumped him out of his hammock, and rolled on top of him as he lay on the ground. The large woman grabbed his genitals. She was enjoying her advantage over the temporarily hobbled Macaw's Bone. The struggle went on for at least a minute until the Indian Service agent with another outsider barged in.

Fun had been had by all, except for the children of the household, who watched silently, unable to laugh when their own father was the butt of the joke. Nevertheless, the children witnessed the amusement and joy associated with sex, even if they could not participate in the joking. Assistants said that in these sex games between "other spouses," "aunts" and "nephews," or "uncles" and "nieces," the women try to grab penises and the men attempt to suck breasts. These games occur only when many relatives are watching, ensuring that the fun does not go beyond culturally allowed limits. Nobody must get seriously hurt—either physically or emotionally.

In the village of Sardinha during my fourth stay, I had built up a group of Canela research assistants whose veracity I could count on. I was undertaking the sensitive quest of reconstructing what their sexual mores had been in earlier times. I inquired into sexual behavior for several days with a group of both sexes, selected for their good memories and their superior abilities of expression. About six of us worked in a room with a window, with coffee and crackers brought to us in the middle of the morning and afternoon sessions. By this time it did not surprise me that little tykes of 3 and 4 years repeatedly came to the window to listen for minutes at a time, and that children of 8 or 9 spent longer periods hanging on the window sill, attempting to follow our debates. Their parents were not concerned about what their children might hear.

One time, the younger Thunder got on the table in our room and demonstrated the positions used in sex, squatting for male ones and lying on his back with his knees spread for female ones. It happened that the table was near the window, so that Thunder's little "niece" of 9 years, Star Girl, could reach him through the window with a pencil in her hand. When she began poking him with it, while he was on his back demonstrating the female position, the group erupted into laughter. Within two to three years she would be doing what Thunder was demonstrating.

Certain festival situations call for public parodies of sexual behavior which, while intentionally ridiculous, are really an expression of great joy. The joy is acted out to honor one's Formal Friend. The sexual behavior thus mimicked, simultaneously comic and ecstatic, is witnessed by children and adolescents. During my first year with the Canela, an old man in his late 70s tried to take off an equally old woman's wraparound skirt in the boulevard during the Warriors' festival. He was doing this with exaggerated clumsy motions, expressing joy to honor his Formal Friend, an adolescent boy. Standing on a mat nearby, this initiate was being ceremonially presented to the adults at the end of his internment. Children and adults had gathered around, enjoying the ridiculous pantomiming of the couple. However, the game was stopped when another old woman came up and hit the old man lightly on the backside with a stick. The second woman, as the old woman's Formal Friend, was protecting her.

During the Closing Wè?tè festival of my eighth Canela trip, a Formal Friend of one of the two ceremonial girls performing in the festival expressed her joy for her Formal Friend. She jerked her hips, thrusting an artificial male genitalia, made of two gourds and a graphically carved stick. During earlier times on such occasions, some men, contrary to the rule of modesty, pulled back their foreskins for everybody to see the glans of the penis, as Nimuendajú wrote[5] and my Canela research assistants confirmed. Although some of the young people may be embarrassed by witnessing these public displays by their close kin, they cannot avoid the realization that the displays are expressions of joy and honor.

Socialization of Virginal Girls for Sex

The socialization of virginal girls into extramarital sex proceeds by steps. During the Facsimile Warriors' festival of my second year, Amkro-?khwèy (sun-light girl), 11, was the younger female associate. She was treated as a virgin because she had had sex only recently with a young man, Khrúwa-tsè (arrow-bitter), who thereby had become her husband, but she had not yet had sex with a number of her "other husbands." In contrast, Tsêp-khwèy (bat-girl), 13, the older nonvirginal female associate of this men's society, gave herself on traditional occasions to her other husbands in the group.

During the Fish festival, Hand's Blossom Girl (hũ?kra-lã: hand its-blossom), about 10 and still a virgin, but already an associate (kuytswè) of a men's Fish society, was ambling by the men's fire on the western edge of the plaza with other Fish society women just after running along the men's log race. One of the older men Warrior Traversed (pep-lêl: warrior crossed-over), age 45, teased her, saying that she should not have sex with adolescent youths, but only with older men like himself. He added jokingly to me that she looked tired because she was having sex with adolescents.

The man was indirectly teaching Hand's Blossom to expect and desire sex with older men by the enthusiasm of his manner. Ironically, Warrior Traversed was one of the three homosexuals in the tribe, and the one of the three who was not able to have erections with women, as assistants had explained in one of our group meetings. Hand's Blossom must have known this too, but she accepted the admonishment anyway in the usual joking spirit.

At the log racing site of the Red versus Black ceremony, during my second year, Kô-?kaprôô (water-blood) carried off a young female nonvirgin toward the woods to the amusement of all present, as if she were a racing log held over his left shoulder. At first she was struggling and screaming loudly in delight, but when her screams turned from joy to fear, Water's Blood released her. Then the two returned slowly together to the group. Although she had not agreed to go with Water's Blood, she had not objected at first. However, since no observers were in the woods to limit the sex game, she began to become fearful and objected seriously. A number of virginal girls helping their mothers prepare food witnessed the joking abduction. They were thus exposed to the appeal of single, non-sequential sex, but also witnessed the limitations provided by consensus.

Another occasion I observed, when virgins witnessed sequential sex and anticipated their involvement in it, was a Wild Boar day. The male log racers and observers lunched and rested by a hut near a family farm away from the village. Four young women went off into the woods while the still virginal girls around 10 years old remained, helping their female relatives prepare food for the racers. About 20 racers ambled off into the woods after the young women and returned with them about 45 minutes later. The carelessly applied black charcoal on the participants' bodies told the virgin girls what had taken place in the woods.

Steps into Full Marriage

Marriage (*më hikhwa:* they lie-down-together) may be arranged ahead of time by the mothers of the couple. The couple may be brought before their kin for a marital meeting (më aypën pa: they to-each-other listen) during which their uncles lecture them on the responsibilities of marriage. Then the couple are engaged (*më aypën tê:* they for-each-other reserved) and are left alone together much of the time so they may have sex, as their mothers hope they will.

One Canela assistant reported that after his marriage had been arranged, his mother took him and his future wife on an extended visit to a backland community. Eventually, after two weeks of living close together and some *cachaça* (cane alcohol) on the final night, he and his fiancée finally had sex. Thus, they had become married, according to the Canela definition. In contrast, a girl may have first sex with an adolescent of her choice without being engaged, which is referred to by the parents as the youth "having stolen" (*to hà?khíya*) the girl. In either case, they are married by the act of sexual intercourse, and the marriage continues unless the boy's extended family pays a fine for his release, if the couple has not yet conceived, the amount being set in an open interfamily trial.

Virginity loss is only the first step into full marriage for a woman. Other important steps are (1) the ceremonial purchase of the son-in-law by the bride's extended family; (2) the bride's winning her social acceptance belt through her service in a festival men's society, which includes sequential sex; (3) the painting of the bride's social acceptance belt by her female in-laws; (4) the mother-in-law's receipt of meat earned by the bride through extramarital sex on a Red and Black racing day; (5) the birth of her first baby and its survival; and (6) the celebration of the postpartum rite about 40 days later by the extended kin of the couple. After the birth of a baby, unless the baby dies, the marriage is unbreakable until the children of the marriage are mid- to late adolescents. Divorce is customarily not allowed until then, although in the 1980s "divorce from children" began to occur.[6]

Stinginess, Jealousy, and Sharing

After a girl has been married for several months, her other husbands begin to ask her for private trysts. If she refuses them too often over a period of several weeks, the rejected other husbands develop a plan to "teach her to be generous," as they say, or to "tame her." They usually seek the cooperation of certain of her female kin, aunts or sisters who have been warning her about what could happen if she did not comply with the ancestors' custom of sexual sharing.

Hill Climber reported dramatically on herself in a research assistant group session that she was too slow in becoming generous with men after she was first married. One day she was gathering buriti palm fruits with several members of her female kin, when all except one left her. The remaining woman physically restrained her from leaving the spot where they were gathering fruit. Soon about six of her other husbands appeared, and she knew immediately that she was in trouble. She did not struggle, because she recognized the inevitable. Besides, her aunts had warned her that if she were physically hurt under such circumstances, her uncles would not be able to bring her case to trial. She had already broken the customary law of sexual generosity, so she would have no case against the men forcing sequential sex on her.

Some ethnologists call such an action "rape," but I prefer not to use such a negative word when the individual involved could have avoided the forced sequential sex experience by obeying the mores of the tribe. Hill Climber's other husbands were not forcing sequential sex on her to humiliate her or to express any hate or disrespect for women. They were bringing her a step closer to accepting sequential sex as a female associate of a men's society.

The Canela believe that husbands have to be taught not to be jealous of their wives. Canela assistants reported that during a Ceremonial Chief sing-dance day one morning, a young husband, Three Forests, saw his wife of a few months in a dancing line consisting of men of his opposing age class moiety. He knew this meant that by the afternoon most of her other husbands in that line would have had sex with her. When the dancing line snaked along the boulevard close to his house, he dashed out, consumed by jealousy, and grabbed his wife by the wrist, dragging her into their house to keep her for himself. Then he stood by the door and waved his machete in defiance at the men of the other moiety. (This is Pedro in the video *Mending Ways*.[7])

He succeeded in indulging his personal jealousy that day, rather than following the demands of his society. However, several days later when he was away at his family's garden, members of his opposing age class moiety entered his house, abducted his partially compliant wife, and ran with her far into the woods, passing her from shoulder to shoulder like a racing log. Once in the woods they enjoyed her sexually in turn. Her mother followed them, running with a machete in hand, but could not keep up.

Women who cooperate in group sequential sex on tribal work days or even "daily" work situations receive small gifts from each of the men. But the jealous husband's wife receives no gifts at all to take home to help her support her female kin. We may feel that she is being unfairly punished for her husband's error, but Canela men know that wives and mothers-in-law have much to do with whether a husband or son-in-law can get away with being sexually selfish. Surely the machete-wielding mother-in-law in this case was violating custom and supporting her son-in-law's wishes in order to keep him for her daughter. She had not been telling her daughter, and especially her sons, to advise her son-in-law well.

Stinginess by men with their own sexual assets rarely occurs. When they are somewhat sick or undergoing food and sex restrictions, they can say no, with appropriate and acceptable justifications, to desiring women (*më khraakhrak to mõ:* they itching/desiring with go-along). Otherwise, men are required by the culture to share in all respects, far more so than women. This is the case with their material possessions (bows and arrows), the game they just killed (venison), their special skills (sing-dance leading or curing), or their sexual abilities. Granting sexual favors is really more a matter of obligation for men than a matter of generosity. It is also an expression of empathy with the strongly expressed needs of a demanding and desirous woman.

Socialization of Nonvirginal Girls for Sequential Sex

Amyi-kaarã (self-clarifier), 13, was appointed during my fourth year by the Council of Elders as the older and therefore the nonvirginal female associate to the men's festival Society of Masks. The younger female associate she was paired with in this society, Te-tsêê (leg's-decoration), 10, was still virginal, and so could not be drawn into performing in the society's several sequential sex occasions. She could only observe them, and most likely was developing expectations for the time when she could enjoy them also. In contrast, Self Clarifier, on prescribed occasions, had had sex with most of her other husbands among the membership of the Masks' society during earlier trysts.

Self Clarifier was well prepared for sequential sex occasions. She had grown up hearing that sex was fun and joyous. She had been sent as a messenger between lovers many times, and she had witnessed an older female associate to a men's society enjoy group sequential sex. Most important of all, Self Clarifier had shared herself with her other husbands several months after first marriage, so she had already had sex with many different men, but only one at a time in private trysts. Nevertheless, Self Clarifier was surely apprehensive of receiving as many as 15 to 20 men in turn for the first time. Female research assistants said that young girls about to have their first sequential sex are afraid that some penises would be too big for their still small and tight vaginas. They were afraid they would dislike some of the men who would approach them so that their feelings would be inhibited. But Self Clarifier could reassure herself because she knew that all of the men coming to her well-prepared nests in the woods would be other husbands; and that she would have had relations with most of them in private trysts already and would continue to do so until much older. Moreover, most of them had joked sexually with her since she was about 3 years old.

Self Clarifier had been brought up to share everything, but if she refused any of the men, she could develop a reputation for being stingy. Then she would have few or no lovers, and eventually a witch might "throw" some disease into her that could lead to her death. Besides, her aunts had made it clear to her that she simply had to go through with this generosity to men, even if it were unpleasant. However, the aunts had said it was fun to please men sexually, and that after several men had come in her, her sexual feelings would get better and better so that she might even begin to "cry" (nkwèl/amra) with pleasure and delight.

Sequential sex was something you had to get used to doing before you could really like it, the aunts had said. It was a way of becoming popular and sought after by your other husbands for private trysts. Then several of your other husbands might become special lovers, and this was really enjoying life at its best. The aunts emphasized that if she did not submit herself to sequential sex, she could not win her social acceptance belt. And if she had not won such a belt, her mother-in-law and sisters-in-law could not paint it red, thus securing her husband for eventual babies and a family of her own. After securing her husband and before having babies, she would have a good time sexually as a "free" young woman.

It encouraged Self Clarifier further that the older Endures Water, the head of the Masks, was kind to her, as were the other male members of the Masks' society. They always had a lot of fun and jokes with their two female associates for most of the morning before a sequential sex occasion, building enthusiasm before involving the nonvirginal one in the group bonding activity. Referring to the activities leading to sequential sex, one of my female research assistants explained, *Ampoo kwèlyapê kahãy koo, kuupên kwèlyapê* (what because-of a-female wet, handling because-of: Why does a woman get aroused? It is from [male] caressing). After all, they were all members of the same tribe, and she had known them all since childhood. Sometimes, the virginal girl associate to a men's society in such a three-month-long festival had sex with a young man privately and then, married to him, became available sexually to her other husbands in the same men's society.

I still had trouble believing young girls could get involved voluntarily in sequential sex until a female assistant gave our research assistant group her story. Hô-?khrã (palm-straw balled) was married to a chief and was a classificatory wife to me. Thus she was not even slightly embarrassed by my presence. We had to throw sex-flavored jokes at each other every time we met, as classificatory spouses do. Balled Straw's account about how she first experienced sequential sex was a moment in field research I will never forget. She had been one of the two girls of highest honor in the tribe, a Wè?tè girl, and so was related to her male society—half of the men of the entire tribe—as a classificatory sister instead of as a classificatory wife or an "other" wife. Therefore, having sex with the men of her group was forbidden; it would be ceremonial incest. These men called her "sister" and her parents "father" and "mother," and they rested and drank water in their "parents'" (her parents') house before every log race and were often served water and food by her. On a Ceremonial Chief sing-dance day, Balled Straw, nevertheless, felt desire for her "brothers." When her brothers had danced around the boulevard with the young wives of the men of the other half of the tribe, they brought these young women, dancing, into their (her) parents' house and placed them in prepared cubicles for sequential sex. Balled Straw, hearing what was going on in her house, was overcome with sexual desire and joined the other women. She told our research group, *Më ha?khrã te i-nin pal* (plural group did me-fuck all: All the society's members had sex with me.)[8]

Young girls very rarely resisted carrying out their sequential sex obligations to an assigned ceremonial men's society, but when they did, they were taken forcefully into it anyway. Research in 1999 indicated that force only very rarely had to be used during the 1930s and 1940s, but that force was used increasingly during later decades until this ceremonial practice was abandoned in the mid-1980s.[9]

Winning the Social Acceptance Belt[10]

Just after the termination of a great summer festival in which a girl has performed as a female associate to a men's society, including involvement in group sequential sex, she is secluded in her maternal house to facilitate the "growth" and "coming into maturity" of her newly won belt. (See Chapter 3 for a description of the belt.) She is considered the "mother" of the belt and therefore has to undergo food and sex restrictions to enhance the growth of her "daughter." To achieve this purpose, the "mother" and "daughter" are placed in an enclosure of mats in a corner of the house of the belt's "mother" and "grandmother," where the consumption of food and the abstention from sex can be enforced. This internment is similar to the much longer postpartum seclusion for the health and growth of a newly arrived baby. After about four days of seclusion, but really when her "uncles" have managed to kill a small deer and have deposited it with her mother, the girl's kin send her out alone toward the plaza carrying the deer on her shoulders, holding its legs around her neck.

As the bride emerges from her maternal house, walking down her radial pathway toward the plaza and carrying the deer on her shoulders, her husband's sisters and "sisters" sprint from their arc of houses, each woman competing to reach her first. They race directly to her, running in the disorderly manner (*më ?prõt:* they scrounge) symbolic of extramarital sex. They dash joyously across the radial pathways through the grass. These competing sisters-in-law take the deer from the bride's shoulders and escort her slowly back to her husband's maternal house, where her mother-in-law receives her. The bride delivers her still green belt to her mother-in-law, an act that is symbolic of the passing of considerable responsibility from her kin to her affines. As described earlier, under the direction of her mother-in-law, her many "mothers-" and "sisters-in-law" from several houses paint the belt and wind it around the bride's hips. The social acceptance belt rite is followed by the sexual exchanges of the Red versus Black moiety day.

After the belt painting, the bride has become an adolescent woman and is recognized as an *nkrekrel-re* (slippery), "free" person, who should participate in most of the festival and other extramarital occasions to keep the morale of the men high, especially during their morning work activities when they work in moiety groups for the good of the tribe as a whole. However, she is not completely married, nor a fully responsible adult, until she has produced a baby.

The "Free" Adolescent Years

The young woman, now a "free" adolescent, is usually from 13 to 17 years old, though women who cannot bear children remain in this stage of life much longer. The adolescent is in this "slippery" period from belt painting to childbirth. She is said to be slippery because she is hard to catch, like the greased pig in a game backlanders play. They mean that she is hard to catch for sex trysts, that she is relatively free but very busy sexually.

Some of the extramarital sex occasions allow the free adolescent woman to accept or reject sexual participation. The Red versus Black hunting ceremony, which occurs once a year, involves her with only one hunter of her choice, but having sex then is not compulsory. The Wild Boar days, which take place about six times a decade, allow her to choose whether she wants to have sex or not, but if she goes into the woods at all with several women, the female-male ratio on these occasions almost requires her to be generous with several men. On the Ceremonial Chief sing-dance days, occurring three times a year at most, when men of the opposing age class moiety to her husband's entice her from her house into their dancing line, she can simply refuse such invitations. If she chooses to go on the 7-to-10-day long Festival of Oranges trip, which occurs once a year, she can involve herself in sex to the extent she wishes.

Three occasions present the adolescent woman with more of a challenge, because she has been appointed to be a female associate in each one; she has not volunteered her sexual services. Usually, she has been appointed by one of the principal chiefs of

William H. Crocker

Figure 5.4 Her sisters-in-law take the deer from the shoulders of the bride. She is wearing her still-green belt with leaf apron, which she will deliver to her mother-in-law.

the tribe, who will designate only women with belts but without children at the morning meeting of the Elders.[11] She can always refuse, but it is difficult to refuse the sitting Elders when summoned to appear before them in the center of the plaza. Moreover, if she refuses too often without sufficient reason, she will be considered stingy and could become the target of witchcraft.

The first of these occasions, which occur once a year, is the two-week hunting trip to catch game for the terminal phase of the summer's great festival, when the two age class moieties take about six women each to cook the game. The second occasion, taking place several times a year, is when the two age class moieties go out in work groups to clear roads or boundaries. Each moiety takes along two to four "free" women for the day. The third occasion occurs when there are enough men working close together in gardens to assemble for a log race. The two age class moiety leaders, themselves tribal chiefs, try to convince several "free" women to come along with each working group of men to encourage them and have sex with them while they are resting before the log race. In each of these occasions, the women receive small presents of meat or other items to please them. These items are not considered payments. Young women without babies owe their people these kinds of services.

Though technically married, a woman in her "free" state may move from man to man, according to her inclinations. Each new man she settles with becomes her new husband. While these men have to pay a fine set in a public trial to leave her, she pays nothing to leave one of them. She follows her feelings, trying and testing each man she likes. This marital musical chairs is stopped by the conception of a child. Then, the man she happens to be living with is her husband until all their children are grown, unless she has a miscarriage or the baby that is born to them dies. If they have no baby to cement their marriage, the husband's family can pay a fine, set in a trial, for him to leave her. A female research assistant in her 70s in 1966, Striped Earth, said that in earlier times this adolescent marital partner changing was far more extensive.

The jealousy of a young husband after his mother has painted his wife's belt can be well understood and sympathized with. Nevertheless, he can only wait patiently and hope that his wife does not turn to some other man as a husband before she becomes pregnant. If she continues to consider him her husband, he remains such. But she may have to name certain of the other men "contributing fathers," if she has had sex with them while pregnant. She must declare them for the sake of her baby, because most men who have contributed semen during her pregnancy must hold postpartum food and sex restrictions for the health and survival of the baby, just as the social father and mother do.

Canela research assistants insist that a young woman must have all the sexual fun and experience she can get at this free stage in her life, because later as a mother she will be heavily burdened by the responsibilities of a household from which she will find it difficult to get away even to have private trysts. Moreover, assistants say that women age faster than men through bearing many children, so they must have their fun while they are young and physically beautiful. Women who become pregnant just after winning their belts are pitied. It is said that such a woman will not be as contented in domestic life as the one who had several years of sexual freedom. She may want to have too many extramarital trysts to make up for the fun she missed, possibly embarrassing her husband's family.

Childbirth and Its Limitations

Childbirth comes as a shock to both sexes. The free young "slippery" adolescent is confined with her infant and husband to an enclosure made of mats within her mother's house for about 40 days, though she is allowed to make some excursions. This confinement, or couvade, is enforced on the couple partly to prevent their eating foods that would pollute their blood, as explained in the preceding chapter.

This first postpartum confinement contrasts sharply with a woman's recent adolescent phase of life. During her free adolescent period, she is not allowed to hold babies because the smell of the secretions of her recent sex acts would be about her. This smell could make the baby cry and eventually become sick. Residues under her fingernails could harm the baby if she scratched it even slightly. Older women could be trusted to wash well and wait a sufficient time before holding a baby, but an adolescent in her free stage is believed to be spontaneous, thoughtless, and irresponsible, so she cannot be trusted to be careful. The free adolescent is left to her own devices and activities, relieved of many of the household activities she had carried out while still a virgin.

Quite obviously, a sharp social discontinuity exists for both sexes between adolescence and parenthood. The "slippery" and free adolescent female has become an adult woman through childbirth. She must look after her baby first of all. Later she must join her sisters and mother of the household, and often her "sisters" and "mothers" next door on either side or behind, in carrying out the chores necessary for the maintenance of the group of households of her extended family, her longhouse. In compensation, the new adult can find many baby-sitters among her several sisters in her house and her numerous "sisters" in the neighboring houses of her longhouse. With their cooperation in tending her baby, she can still slip off for a private tryst with her husband, or a lover, when she is no longer breast-feeding her baby after a year or two. Of the various festival extramarital sex occasions, the Wild Boar day is the only one that is constructed so that she can still participate easily. While her sisters and "sisters" are preparing the food for the whole group at a garden hut, she can slip off into the woods with women to join one or several of her other husbands.

Socialization of Boys for Sequential Sex

Boys as well as girls experience sexual joking and teasing from an early age. One morning in the house of a ceremonial Wè?tè girl, I observed the middle-aged Standing Water teasing a young boy, his "nephew." Standing Water was sitting on the platform bed on which the boy was lying. He was repeatedly grabbing at the boy's testicles, penis, and nose, while the boy protested loudly, though not desperately. The 7-year-old boy was trying unsuccessfully to fend off his uncle's thrusts and was distressed, but he liked the attention; he was not running away. He could have easily escaped his tormentor. As Standing Water asserted his customary authority over his nephew, he was softening it with sexual teasing and fun. Moreover, many others were present to limit the game in case it went too far for the boy.

During the terminal phase of the Warriors' festival on the Wild Boar day, the commandant of the troop of male initiates requires all the nonvirginal youths to have sex in the sequential style with one of the older women who are summoned for the occasion. The strength of these older women gained from their years of survival is transmitted through sex to the boys. In the first of the four or five festivals required for initiation, which take place one or two years apart over a period of about 10 years, none of the boys is old enough to have had sex, being between one and 10. However, at the time of the subsequent festivals more of them will have had sex, and so are *required* to have sequential sex once on each Wild Boar occasion of an initiation festival, three times for the oldest boys. The younger boys become used to the expectation of sequential sex by being near the scene of the action. By the time of the last performance of an initiation festival, all of the adolescent youths, ranging from age 13 to 23, are at least somewhat experienced at paired sex and must have sequential sex on this occasion.

Some of the youths may be relatively inexperienced even in private paired sex and may be having semipublic sequential sex for the first time. When there is some doubt about whether a youth will carry out such orders, the troop's commandant sends one of the troop's two messenger boys to watch the act from an appropriate distance, so the commandant can be sure whether it really took place and in what way. How any female or male in the tribe performs sexually is public knowledge and talked about generally, though not in the presence of the subject or to embarrass her or him directly. However, age class mates do joke with each other about their abilities, especially if they are Informal Friends.[12]

CONFORMITY TO SEXUAL NORMS

Occurrences of uncustomary sex with adults are minimal, though a few instances caused by alcohol have been reported. Child abuse, as the Canela would define it, hardly exists, since violations of their incest mores (closer in than the second cousin range) rarely occur. Thus, young girls growing up are not likely to be traumatized by acts that violate their prevailing sexual code. The general U.S. concept of child abuse includes the destruction of the child's trust in kin and others who are supposed to be the child's protectors. Also, the Western world generally thinks of such abuse as involving pain and injury to the sexually immature child. The clear and public definition of kinship roles in Canela society makes incest, as they would define it, very infrequent. Canela claim that little pain is involved in first sex. Although girls had some anxiety before their first sequential sex, painful experiences were not usual. Here again, cultural expectations heavily influence the physical experience.

Masturbation for both sexes is strictly forbidden. A girl is warned by her aunts that she might lose her virginity payment if she were to stretch or break her hymen (*kuror:* thin skin, paper). Such a loss would make a preferable marriage more difficult. (If presented by her family as a virgin, an adolescent youth could leave his bride without a payment if she were found through a trial to have been nonvirginal.) If the girl had even the faintest odors of sexual secretions on her hands, they would cause babies to cry, foods to become tasteless, and crops to wilt. Young girls are seldom left alone and are continuously kept involved in domestic activities, so that the time and place for self-fondling would be difficult to find.

Uncles warn their nephews that handling themselves may loosen their foreskins and thereby cause the loss of their virginity payment. (A woman who takes a youth's virginity must make a small payment to his family, though it is less than the payment a man makes when he takes a girl's virginity and leaves her.) The youth's transgression would become generally known and an embarrassment to his family. Any slight male sexual odors on hands cause arrows to fly off their courses and axes to miss their marks, as well as leg muscles to become cramped during running. Much of the time boys are kept in age class groups to which older men tell myths on various topics, some exemplifying the traditional parameters of sex. They also tell stories about their sexual experiences as youths or about their current ones. It is feared that letting boys be alone will allow them to develop antisocial attitudes. Activities requiring long periods of time alone, such as hunting and fishing, are generally for adolescents and grown men.

Because of the practices described above, sexual use of the genitals for both sexes is largely confined to heterosexual intercourse at the age when this first becomes possible. Though some masturbation and boys' handling of each other's genitals surely occurs occasionally, such activities are not frequent enough to influence the course of maturation. This narrow channeling of the sexual drive is what we might expect for such an action- and group-oriented society.

Canela socialization also seems to suppress homosexuality. A relatively permissive atmosphere during the maturing of the age class of older Thunder (the 1930s) allowed two homosexuals to express their orientation. They wore wraparound skirts to just above their knees, while women wear their skirts to just below the knees. Research assistants said that one of the homosexuals was used as a passive sex partner by members of his age class several times when they were all in their twenties, but that the practice did not continue. This individual was said to be an ineffective worker, and his wife told him to leave even though their children were still young. Evidently his wife had conceived children while married to him. The other homosexual, after a short marriage with no children, worked effectively in the household of his female kin. Both males worked on their female kins' farms, but neither joined the log races or met often in the plaza with the Council of Elders. Thus male homosexuality was expressed in the assumption of certain female roles and the rejection of certain male activities.

A third homosexual emerged in the age class of younger Thunder 20 years later. He was one of the men who emigrated from the tribe after the messianic movement of 1963 and worked for several years as a cook's assistant in a coastal city hotel. Before he left the tribe, he had worked at the Indian Service post, where he excelled at sewing. He enjoyed helping visitors to the tribe, almost as a servant. He married and had children whom even he indicated were made by his wife's other husbands. He wore shorts or pants and carried out most male roles, but not log racing or sitting in the plaza with the Elders.

During the 2001 census, I noted several unmarried men in their 20s and 30s. Canela research assistants said, nodding knowingly, that they could not keep wives. With extramarital sex largely gone, wives with homosexual husbands leave them to seek satisfaction elsewhere, keeping any children. Due to backland Brazilian influences, Canela no longer allow homosexual manifestations, though they tolerate individuals with such orientation.

Judicial Resolution of Sexual Disputes

We have seen how social pressure works on individuals to suppress most jealousy they might feel when their spouses engage in extramarital sex. In addition, daily tribal council meetings may take up marital disputes that involved more than one extended family.

The Canela have tribal meetings twice a day when they are assembled in their village, at about 7:00 in the morning and 5:00 in the afternoon. These meetings of male Elders—any men from about 45 to 75 years—take place in the center of the village plaza and are led by one of the tribal chiefs. A principal purpose of such meetings is to pick up contentious issues between extended families, which might disturb the peace, and to resolve them.

The first part of a meeting of the Elders in the center of the plaza is quite informal. Men simply exchange news of the day about the tribe, about the backlanders, or even, though rarely, about the Brazilian nation. Much of what is discussed is simple gossip and serves the purpose of amusement. Men enjoy sharing stories, often at the expense of women and backlanders, during this informal part of a meeting.

When the first chief[13] comes walking slowly down the radial pathway from his house and joins them, the small talk stops and the seating is rearranged, so that no significant speakers are sitting behind the chief. The first chief opens the formal part of a meeting by changing the tone of the discourse and, formerly, by using a somewhat archaic vocabulary. He imposes the power of his office on the Elders through his commanding manner. Nevertheless, he cannot take initiatives that fall far outside the opinions of the Council of Elders, the dominating age class of the Elders. He must convince this Council of the worth of his opinions; they definitely limit his power.

After the first chief has spoken at the meeting, the second chief and lesser leaders speak in descending order of political importance. Then any man speaks who has a topic of interest, each one using formal tones and language. Because the center of the plaza is a sacred place, little dissension can occur there. The tendency of the Council of Elders is to follow the chief or to make indirect statements offering alternative points of view, which the chief listens to carefully. These additional points

William H. Crocker

Figure 5.5 The chief exhorts the Elders in the center of the plaza in the morning. A few younger men look on.

may change the chief's point of view by the time he brings up the topic again at a later meeting.

I was impressed by the tones of goodwill that I almost always heard voiced at these meetings. Individuals who could not express goodwill usually stayed away or remained quiet.[14] For instance, the older Thunder, the second chief during the 1970s, often held opinions that ran counter to the programs of the first chief, Jaguar's Coat. Thus, the older Thunder usually did not attend meetings led by Chief Jaguar's Coat, but he often led meetings in Jaguar's Coat's absence. Personal avoidances to prevent conflicts or unpleasant situations are typically Canela.

Topics that come up as gossip during the informal part of a meeting of the Elders, if thought sufficiently disruptive of the peace, may be introduced at the formal part of the meeting or at a later formal meeting. Problems within an extended family are settled by the family itself, but problems between extended families are first discussed informally by principal older representatives of the two families, usually "grandfathers" or "uncles" of the plaintiff and the accused. If these family representatives cannot resolve the problem among themselves, or swiftly among the Elders, they take the problem to a meeting in a convenient house of the extended family of either the plaintiff or the defendant. There a "hearing" takes place, which lasts for as many mornings as are needed to resolve the situation.

The Trial of a Wayward Husband

One of the most notorious hearings between two extended families I ever recorded was between the family of a virgin of 11 or 12 years and the family of a married man of 25 with two children. I will not use their names, even translated ones, to avoid considerable embarrassment for the married couple in this account, who are still alive; the girl has since died. Let us call the husband "Horse," the wife "Wind," and the virginal girl "Violet."

I felt sorry for Horse because Wind was such a loudmouth. Extramarital sex was the custom, but Wind made a big fuss over any suspicion she had about her husband's activities with other women. Nevertheless, I was quite surprised when I heard that Horse had taken the virginity of young Violet, who was very beautiful and light of frame. Her breasts were barely coming out. I would have thought it impossible for any man to have sex with her—she was so small and fragile—but I knew that girls had first intercourse at 11 to 13 years of age, or among some other Brazilian Indian peoples, such as the linguistically related Kayapó, at still younger ages.

When young Canela women are behaving "correctly," they have sex first with a man who is unattached. Through this act young women become married, but the man's family can pay a fine to get him out of the marriage. "Unattached" here means a man without a child of his own "fathering" in his marriage, not a man without a wife. Unattached men may be married, and they may have been contributing fathers to children in other marriages, but if they do not have a child with the woman they are married to, they are considered unattached. If an unattached married man had married his wife as a nonvirgin, and if he then took the virginity of a young woman, he would have to leave his wife. He would have to marry the young woman whose virginity he had taken, according to custom. However, if the married man had children with his wife and then took the virginity of another woman, he created a dilemma for himself and for the young woman. This was the situation of Horse, Wind, and Violet. Trying to resolve this problem, the leading uncles of the extended families of these three individuals held at least a dozen hearings (*më aypën pa:* they to-each-other listen: *audiências*) over a period of six months.

Since Horse had two children with Wind, the usual way out of the conflict of loyalties would be for Horse's family to pay an acceptably large fine to Violet's family. Having lost her virginity, but not having gained a husband, however, Violet would find getting married more difficult. Horse made the situation much more problematic, however, by going to live with Violet in her family's house. By not paying the fine to get away from Violet and by going to live with her, Horse became married to Violet as well as to Wind. The Canela have no tradition for polygyny; they think it is ridiculous. I used to hear Horse's age class mates, as well as his "other wives," teasing him as he passed along the boulevard, calling him "Tomas." Tomas was a backlander who, as a traveling salesman, lived in two communities several mule-traveling days apart. He had a "wife" and children in each community, though he was legally married to neither woman.

After Horse went to live with Violet and was accepted by her family (he was a good financial catch), the problem became compounded because Wind refused to have him back. She gave him a tongue-lashing whenever he returned for equipment or to see his children. His position was untenable, because the Canela do not allow divorces to occur while a couple are raising their own "biological" children. The Canela held many hearings between spouses who were raising their own children. I assumed that even though such estranged spouses could separate only temporarily, their families nevertheless held hearings so the plaintiff could thoroughly air the complaints against the accused.

Since the Canela had made me a ceremonial chief, the Council of Elders sent me to visit Wind to get her to accept Horse's return for the sake of their children. I thought this assignment would be relatively easy to carry out, because I was on a joking footing with Wind, since by a quirk of kinship, she was one of my "other wives." I asked my uncle Sticky Boar to see if she would accept a visit from me, and he returned saying that she would. Wind quietly listened to my explanations and request; nevertheless, she seemed more interested in using me to get back at Horse. She turned her loudmouth on me, demanding that I make him hear her objections. Obviously, I did not comply.

While it was within my role as ceremonial chief to help resolve such problems, I nevertheless decided to decline further requests to act as an intermediary. It was clear to me that I could not understand their personal problems sufficiently well, considering all the shadings and subtleties such problems always have. It was more important to my research to see how they resolved their problems by themselves. I could learn their ways better if I did not add my foreign influences. Besides, if I let an active role as a go-between develop, such activities would consume more time than I could afford to give. If matters happened to go wrong, my prestige among the Canela could plummet, and then the chief and the Council of Elders would terminate my stay.

After many hearings led by uncles of the three parties, who summoned witnesses on all sides, and after we had heard the vitriolic complaints of Horse against Wind, Wind against Horse, and Violet against Horse many times, Horse returned to Wind, as everybody knew he would have to eventually. A man *cannot* leave his children who were born to the woman he is married to, for the sake of the children. The uncles decided that Horse had to give everything he owned to Violet's family, which in Horse's case was a substantial amount, including a horse and its equipment, machetes, axes, and shotguns. He also had to deliver a suitcase of city clothes, which in those days were rare possessions. Wind had to turn over half of her manioc crop to Violet's kin.

These interfamily hearings can be seen as responsibly run trials, if the premises on which their decisions are based can be understood and accepted. All the hearings in this case took place in Wind's house, because it had a large room with two open sides, so many people could assemble inside or just outside in the sand to witness the proceedings. The location did not give one side or the other an advantage.

The main purpose of such hearings is to keep the peace between extended families. The Canela abhor and fear dissension. Justice is a lesser consideration than placating indignant and vocal plaintiffs. Moreover, the more ceremonially prestigious families are expected to give in to the less elite ones. Relative material wealth was also just beginning to become a consideration in 1959, when this hearing took place. Given these cultural assumptions, Horse and Wind did not have a chance of avoiding the payment of immense fines to Violet's extended family. Everyone knew this, but everyone also wanted to let the hearings run their course. The full public airing of injured feelings—from personal mistreatment to deeply felt shame—seemed to me to be what these hearings were arranged to provide.

During the first hearings, it seemed as if no one would give ground. Horse scored strongly on his numerous examples of Wind's harsh tongue, and several witnesses of both sexes supported him. Horse's numerous extramarital trysts had been carried out in a discreet manner, so Wind's complaints fell on largely unsympathetic ears. Wind's accusations were based on suspicions rather than on what anyone had seen and gossiped about. Thus, she had no reason to experience shame. Moreover, her picky and unloving nature came through clearly, as she stood and made her unsupported accusations before 50 to 60 people.

Violet said very little, being so young and shy. Nevertheless, her uncles and mother presented her case well. They spoke repeatedly about the point, well known to everyone, that Violet would be *na rua* (in the street), which they always stated in Portuguese, leading me to think this was a recently developed belief. They spoke of her as becoming a *rapariga* (whore), again in Portuguese, which to me was clearly an inconsistency with what I knew of Canela custom. Her uncles were playing on our sympathies by calling on backland customs.

Violet's uncles also spoke of her loss of virginity and that she would have gained nothing from this loss if Horse did not stay married to her. This point made more sense to me, according to my understanding of Canela custom. Young girls gave their virginity to gain marriage—it was traded—as was everything in Canela life, except between close kin and married couples. Violet's uncles also expressed how ashamed they were—shame had been "passed onto their faces"—because Horse was not offering to pay a sufficient amount to leave Violet.

What clearly "won" the case for Violet's uncles—though according to the premises of the culture they *had* to win—was the vehemence of their presentations, characteristic of people of low ceremonial honor. They were disturbing the peace of village life, hoping to get their way; they were capable of going around moping and complaining, if the case were not resolved very much to their favor. My research assistants expressed it this way: Violet's family had to be placated, so that all the uncles of the tribe, essentially all the Elders, could meet face-to-face every day in the plaza, enjoying each other's company in peace and harmony.

I remember well that I felt I had to account for my own subjective reactions to these hearings. Wind had rebuffed my efforts at mediation, and I found her personality unappealing. These two facts may have accounted for my lack of sympathy for her. I felt sorry for Violet but knew she would eventually get a husband. She was so young that her family could still keep her at home (i.e., off the street) for several years to improve her chances of getting a more reliable husband. They could keep her like a widow, not allowing her to go on the extramarital sex days. The first man to have sex with a widow after her loss, as with a virgin, is married to her by custom.

My own interpretation of the imbroglio was that Horse had managed to put Wind in her place during those hearings, so that their marriage could become more tolerable for him. Or, is my male bias showing here?

In her March 2000 diary on tape, my research assistant Relaxed-One, harshly criticized Horse's wife for having, through the decades of her marriage, been a shrew who had damaged Horse's career with her unjustified accusations of others. Maybe my earlier point of view about Wind was justified.

Social Control and Balance of Power between the Sexes

I find that the extramarital sex system of the Canela may have been their most immediate and therefore their most effective institution of social control, and that this system was enforced mainly by young women during their almost daily extramarital
contacts with men. Many other forms of social control exist among the Canela. To
reiterate some examples: first, the principal chief issues orders to determine which
groups of men work on which family fields during the occasional tribal work days;
second, the Council of Elders gives good youthful performers in festivals highly
prestigious awards—artifacts such as special gourds for girls and feathered lances for
boys—to reward positive behavior; third, the uncles or grandfathers of extended
families, as the result of trials, levy fines on uncooperative individuals, who in this
case are almost always young males; fourth, shamans, backed by ghosts, decree who
has broken certain customs, explaining illnesses and mishaps at the expense of
socially uncooperative individuals; fifth, strong middle-aged women impose order on
their domestic households and on their farms, providing more advantages and food,
including preferred cuts of meat, to cooperative individuals. Finally, we must consider a sixth form of social control: uncooperative individuals of either sex experience far greater difficulty in acquiring partners for extramarital sex.

While the first four examples of social control are applied *occasionally* and by
men, the last two examples, the domestic and extramarital ones, are likely to be
applied *every day* and by women, especially to young people. Thus, the domestic and
extramarital rewards and disappointments, which occur largely between two individuals—may be among the most effective forms of Canela social control, and they
are enforced by women. Again, such direct person-to-person checks and balances are
what we would expect to find among a people who know almost all the members of
their group very well and who will be living with each other for the rest of their lives.

A crucial aspect of the system is the following: Every time a person has extramarital sex, any different or unusual activities of the tryst are likely to be topics of
conversation among the women down by the stream washing clothes, or among the
men in the plaza waiting for a meeting to start. Most certainly, a person's awareness
that what he or she is doing during a tryst may soon become public knowledge
restrains this person's behavior. The person would not want to have a tryst at all with
an individual well known for his or her antisocial behavior, because most of the tribe
might soon know about the tryst and surely would disapprove of this person's com-
forting and abetting an individual who, in the tribe's terms is almost a "criminal."
Thus, the setting of the tryst holds great rewards and effective punishments, especially for young men. In contrast to the behavior of individuals catching each other
in frequent quick trysts, those couples involved in long-term affairs were more likely
to keep the details of their relationship a secret.

Men are more controlled by the context of the quick extramarital tryst than young
women, because Canela women use sexual negatives far more often than men. The
culture allows women to say no, or to be evasive, while men must be immediately
generous and serving or be branded as stingy. While I often heard and saw young
men singing all day around the boulevard with ceremonial lances to help forget a
woman's rejection, I never heard of women turned down by men. The culture allows
strong female initiatives; women go out and get what they want.

Considering changes through time, it is clear that warfare during the 1700s
favored male over female power and that peace and stability since 1840 have favored

women, redressing the balance between the sexes to some extent. Closer contacts with backlanders and with personnel of the Brazilian Indian Service since 1940 have favored men, however, since the Brazilian backlander is distinctly male-oriented. Especially the young men who carry out the recently more extensive practice of slash-and-burn agriculture are more valued now as young sons-in-law in their domestic units than they were formerly. In addition, since the 1970s, they can leave wives with their children, which means they have even more leverage against their in-laws than earlier. Thus, young husbands are no longer as completely subjected to the whims of females of the domestic unit they married into as they were even in the 1930s, during the time of Nimuendajú.

ADVANTAGES OF THE SYSTEM FOR CANELA SOCIETY

If we keep in mind the deepest values of Canela life, the practices of extensive extramarital sex and group sequential sex seem less bizarre and repellent than they might seem at first glance.[15] In Canela society, which no longer experiences economic self-sufficiency or the male opportunities for military activities, sex is a paramount pleasure and gratification. It is immensely important for the ease and assurance with which the Canela carry out both extramarital trysts and sequential sex that these acts are legitimized in a number of traditional ceremonies.

A man of elite standing who is also good at sex finds it easy to "catch" (*to pro: pegar*) an abundant variety of women for private trysts. Thus, he need not be involved in sequential sex; he is above it. In contrast, a man of poor standing with limited sexual abilities finds it harder to arrange personal trysts. Sequential sex on workdays gives this less gifted man a chance for frequent sexual outlets, and it also motivates him to work on tribal projects. Like so many other Canela institutions, group sequential sex tends to equalize relative advantages, in this case disparities among men, and thus contributes to male bonding and tribal morale.

Men appeared to be exploiting women through group sequential sex, and to a certain extent this may have been the case. Why did women continue to let themselves be used in this way? A girl was drawn into the experience of sequential sex by the expectations of gaining a belt, a husband, and a family of her own. Moreover, she knew that this was the favored route to a plentiful source of private extramarital trysts and general social popularity and respect. Women in their 20s and 30s continued to cooperate with this practice. If they lacked children, they could contribute in this other way to societal morale. Moreover, some women came to enjoy the sexual side of a sequential sex day as well as its festive side. Finally, it is clear that full intromission was the only permissible sexual outlet; masturbation was not an alternative. This lack of an alternative sexual outlet helps explain the value of sequential sex for both sexes, especially for those who found private trysts difficult to obtain.

It is difficult for members of a modern individualistic society to imagine the extent to which the Canela saw the group and the tribe as more important than the individual. Generosity and sharing was the ideal, while withholding was a social evil. Sharing possessions brought esteem. Sharing one's body was a direct corollary. Desiring control over one's goods and self was a form of stinginess. In this context, it is easy to understand why women chose to please men and why men chose to please women who expressed strong sexual needs. *No one was so self-important that satisfying a fellow tribesman was less gratifying than personal gain.* Another great Canela value, besides sharing generously, was having empathy and compassion for a person in need. Thus, a self-respecting, generous, and caring Canela woman or man found it extremely difficult to turn away from the strongly expressed sexual need of another.

The intricate pattern of socialization for extensive extramarital trysts and group sequential sex that we have traced in this chapter may seem to the outsider to amount to severe coercion. However, we are all coerced in our own cultures while undergoing the pressures of various stages of socialization. In most societies, there are penalties for not conforming to custom. In the Canela case, the stingy person received few favors from others and might have found it difficult to borrow foods when hungry, especially pieces of meat. Obtaining partners for extramarital trysts became extremely difficult. The ultimate penalty was extreme. Some rejected shaman threw a spell of illness that might have eventually resulted in death. On the other hand, the Canela social coercion was ameliorated for children by good fun and sexual joking with aunts and uncles. For adolescents, the compulsory aspect of socialization was ameliorated by long flirtations and sexual activities with familiar and friendly other spouses.[16]

In the final analysis, if we consider the extent to which Canela society provided the support for a strong ethic of caring and generosity, partly through extramarital trysts and sequential sex, we may find these customs more understandable.

THE DEMISE OF THE EXTRAMARITAL SEX SYSTEM

I have been describing the Canela extramarital sex system as I found it in the earlier years of my field research. No cultural institution is static, nor is it possible to say at what moment it reaches its apogee, or moment of greatest benefit to the society. Prolonged and ever-increasing internal and external forces have eroded the extramarital system until it is almost nonexistent today.[17]

In March 2000, I faxed a page of questions to my agent in Barra do Corda to solicit the thoughts of my research assistant diarists[18] on the loss of the extramarital sex system. Relaxed-One, 37, one of two female diarists, responded as follows:

> Group sequential sex was good during early times. It was lost because the young people did not want it anymore. . . . It is just like what the beast of the forest, the peba [one of their four armadillos] does. They love to do group sequential sex. The fox does it in the same way as the peba. It seems that, in earlier times, we did it in the same way as the animals do. Women these days are free of this group sequential sex. They might do it occasionally. . . . It was all wrong because there was no certain payment. It is for this reason that the young do not want to have anything to do with it. Today the young do things that have to do with sisters, relatives, and husbands. And for me, the Believers [Protestant missionaries] talk about the word of God and read the Bible. They keep pointing out the good things of God for the Canela's future. And so today, we have to love and obey God. We have to keep the message of God and stop doing group sequential sex. Doing it just creates shame for the Canela people.

Most of Relaxed-One's comments are what I would expect, mingling missionary influences with commercial considerations. She may not realize from her young perspective that in earlier times, women engaged in group sequential sex to advance their reputations, to have fun, and to serve the community, a service for which they expected only token presents. Relaxed-One was not involved in sequential sex herself during her adolescence. Most of the practice had died out when she was old enough to participate, and she was also away attending school. Most interesting is her statement that Canela still engage occasionally in sequential sex, but she implies that this would have to be for sufficient payment. This demonstrates *the* great change that has come over the Canela. Individuals do things for pay rather than as part of the social fabric of orders, services, and desire to please others.

During the Facsimile Warriors' festival in July 1999, I was working with my research assistant group, including Relaxed-One, when they told me that the Wild Boar day activities were being held near my old swimming spot just upstream . Since this festival day was formerly held at a farm several miles away, I had not expected to attend it, but this time it was so close that I could walk out to it during our lunch recess. While there, I jokingly lamented along with the men that they no longer had sequential sex on this occasion. They confirmed that these days the women can be stingy.

Back with my group during the afternoon session, one of my research assistants took the initiative and commented that sequential sex had indeed just taken place out there, but for a high price, a quarter of a large hog, half a big sack of rice, and half a large sack of manioc flour. They gave the names of the two women who had gone out to provide sex, but said that one of them had turned back in fear, leaving just one woman in her 30s for the men to "use." Another surprise was that only the younger men had sex with her, because only their group had made the payment. Thus, the younger men did not allow the older ones near the lone woman's area, just across the stream from where I had been scouting out the situation at noon so unsuccessfully. I noted to myself how well I could trust my research assistant group in contrast to Canela at large who would still keep their secrets from me—or by now, their shame from me.

Relaxed-One was less disapproving in her diary on the almost lost custom of extramarital trysts:

> Trysts were good. There are a few who still have trysts. They always made for joy and cre-ated courage to help people work. But it is something else today. Trysts serve to hurt spouses. Why? Because when jealousy is created, you are not going to like it. You will be disgusted and [the chance for] the same tryst will never appear again.

Many of the changes that contributed to the virtual loss of the extramarital system have been described in Chapter 2. We know that the Canela were a quasi-military society governed by chiefs who gave orders that were obeyed because of custom rather than force. However, when three generations had passed since anyone had experienced warfare, the training to be warriors made little sense to young internees in the Warriors' festival. These warriors-in-training violated the customary rules of celibacy while interned as early as 1912. The grip of the older generations over the younger ones was already being loosened 90 years ago. The next loss was the practice of adolescents having sex largely with old people of the opposite sex to gain their strength, a custom that the older generations were no longer able to enforce by the 1930s. These changes were internal ones, which were evolving gradually without damaging the social fabric significantly. The next ones, however, came from the outside and with such suddenness that they did cause irreparable damage.

During the early 1940s, the presence of the Indian Service personnel, as reported in Chapter 2, caused the abandonment of the hazing rite through which the older generations maintained their ultimate control over the youths. Additionally, a strong, well-intentioned Indian Service agent took over the political control of the tribe to ensure that they would put in large enough farms to feed themselves. He succeeded, but in doing so he created a political vacuum. No chief was strong enough to take back the control when he left in 1947. An age gap was evolving. The older generations could no longer control the younger ones. The aunts and uncles could neither cajole the girls and women to perform during the sex occasions nor could they suppress the jealousy of the youths and men.

The next intrusion of the Indian Service personnel of the early 1940s was their spying on unmarried pairs sleeping in the plaza at night and their scolding them about their infidelities the next day. Thus, women without babies ceased to sleep in the plaza with men of the other moiety from their husbands' moiety. I consider this practice in the plaza the basis for the maintenance of the Canela's extramarital sex system, because young women who had just won their social acceptance belts slept there every night getting more and more accustomed to sequential and paired extramarital sex. It is my understanding that after they had gone through this formative experience for learning extramarital sex, any other customary sexual experiences would be easy and enjoyable. Once this practice was abandoned, the rest of the system became increasingly difficult to maintain during the ensuing generations. Relaxed-One was born in 1963, so she missed sleeping in the plaza during her adolescence by a generation.

The high evaluation of commercial goods, which flowed into the area starting in 1956, was another significant factor in the loss of the extramarital sex system. During the much earlier times that were formative for their culture, Canela households possessed so few items that sharing them amounted to little sacrifice, as was sharing their bodies. However by the 1960s, and certainly by the late 1970s, sharing such goods became too costly. Similarly, sharing one's body became too costly in terms of spousal jealousy, which the Elders and the uncles could no longer suppress. Commercial goods and the addiction to them—they had become a "necessity"—considerably raised a person's sense of separate self-worth. Relatively speaking, the individual's former orientation was to the good of the tribe—for the always precarious survival of the whole foraging society—rather than to personal satisfaction.

Agricultural economics also influenced the Canela sex system. When the strong, well-intentioned Service agent left the Canela and no strong chief took over during the 1940s, the Canela failed to put in large enough farms to support themselves. The general loss of authority of the Elders contributed to the same problem—the prevalence of hunger. Earlier, the preparation of uncompleted family farms was finished quickly by the "warrior" age class sent by the chief to do the job, but by the 1950s, neither the chief nor the warriors' age class leader was strong enough to carry out such assistance. The warriors had been rewarded for their work with sequential sex, but by the 1960s and 1970s this was becoming more difficult to bring about. Consequently, many farms were not completed and their owners begged crops from the more successful family farmers, dragging them down too. The Canela were no longer able to feed themselves and became dependent on handouts from the Indian Service and on working on backland farms for food. Hunger set in for the months of September through December, and women began demanding a considerable amount of meat for their involvement in sequential sex and even for trysts, raising jealousy and creating friction between families about who got the ever dwindling supply. To eat reasonably well during these lean months, Canela families had to sell most of their commercial goods at ridiculously low prices and buy them again in February or March.

To meet this demand for goods, young men worked harder during the 1980s on their farms, putting in larger ones. Thus, the sons-in-law of families, their farm workers, became more valuable. When they became jealous of their wives' extramarital activities, the mothers had to keep their daughters at home so as not to lose the sons-in-law. These sons-in-law became stronger in enforcing their grievances against their wives' families because since the mid-1970s, divorce was becoming possible even when children were involved. Earlier, the Elders were strong enough to prevent this. Thus, the family dynamics were completely changed. First, the uncles and aunts had lost their authority to send their nieces out to perform sexually in ceremonial activities, so that the control over young girls and adolescent women fell to their mothers. Then, the mothers had to restrain their daughters for fear of losing their sons-in-law through whose farm work they could buy more and more commercial goods.

While many feel the old sex customs are now shameful, others feel nostalgia for them, and appreciate the role they played in the morale of the tribe. One of my research assistants, His Water, 52, wrote me in his March 2000 diary:

> Group sequential sex was very good because it brought a great deal of value to the older people during past times and gave much joy to groups in general. Besides serving one particular group on an occasion, it served all the four age classes at other times, giving them strength, a lot of courage, great joy, and much animation. . . . The age classes . . . went singing in the boulevard [before the circle of houses] because they had just had sequential sex, and they passed on this animation to the entire population. This is what group sequential sex provided.

Yomtam, Pedro's wife, made several regretful comments about the loss of extramarital sex that were recorded in the video *Mending Ways:*

> I loved all the men. They were so handsome, in their wristlets and other decorations. They were so beautiful and there were so many of them. . . . I had many lovers who were seeking me out. . . . I wanted to go with the group of men. I like the other men. . . . Yes, it's been lost. The custom has been lost. I miss it, but what can be done about it?

NOTES

1. See Nimuendajú (1946:169) and Crocker (1990:280–281) for a more complete description of the Wild Boar day, when the Canela kill a tame peccary and have sequential extramarital sex.

2. See Nimuendajú (1946:129) for his views on Canela infidelity, adultery, and divorce, which differ considerably from those reported by my Canela research assistants even for his decade of the 1930s.

3. Canela research assistants associate *?-hê* (her vulva) with the vertical lines of house posts and with the single, thin straight line of a stalk of sugar cane.

4. See Crocker (1990:283–284) for a description of Ceremonial Chief days and their Më Aykhë style of dancing.

5. See Nimuendajú (1946:102) for his account of this mock-erotic behavior.

6. For a full account of Canela marriage, see Crocker (1984), Crocker (1990:292–295), and Nimuendajú (1946:119–125).

7. For a video comparing the Canela scene during the 1970s with the late 1990s, and sex jealousy, see Schecter and Crocker (1999).

8. In contrast to the Canela spirit of joy, sharing, and female maturation surrounding sequential sex, Sanday (1990) presents American fraternity gang rape as thoroughly degrading for women.

9. For sex forced on women in Amazonia, gang-rape, or ceremonial rape, see Maybury-Lewis (1967:255, 266) and Murphy and Murphy (1985:126, 161–2).

10. The belt won by young women through service to a men's society I call a "social acceptance" belt in an etic interpretation. This is how in my overview of the Canela system, I see that the belt serves young women. Canela merely say that the belt serves as a bond between the owner's female kin and her female in-laws.

11. The distinction between "Council of Elders" and "Elders" may be confusing. The Elders are not just the elderly men; they are the men who meet in the plaza, a group that is composed of the three oldest age classes. The Council of Elders comprises just one age class, the dominant one that governs the festivals, awards honors, and balances the power of the chief. The Elders are an informal body, while the Council of Elders are like a senate.

12. The discussion of girls' socialization is longer and more detailed than that of boys' socialization because the training of girls is likely to be stranger to the Western reader and therefore needs more support.

13. For a classic on leadership in the Amazon, see Kracke (1978). However, leadership among the Canela differs significantly. Compare with Crocker (1990:210–225).

14. The Waorani of Ecuador (Robarchek and Robarchek 1998) contrast dramatically with the Canela. While a Canela lived, largely, as a small part of the whole tribe, subjugating him- or herself to the survival and welfare the people, a Waorani lived more for him- or herself, experiencing rage and even committing homicide when a situation was not within sociocultural compre-hension. Again, in contrast to the Canela who practiced little internal violence though much external warfare, the Yanomáma—according to a Venezuelan girl abducted at age 12 (Biocca 1969) and forced to live with them and become a wife three times before escaping at around 30—practiced both inter-nal homicide and intervillage raiding.

15. The anthropology of sexuality is becoming a new subfield of anthropology. Suggs (1999) furnishes a set of sophisticated and current essays on this new field's his-tory, its biological basis, and its relationship between romantic love and sex. The World Health Organization has published a study of various sexual practices in relation to the health of peoples all over the world. For this readable, colorful atlas, see Mackay (2000). For a variety of the forms in which human sex may be practiced from a cross-cultural point of view with psychoanalytic interpre-tation, see Endleman (1989).

16. See Gregor (1985:3) for an anxious rather than a joyous orientation to sex. Gregor and Tuzin (2001) furnishes a collec-tion of excellent papers comparing gender in Amazonia and Melanesia.

17. A more complete analysis of the demise of the Canela extramarital sex system is in Crocker MS.

18. I have collected diaries as "voices" of an indigenous people since 1964. Other ethnog-raphers have collected indigenous oral histo-ries (Basso 1995), discourses (Graham 1995), and stories (Mindlin 2002). Such raw materials of indigenous self-representation may be found important for later studies as indigenous ways disappear.

Epilogue
The Future of the Canela

The Canela realize that they must adopt some of the ways of the modern world, or the world of the "whites" as they call it. They also are consciously wrestling with the problem of how to do this without losing their Canela identity. They are moving from a culture of obedience to chiefs and Elders to one of individualism; from a culture of sharing to one of money and competition. So far the Canela have not been able to translate their practice of sharing into a system of taxation for the benefit of the community, though they know this happens in the towns of the whites. They understand how they might contribute money to pay for a truck, for instance, but they do not trust their leaders with the funds.

Several failed projects help illustrate the difficulties the Canela face in adapting to modern economy and governance. During the mid-1990s, the Banco do Nordeste in Fortaleza, Ceará State, granted the Canela a gasoline-run, rice-hulling machine from World Bank funds. To maintain this machine, money is needed for gasoline and occasional repairs. Individuals with Indian Service salaries or farm retirees' pensions usually chip in to buy some gasoline, but repairs are too expensive for any one person to afford. They look to the chief, who looks to the Indian Service, to the mayor of the municipality, or to any outsider rather than to themselves. There are several points in the general flow of goods and services at which chiefs could impose taxes from individuals or families to pay for repairs. Even when Canela leaders see these possibilities, however, they do not have the power or the trust of the people to raise money in this way for the general good. Instead, the rice-hulling machine remains inoperative for months, and the women return to the customary way of pounding rice with wooden mortars and pestles. After five years of sporadic use, this machine has become inoperable.

Besides the rice-hulling mill, the Canela have manioc-root-grating machines driven by gasoline-run motors in three different farm areas. These mills break down occasionally requiring expensive repairs. Various outsiders, including myself, have pointed out that if an individual designated by the farm community's leader and the Council of Elders were to take the tenth or twentieth sack of grated manioc from each family to store and sell later on the regional markets, they could fund the repairs of these machines quite easily. The younger Thunder tried this at his farm community in 1997 with only sporadic success. Either the family member using the machine refused to surrender sacks of manioc flour or the appointed managers were accused of pocketing most of the funds raised in this manner. Or, still worse for morale, the younger Thunder was blamed for spending the money for other purposes whether or not he had done so. Leaders soon gave up the project after encountering such difficulties. The women of the farm communities could easily return to processing manioc roots on punctured can graters for months, until some outside organization funded the necessary repairs.

Optimistically one may see the failed attempts at modern economy and governance as practice runs. Eventually the Canela may gain the attitudes and skills to make the projects work. His Water, the current chief, expressed his hopes for a solution in his diary of May 2000. He favors high school education in Barra do Corda for bright young men who could become trained in money management:

> The chief and the Council of Elders do not have money to spend like a mayor of a city for one reason, namely, that we do not have a person of great experience and training to collect money from us to put in a bank so that the chief and the Elders can spend it just as a mayor does. [I want] for us to have a high level person of much experience so that he would know how to economize and maintain the procedures, [enabling] the chief and the Elders to spend like the mayor of a city. It is for this reason that we need schooling very much . . . for our children so that some of them can learn profoundly how to maintain their community in an approved [financial] condition.

The Canela inability or reluctance to manage money and especially to save it may be hard to understand unless we remember that aboriginally the Canela were basically food collectors with little horticulture and that they were certainly not settled agriculturalists. As recently as the late 1950s, when individuals exchanged goods with each other, most of them gave to please the other party and expected to be pleased in return. They did not try to bargain down the other person or get the better deal. Until the 1990s, the Canela could not raise cattle, because they did not have the values to resist hunger for meat, so they killed the calf before it could grow up to reproduce. They lived very much for the present and expected somehow to survive in the future. In her diary of May 2000, Relaxed-One expressed the Canela attitude:

> The Canela like to give manioc to others, to relatives. They like to give to those who do not have any manioc. . . . Moreover, during a big festival the Canela know only how to hurt themselves, because they consume too much manioc flour, feasting. They make large manioc meat pies so that the supply of manioc dwindles until there is no more, so then, where is the manioc for them to sell? . . . The Canela do not sell manioc flour in Barra do Corda because we use it all up in the village festivals.

The propensities she describes are customary; her awareness of their harmfulness is modern.

As the Canela give up wasteful feasting and keep their families' produce for themselves, they wonder if they will maintain their Canela identity. As they study in school in Barra do Corda, they are keenly aware of the Brazilians' perceptions of them. Carampei wrote an especially poignant entry in his diary in April 2002 concerning the dilemma of his identity. He was the little boy who is portrayed in the Canela video, chopping on a banana tree with a machete and holding back a blow to avoid hitting his little sister. He appears later in 1997, as a young father lamenting

Myles Crocker, 2001

Figure 6.1 Angelo Carampei Canela

the loss of extramarital sex in the festivals. He now studies in Barra do Corda in the 7th grade at age 27. He makes Canela artifacts to sell in downtown Barra do Corda to earn some funds to help support his family. As my newest diarist, Carampei wrote the following in Portuguese:

> [T]hese artifacts that we make for sale produce little profit, not enough to support a family in 2002. It is not the way it used to be years ago, when it was easy to trade our artifacts for clothes. In 2002, we wonder: is one an Indian or is one not an Indian?
>
> So, with artifacts, I took a bus headed for the plaza of Barra do Corda. . . . It gave me a special pleasure to show myself off, to feel the reactions of the people when they saw me pass by. I wanted to be able to be sure whether people identified me as being Indian to form my image of myself.
>
> On this occasion . . . I heard the following dialogue between two ladies who looked at me from top to bottom when I got on the bus:
>
> "You see that boy. He looks like an Indian," [said lady A].
>
> "It seems so, but I am not sure," [returned lady B]. "Didn't you see that he is wearing long pants, jeans? It is possible that he is an Indian, wearing clothes of the whites."
>
> "I think that he is not really an Indian," argued the other lady. "But it is possible. Did you see his hair? It is very smooth. Only Indians have such hair, yes," said the lady, defending me.

"Didn't you see that he wears a watch? The Indian tells the time by looking at the day. The clock of the Indian is the sun, the moon, and the stars. So, it is not possible that he is an Indian," argued the other lady.

"I know, but he has a withdrawn look," said the lady. "Also, he wears shoes and a shirt," the lady returned with irony.

"But he has prominent cheeks, and so, could only be an Indian, and he seems to be a pure one."

"I do not believe this. Pure Indians do not exist," the lady affirmed, full of wisdom. "Finally, how could an Indian be riding this bus? Real Indians live in the woods, carrying bows and arrows, hunting and fishing, and planting manioc. I think he is not an Indian in any way. You saw the necklace that he is wearing. It seems to have teeth in it. Could it be that these are the teeth of people? Recently, I even heard that Indians who eat people still exist."

"Didn't you say that he was not an Indian? But now it seems that you are in doubt and even afraid. How do you think it would be if we talked with him?"

"But what if he would not like this?"

I was listening to this conversation of the two ladies behind my back, and from time to time, I turned around. Unfortunately, they delayed speaking to me and my getting-off point was arriving. [So I stood up,] I looked at them, and smiling, I said, "yes."

This gave me great satisfaction.

The ambiguity of Carampei's story reflects the ambiguity of his position among the Brazilians. Was he proud to announce himself as a Canela to the ladies on the bus? Or was he proud to have been confused with the whites? In either case, the economic deprivation of the Canela, their social isolation, and the lingering prejudices of the Brazilians are all present in his account. It shows how the Canela are able to move in the Brazilian world and learn many of its ways. But Carampei can return to the Canela village, a refuge that the Canela seem determined to preserve. As long as the Canela keep their circular village, they will not have lost the essence of their way of life.[1]

NOTE

1. For more on the Canela, go to the Canela website, http://www.mnh.si.edu/anthro/canela (Crocker and Watanabe 2002). Also see Appendix C, "Comparison of Topics Across Various Media" to compare materials in this book with similar ones in the Canela video, *Mending Ways*, in this video's study guide, and on the Canela website.

Appendix A
Mythology

CREATION MYTHS

Sun and Moon

Sun (Pùt) created the Canela by walking out of a pool of a savannah stream, followed by a file of Canela individuals. He established the intelligent, ideal life in which work was carried out without effort: axes and machetes swung on their own, felling trees, cutting brush, and clearing the ground for gardens. Moon (Putwrè) modified the ideal world through his clumsiness and individuality, creating death, floods, forest fires, and work. Because of Moon, men, by their own efforts, had to swing axes and machetes for the first time to prepare the ground for planting gardens. Because of Moon's intervention, short fruit trees grew tall, so their fruit became harder to harvest. Moon also created the individual body characteristics that are less preferred by the Canela—kinky instead of straight hair, darker instead of lighter skin, and squatter instead of taller bodies—by walking out of a pool with a file of these accepted but less prestigious types following him. Sun ascended to the skies, taking Moon along with him, because he felt badly about the incest and fighting occurring among his people. Sun wanted to distance himself from the partially evil Canela nature, caused by Moon's intervention.

Star Woman

Star Woman (Katsêê-ti-?khwèy) came down from the skies and showed the Canela all sorts of edible fruits and plants, which they began to collect or cultivate for the first time. Then she returned to the skies with one Canela male she loved, and they became the twin stars known to us as Castor and Pollux.

Awkhêê

Awkhêê was born of a Canela mother, but he had remarkable other-worldly powers, which he used playfully as a child. For instance, he turned himself into a jaguar to scare his siblings, and then into an anaconda (a large constrictor water snake) to scare them again. However, his "uncles," the Elders, took a dim view of such activities. Awkhêê's remarkable abilities threatened the uncles' power, so they connived to kill him. They pushed him off a cliff, but Awkhêê turned into a leaf and floated to safety. He saved himself in similar ways several times. Finally, the uncles pushed him onto a bonfire, but Awkhêê jumped out. Then, they surrounded the fire and kept pushing him back onto it from every side. Seeing how determined they were, Awkhêê let them succeed. So he turned himself into a cinder and disappeared from view.

Several days later, Awkhêê's mother, longing for him, went to see the location of the bonfire. Instead of ashes, she found a farm with a white house. Horses, cattle, pigs, and chickens were roaming about. Awkhêê had turned himself into the first *civilizado* and had created the backland society and economy. Awkhêê welcomed his mother and showed her the new world he had constructed. He told her to go back to their people to summon his uncles.

When the uncles arrived at the white house, they became afraid of Awkhêê and the new world of the backlanders. Awkhêê welcomed them and told them not to be afraid; he wanted to help his special people, the Canela. At this point the myth continues with the offer of the shotgun which the Canela rejected in favor of the bow and arrow.

WAR STORIES

Flint Revenges the Death of His Uncle

Khrùt (flint) persuaded an "uncle" to go with him on a raid of an enemy people to avenge the death of an uncle (his mother's brother), but the real reason was to prove his manhood and to gain the status of war leader. Flint and his uncle traveled inconspicuously and swiftly for several days and penetrated enemy territory successfully without being discovered. Leaving his uncle behind on a knoll, Flint slipped into the enemy village at night and killed one man, taking his war bonnet of macaw tail feathers. As he was leaving the village, enemy warriors shot at him, but, using his shamanic abilities, Flint dodged all the arrows and escaped into the darkness. Flint found his uncle waiting on the knoll, and, running all the way out of enemy lands, they returned to the Canela village safely. Arriving home in the late afternoon, Flint laid the enemy's war bonnet on a mat before the Elders and showed the blood still on his hands. After a number of weeks of seclusion and diet to rid his system of the blood pollutants introduced by killing a man, Flint presented himself to the Elders and they declared him a *hààprāl*, a war leader.

TALES ABOUT THE ORIGINS OF FESTIVALS

Origin of the Fish Festival

To obtain most of the festivals, a young Canela male (or two youths) went off to an other-world of the past where they saw a festival that they then taught to the Canela after their return. For example, Pore-?tèy (ear-plug capable) and his companion were sent by the Elders across a great river to check on the growth of their people's vegetable gardens at the winter village. While Ear Plug and his companion were swimming, Ear Plug was swallowed by a large water snake, but his companion escaped to return to his people. As Ear Plug lay in the great constrictor's stomach being digested, the Fish people around the anaconda felt sorry for him. They entered the snake's mouth to introduce slime, which caused Ear Plug to pop out. Then, the Fish took Ear Plug to the world of their village under the river, where their festival was just beginning. There, Fish were dancing in human form. Ear Plug carefully memorized all that the Fish were doing and taught the Canela the Fish Festival upon his return.

Appendix B
Orthography

The orthography used follows Crocker (1990:9–10) for consistency, except for the phonemes *a, i, e,* and *ù* when they are nasalized phonemes. Then they are written as the nasalized phonemes *ä, ï, ë,* and *ü*. Only the tilde and the diaresis are used to indicate phonemic nasalization. Each letter in italics represents a phoneme in Canela, or its equivalent or approximation in another language.

17 VOWELS

There are no nasalized vowel phonemes in English, so examples in Portuguese are used.

Unnasalized	English	Nasalized	Portuguese
i	b*ee*t	*ï*	p*i*nto
ê	b*i*t		
e	b*e*t	*ë*	p*e*nte
a	hurr*ah*	*ä*	
u	b*oo*t	*ü*	j*u*nto
ô	b*oa*t		
o	b*ough*t	*ō*	p*o*nto

The following vowel phonemes have no equivalents in English, Portuguese, Spanish, or French, but approximations are included. For the linguist, these five phonemes are "back" and "unrounded," and the varying placements are indicated.

	Unnasalized		Nasalized	Placements
ù	t*u*	French	*ü*	high and closed
è	p*eu*	French		mid and closed
à	p*u*ddle	English	*ā*	mid and open

2 SEMIVOWELS (GLIDES)

w	*w*est, pe*w*
y	*y*es, co*y*

11 CONSONANTS

Stops

Unlike in English, the phonemes, *p, t,* and *k* are unaspirated; they are found both unvoiced [p, t, k] and voiced [b, d, g]. The phoneme *kh* is aspirated and unvoiced.

(English approximates)

p	[p varies with b]	*p*ill and *b*ill
t	[t varies with d]	*t*ick and *D*ick
k	[k varies with g]	*k*ill and *g*ill
kh		*k*iss
?	[glottal]	bo'le (as sometimes in "bottle")

Affricative

ts	cen*ts*

Fricative

h	*h*ome

Lateral

r	[r varies with l]	o*r*ar, Isabe*l* (Spanish)

Nasals

m	*m*et
n	*n*et
g	*g*aunt

VOWEL LENGTH

Vowel length can be phonemic: k*a*tswa: night

                                                 k*aa*tswa: salt

STRESS

Word stress almost always falls on the last syllable, though it is ultimately determined by the phrase and sentence.

Appendix C
Comparison of Topics across Various Media

Use the following table to compare topics in the text, video, video's online study guide, and Web site. To guide your use of the video, timing and opening sentences are included in the table. Note that timing starts from the beginning: "Deep in the grass lands . . ." at 00 min. 00 sec. (00' 00"). To locate relevant material in the online Study Guide, major headings are in all capitals and you may also use the "Find" feature on your Web explorer to search for the unique phrases listed here. If you choose to print out the Study Guide, page number and paragraph references are listed in the table as well. To locate corresponding material on the Web site, click on the major headings as listed in the table below.

Topic

Text	Video	Online Study Guide	Web Site
	Distributed by: Films for the Humanities and Sciences www.films.com search "Canela"	http://www.films.com /Films_Home/ MendingWaysGuide. cfm?s=1	http://www.mnh.si. edu/anthro/canela/
Women prepare food, sisterhood, pp. 48, 124	". . . the women rule the roosts in the domestic situation." 32' 25"		Daily Life, Cooking (photo); Manioc Processing
Circle of houses, p. 56	". . . to keep the other people happy." 00' 55"	p. 2, par. 2 OVERVIEW, semi-circular	About Canela (photo)
Legal payment to keep peace not justice, pp. 69, 122	"The payment of a horse . . . satisfied . . ." 21' 40"	p. 5, par. 3; p. 6, par. 3 MENDING WAYS, mending them, internal peace, resolve problems p. 7, par. 1	About Canela, paragraph 13

Topic

Text	Video	Online Study Guide	Web Site
Ear-piercing rite, p. 72, cover	"A boy learns obedience through ear-piercing." 25' 05"	p. 5, par. 4 MENDING WAYS Earlobe piercing	Rituals, Body Adornments
Live for group, share sex extra-maritally p. 125	"They lived for the tribe, for the survival . . ." 0' 45"	p. 2, par. 4; p. 5, par. 1 OVERVIEW, MENDING her body, creating joy p. 8, par. 3; p.10, par. 2 SEX SYSTEM, cultural support, every night	About Canela, par. 12
Log racing, pp. 4, 81	"A festival day . . . starts with a log race." 9' 35"; 36' 10"	p. 6, par. 2 MENDING WAYS, bonding device	About Canela (photos)
Death and mourning, pp. 75–78	". . . death of my own niece . . ." 15' 40"		
Elders in plaza, pp. 119–120		p. 6, par. 4 MENDING WAYS, Elders meet	Daily Life, Plaza Gathering
Ecology, farms, pp. 59, 70	". . . expanded into large-scale farming." 43' 00"	p. 3, par. 3; p. 4. par. 3 HISTORY, various crops, sufficient surpluses	Daily Life, 7–9 A.M.
Demise of extra-marital sex system, pp. 126–129	"Yes . . . the custom has been lost." 43' 55"	p. 10–12 LOSS . . ., almost lost	About Canela, (last paragraph)
Facsimile warriors singing, p. 80	"In this sacred festival . . . retreat . . ." 37' 05"		
Mediation is the true way of life, pp. 81	"Leadership mends through compromise." 39' 05"	p. 5; par. 3; p. 8, par. 1 MENDING WAYS, to repair, non-confrontational p. 12, par. 5	About Canela, par. 13
Hunter's meat shared, sharing for survival p. 85	". . . distribute meat to all households in the tribe." 32' 55"	p. 2, par. 4 OVERVIEW, welfare of	About Canela, par. 12
Shamanism, pp. 87–93	"So a shaman is bound to be off on his own." 8' 20"		

Topic

Text	Video	Online Study Guide	Web Site
Keeping out pollutants, purifying body, pp. 93–96	"Once the black paint is on, he is shielded." 27' 15"		
Curing ceremony, pp. 88–90	"When a person is . . . sick, the soul . . ." 8' 15"		
Younger Thunder = Raimundo Roberto = ceremonial chief, p. 101	"Raimundo Roberto became Bill Crocker's most helpful guide." 6' 30"	MENDING WAYS, two kinds of powers	
Trials, hearings, pp. 69, 119–123	"The village Elders . . . resolve this . . ." 21' 10"		About Canela, par. 13
Ceremonial Chief day, sideways dance, p. 101	"The day starts with a dance line, snaking around . . ." 18' 00"	p. 7, par. 3 MENDING WAYS, social respect	
Learning restrictions, Warriors' festival, p. 79	"These initiates have just emerged from a long period of learning." 26' 45"		
Wild Boar day, women return painted, p. 100	". . . black paint serves as a memento of the liason." 34' 10"	p. 6, par. 1 MENDING WAYS, paints represent p. 9, par. 2 LOSS . . ., extramarital event	
Pedro's defiance, p. 111	". . . I saw my wife and got jealous." 19' 20"		
Sequential sex for less able men, bonding, p. 125	". . . the women have to yield . . . an honorable custom." 18' 40"	p. 2, par. 3 OVERVIEW, especially known	
Views of savannahs, p. 6 Hunting, p. 48	"To become a man one must become a hunter." 28' 45"		About Canela, log racing
Formal Friendship, pp. 63–64	"Formal Friends transform pain . . ." 13' 30"	p. 7, par. 4–6 MENDING WAYS, mending device	Festivals, Pepyê
Crocker in field, pp. 31, 71, 98	"Bill Crocker first came to study . . ." 5' 00"	p. 12, par. 1; p. 13–16 LOSS . . ., Yomtam unusual FIELD WORK; why did you go	Smithsonian Research

Topic

Text	Video	Online Study Guide	Web Site
Waterfall, pp. 46, 48	". . . he led me to his family house . . ." 6'15"	p. 15, par. 4 FIELD WORK, sister Waterfall	
Relaxed-one, pp. 126, 132	"These days we all need money . . ." 43' 20"		
Yomtam, p. 111	"Yes, I liked the men . . . so many . . ." 7' 40"	p. 12, par. 1 LOSS . . ., women liked it	
Carampei, pp. 132–134	"Carampei . . . runs with the pack." 8' 50"		Research, Mending . . .

References

Arnaud, Expedito. 1989. O índio e a expansão nacional. 485 pages. Belém: CEJUP.

Balée, William. 1994. *Footprints of the Forest: Ka'apor Ethnobotany: The Historical Ecology of Plant Utilization by an Amazonian People.* New York: Columbia University Press.

Basso, Ellen B. 1995. *The Last Cannibals: A South American Oral History.* Austin, TX: University of Texas Press.

Biocca, Ettore. 1969. *Yanoáma: The Story of a Woman Abducted by Brazilian Indians,* as told to Ettore Biocca. Dennis Rhodes, trans. London: George Allen and Unwin.

Castro, Eduardo B. Viveiros de. 1992. *From the Enemy's Point of View: Humanity and Divinity in an Amazonian Society.* Catherine V. Howard, trans. Chicago: University of Chicago Press.

Chagnon, Napoleon A. 1992. *Yanomamö.* 4th ed. In George and Louise Spindler, series eds., *Case Studies in Cultural Anthropology.* Fort Worth: Harcourt.

Chernela, Janet M. 1993. *The Wanano Indians of the Brazilian Amazon: A Sense of Space.* Austin: University of Texas Press.

Conklin, Beth A. 2001. *Consuming Grief: Compassionate Cannibalism in an Amazonian Society.* Austin: University of Texas Press.

Crocker, William H. 1967. The Canela Messianic Movement: An Introduction. In *Simpósio sôbre a Biota Amazônica 2 (Antropologia).* Pp. 69–83. Belém, Brazil: Museu Goeldi.

———. 1982. Canela Initiation Festivals: "Helping Hands" through Life. In V. Turner, ed., *Celebration: Studies in Festivity and Ritual.* Pp. 147–158. Washington, DC: Smithsonian Institution Press.

———. 1984. Canela Marriage: Factors in Change. In K. Kensinger, ed., Marriage Practices in Lowland South America.

*Illinois Studies in Anthropology 14:*63–98. Urbana: University of Illinois Press.

———. 1985. Extramarital Sexual Practices of the Ramkokamekra-Canela Indians: An Analysis of Sociocultural Factors. In P. Lyon, ed. of reissued edition, *Native South Americans: Ethnology of the Least Known Continent.* Pp. 184–194. Prospect Heights, IL: Waveland.

———. 1990. The Canela (Eastern Timbira), 1: An Ethnographic Introduction. *Smithsonian Contributions to Anthropology, No. 33.* Washington, DC: Smithsonian Institution Press.

———. 1994. Canela. In J. Wilbert, ed., *Encyclopedia of World Cultures 7 (South America).* Pp. 94–98. New York: G. K. Hall.

———. 1995. Canela Relationships with Ghosts: This-Worldly or Other Worldly Empowerment. In J. Ehrenreich, ed., Latin American Anthropology Review. *Journal of the Society for Latin American Anthropology 5(2)*71–78.

———. 1999. A study guide for the video *Mending Ways:* The Canela Indians of Brazil. Schecter Films/Smithsonian's Human Studies Film Archives. Princeton, NJ: Films for the Humanities and Sciences. (www.films.com. Search for "Canela.")

———. 2002. Canela "Other Fathers": Partible Paternity and Its Changing Practices. In Stephen Beckerman and Paul Valentine, eds., *Cultures of Multiple Fathers: The Theory and Practice of Partible Paternity in Lowland South America.* Pp. 86–104. Gainesville, FL: University of Florida Press.

———. In press. *War and Peace among the Canela.* Instituto Venezolano de Investigaciones Científicas. Caracas: Fundación la Salle de Investigaciones Científicas.

————. MS. The Canela Extramarital Sex System and Its Decline. In an anthology on South American Indians, Patricia Lyon, ed. Prospect Heights, IL: Waveland.

Crocker, William H., and Barbara Watanabe. 2002. The Canela of Northeastern Central Brazil. A website with eight republications in the "Literature" section, including: (1) The Eastern Timbira by Curt Nimuendajú. Berkeley, CA: University of California Press, 1946; (2) The Canela (Eastern Timbira), 1: An Ethnographic Introduction; (3) Crocker (1982, 1984, 1994, 1995); (4) Greene and Crocker (1995), and (5) a review of Crocker (1990) by William H. Fisher. (www.mnh.si.edu/anthro/canela)

Da Matta, Roberto. 1979. The Apinayé Relationship System. In Dialectical Societies: The Gê and Bororo of Central Brazil. Pp. 83–127. David Maybury-Lewis, ed., *Harvard Studies in Cultural Anthropology 1.* Cambridge, MA: Harvard University Press.

————. 1982. A Divided World: Apinayé Social Structure. *Harvard Studies in Cultural Anthropology 6.* Cambridge, MA: Harvard University Press.

Descola, Philippe. 1996. In the Society of Nature: A Native Ecology in Amazonia. Nora Scott, trans. *Cambridge Studies in Social and Cultural Anthropology 93.* First paperback ed. Cambridge, UK: Cambridge University Press.

Endleman, Robert. 1989. *Love and Sex in Twelve Cultures.* New York: Psyche.

Ferguson, R. Brian. 1995. *Yanomami Warfare: A Political History.* Santa Fe, NM: School of American Research Press.

Fisher, William H. 2000. *Rain Forest Exchanges: Industry and Community on an Amazonian Frontier.* Washington, DC: Smithsonian Institution Press.

Gomes, Mercio P. 2000. *The Indians and Brazil.* John W. Moor, trans.; first English ed. University of Florida Center for Latin American Studies. Gainesville, FL: University of Florida Press.

Good, Kenneth, with David Chanoff. 1991. *Into the Heart: One Man's Pursuit of Love and Knowledge among the Yanomama.* New York: Simon and Schuster.

Graham, Laura R. 1995. *Performing Dreams: Discourses of Immortality Among the Xavante of Central Brazil.* Austin, TX: University of Texas Press.

Greenberg, Joseph. 1987. *Languages in the Americas.* Stanford, CA: Stanford University Press.

Greene, Margaret E., and William H. Crocker. 1994. Some Demographic Aspects of the Canela Indians of Brazil. In K. Adams and D. Price, eds., The Demography of Small-Scale Societies: Case Studies from Lowland South America. Pp. 47–68. *South American Indian Studies.* Bennington, VT: Bennington College Press.

Gregor, Thomas. 1985. *Anxious Pleasures: The Sexual Lives of an Amazonian People.* Chicago: University of Chicago Press.

Gregor, Thomas A., and Donald F. Tuzin, eds. 2001. *Gender in Amazonia and Melanesia: An Exploration of the Comparative Method.* Berkeley, CA: University of California Press.

Heckenberger, Michael J. 1996. War and Peace in the Shadow of Empire: Sociopolitical Change in the Upper Xingu of Southeastern Amazonia, A.D. 1400–2000. Ph.D. Dissertation, University of Pittsburgh. University Microfilms, Ann Arbor.

Hemming, John. 1987. *Amazon Frontier: The Defeat of the Brazilian Indians.* Cambridge, MA: Harvard University Press.

Hill, Kim, and A. Magdalena Hurtado. 1996. Ache Life History: The Ecology and Demography of a Foraging People. *Foundations of Human Behavior: An Aldine de Gruyter Series of Texts and Monographs.* New York: Aldine de Gruyter.

Kensinger, Kenneth M. 1995. *How Real People Ought to Live: The Cashinahua of Eastern Peru.* Prospect Heights, IL: Waveland.

Kent, Susan, ed. 1989. Farmers as Hunters: The Implications of Sedentism. *New Directions in Archaeology.* Cambridge, UK: Cambridge University Press.

Kracke, Waud H. 1978. *Force and Persuasion: Leadership in an Amazonian Society.* Chicago: University of Chicago Press.

Langdon, E. Jean M., and Gerhard Baer, eds. 1992. *Portals of Power: Shamanism in South America.*

Albuquerque, NM: University of New Mexico Press.

Lave, Jean C. 1979. Cycles and Trends in Krikatí Naming Practices. In *Dialectical Societies: The Gê and Bororo of Central Brazil.* Pp. 16–44. David Maybury-Lewis, ed. *Harvard Studies in Cultural Anthropology 1.* Cambridge, MA: Harvard University Press.

Layrisse, Miguel, and Johannes Wilbert. 1999. The Diego Blood Group System and the Mongoloid Realm. *Fundación La Salle de Ciencias Naturales 44.* Caracas: Fundación la Salle de Investigaciones Cientificas.

Lea, Vanessa. 2001. The Composition of Mēbengokre (Kayapó) Households in Central Brazil. In Laura M. Rival and Neil L. Whitehead, eds., *Beyond the Visible and the Material: The Amerindianization of Society in the Work of Peter Rivière.* Pp. 157–176. Oxford: Oxford University Press.

Linn, Priscilla R., and William H. Crocker. MS. The Canela Messianic Movements of 1963 through 1999: A Monograph on World Comparisons.

Lizarralde, Manuel. 1988. Indice y Mapa de Grupos Etnolingüisticos Autoctonos de America del Sur. *Antropologica Suplemento 5,* Instituto Caribe de Antropologia y Sociologia Fundación La Salle de Ciencias Naturales. Caracas: Fundación La Salle.

Lizot, Jacques. 1986. Tales of the Yanomami: Daily Life in the Venezuelan Forest. *Cambridge Studies in Social Anthropology, 55:* Cambridge, MA: Cambridge University Press.

Mackay, Judith. 2000. *The Penguin Atlas of Human Sexual Behavior: Sexuality and Sexual Practices around the World.* Brighton, UK: Myriad Editions Limited.

Maybury-Lewis, David. 1965. *The Savage and the Innocent: Life with the Primitive Tribes of Brazil.* Cleveland: World.

———. 1967. *Akwē-Shavante Society.* Oxford, UK: Clarendon.

Maybury-Lewis, David, ed. 1979. *Dialectical Societies: The Gê and Bororo of Central Brazil. Harvard Studies in Cultural Anthropology 1.* Cambridge, MA: Harvard University Press.

Meggers, Betty J. 1971. Amazonia; Man and Culture in a Counterfeit Paradise. In W. Goldschmidt, ed., *Worlds of Man: Studies in Cultural Ecology.* Chicago: Aldine.

Melatti, Julio C. 1967. Índios e Criadores: A Situação dos Krahó na Área Pastoril do Tocantins. *Monografías do Instituto Ciências Sociais 3.* Rio de Janeiro.

———. 1972. *0 Messianismo Krahó.* São Paulo: Editora Herder.

———. 1978. Ritos de uma Tribo Timbira. *Coleção Ensaios, 53.* São Paulo: Editora Ática.

———. 1979. The Relationship System of the Krahó. In Dialectical Societies: The Gê and Bororo of Central Brazil. Pp. 46–79. David Maybury-Lewis, ed. *Harvard Studies in Cultural Anthropology 1.* Cambridge, MA: Harvard University Press.

Mindlin, Betty, and indigenous storytellers. 2002. *Barbecued Husbands and Other Stories from the Amazon.* Donald Slatoff trans. London: Verso.

Mooney, James. 1896 [1897]. The Ghost-Dance Religion and the Sioux Outbreak of 1890. *Fourteenth Annual Report of the Bureau of American Ethnology* 2:641–1110. Washington, DC: Smithsonian Institution.

Morse, Richard M., ed. 1965. *The Bandeirantes: The Historical Role of the Brazilian Pathfinders.* New York: Alfred A. Knopf.

Murphy, Yolanda, and Robert F. Murphy. 1985. *Women of the Forest,* 2nd ed. New York: Columbia University Press.

Newton, Dolores. 1994. Krikati/Pukobye. In J. Wilbert, ed., *Encyclopedia of World Cultures 7 (South America).* Pp. 203–206. New York: G. K. Hall.

Nimuendajú, Curt [Nimuendajú Ukel, Curt]. 1946. The Eastern Timbira. Robert Lowie, trans. and ed., *University of California Publications in American Archaeology and Ethnology 41.* Berkeley, CA: University of California Press.

Peters, John F. 1998. *Life Among the Yanomami: The Story of Change Among the Xilixana on the Mucajai River in Brazil.* Peterborough, Canada: Broadview.

Picchi, Debra. 2000. *The Bakairí Indians of Brazil: Politics, Ecology, and Change.* Prospect Heights, IL: Waveland.

Popjes, Jack. 1990. Pahpãm Jarkwa Cupahti Jõ Kàhhôc: Seleções da Bíblia Sagrada. Tradução no dialeto ramkokamekra-canela. *Liga Bíblica do Brasil*. Brasília: Summer Institute of Linguistics.

Posey, Darell A. 2002. *Kayapó Ethnoecology and Culture*. London: Routledge.

Ramos, Alcida R. 1995. Sanumá Memories: Yanomami Ethnography in Times of Crisis. *New Directions in Anthropological Writing*. Madison, WI: University of Wisconsin Press.

Ribeiro, Darcy. 2000. *The Brazilian People: The Formation and Meaning of Brazil*. Gregory Rabassa trans. Gainesville, FL: University of Florida Press.

Ribeiro, Francisco de Paula. 1815 [1870]. Roteiro da Viagem que Fez o Capitão . . . Às Fronteiras da Capitania do Maranhão e da de Goyaz. *Revista de Instituto Histórico 10:*5–80.

———. 1819a [1841]. Memória sobre as Nações Gentias que Presentemente Habitam o Continente do Maranhão. *Revista de Instituto Histórico 3:*184–197, 297–322, 442–456.

———. 1819b [1874]. Descripção do Território de Pastos Bons, nos Sertões do Maranhão, *Revista de Instituto, Histórico 2:*6–86.

Robarchek, Clayton, and Carole Robarchek. 1998. *Waorani: The Contexts of Violence and War*. In George and Louise Spindler, series eds., *Case Studies in Cultural Anthropology*. Fort Worth: Harcourt.

Rumsey, Alan. 1971. A Comparative Lexicon and Glottochronology of Some Gê Languages. (Manuscript in the files of W. H. Crocker, Department of Anthropology, Smithsonian Institution.)

Sanday, Peggy R. 1990. *Fraternity Gang Rape: Sex, Brotherhood, and Privilege on Campus*. New York: New York University Press.

Santos, Sílvio C. dos. 1973. *Índios e Brancos no Sul do Brasil: A Dramática Experiência dos Xokleng*. Florianópolis, SC: Edeme.

Schecter, Steven, and William H. Crocker. 1999. *Mending Ways: The Canela Indians of Brazil*. A video, 50 minutes, color. By Schecter Films/Smithsonian's Human Studies Film Archives. Princeton, NJ: Films for the Humanities and Sciences. (http://www.films.com/. Search for "Canela.")

Seeger, Anthony. 1975. The Meaning of Body Ornaments: A Suya Example. *Ethnology, 14*(3):211–224.

———. 1981. Nature and Society in Central Brazil: The Suya Indians of Mato Grosso. *Harvard Studies in Cultural Anthropology 4*. Cambridge, MA: Harvard University Press.

Suggs, David N., and Andrew W. Miracle, eds. 1999. Culture, Biology, and Sexuality. *Southern Anthropological Society Proceedings, 32*. Athens, GA: University of Georgia Press.

Turner, Terence. 1969. Tchikrin: A Central Brazilian Tribe and Its Symbolic Language of Bodily Adornment. *Natural History 78*(8):50–59, 70.

———. 1979. Kinship, Household, and Community Structure Among the Kayapó. In Dialectical Societies: The Gê and Bororo of Central Brazil. Pp.179–214. David Maybury-Lewis, ed. *Harvard Studies in Cultural Anthropology 1*. Cambridge, MA: Harvard University Press.

Verswijver, Gustaaf. 1992. *The Club-Fighters of the Amazon: Warfare among the Kaiapo Indians of Central Brazil*. Gent: Rijksuniversiteit.

Wilbert, Johannes, ed. 1994. *Encyclopedia of World Cultures 7 (South America)*. New York: G. K. Hall.

Wilbert, Johannes, and Karin Simoneau, eds. 1984. Folk Literature of the Gê Indians, 2. *UCLA Latin American Studies 58*. Los Angeles: UCLA Latin American Center Publications.

Wüst, Irmhild, and Cristiana Barreto. 1999. The Ring Villages of Central Brazil: A Challenge for Amazonian Archaeology. *Latin American Antiquity 10*(1):3–23.

Index